in search of a new AFGHANISTAN

in search of a new
AFGHANISTAN

Sujeet Sarkar

NIYOGI
BOOKS

Published by
NIYOGI BOOKS
D-78, Okhla Industrial Area, Phase-I
New Delhi-110 020, INDIA
Tel: 91-11-26816301, 49327000
Fax: 91-11-26810483, 26813830
email: niyogibooks@gmail.com
website: www.niyogibooks.com

Editor: Jyoti Kumari
Cover Design: Aarti Devasher
Layout: Shashi Bhushan Prasad

ISBN: 978-93-81523-42-1
Publication: May 2012
Second Impression: July 2012

Other than actual historical persons and events, portrayed according to the author's interpretation, all characters appearing in this book are a work of the author's imagination. Any resemblance to actual persons is entirely coincidental.

Printed at: Niyogi Offset Pvt. Ltd., New Delhi, India

Contents

Preface

Afghan society is a complex conglomeration of ethnic, linguistic, religious and tribal lineages, more closely united at the local level, than under the banner of Afghan identity at the national level. This fault line has always been exploited by the neighbouring countries to advance their wider strategic interest. The fractured social capital can be attributed to the legacy of civil wars and external proxy interferences, over the past three decades. The country also suffers from a complex set of socio-political and socio-cultural undercurrents. Present day Afghanistan is a result of not only the unending civil wars but also the strategic blunders of its neighbouring countries, including the infamous Soviet occupation spanning the decade from 1979 to 1989.

More than three decades of conflict and war, displacements and social disruption have caused massive destruction and depletion of Afghanistan's infrastructure, sources of livelihoods, housing and agricultural resources. This destruction has further, eroded public and political institutions, thereby severely denting the overall governance process.

After the 9/11, Afghanistan is of prime strategic interest to its regional neighbours, as well as the broader international community. It is a critical link for achieving both regional and international peace and security. Hence, in the contemporary political scenario, every country has incorporated the Afghan reality in their foreign policy matters. The US military forces, in communion with its NATO allies, arrived in Afghanistan to weed out the al-Qaeda and the Taliban militants, and irreversibly degrade their capabilities to control Afghanistan, post 9/11. Massive troops with latest range of arms and equipments were deployed all across the country. The international community pledged considerable military and civilian support and vowed to create a stable, peaceful, prosperous nation—a new Afghanistan.

In the process of embracing democracy, Afghanistan successfully went through two rounds of democratic elections, to elect the president and the parliament. The populace voiced their needs through the Afghanistan National Development Strategy, popularly referred to as ANDS. They expect the State and the international community to fulfill their promise, to strive for durable peace, and to reward them for their trust in democracy.

A series of national priority programmes has also been initiated since the constitution of the first democratically elected government. The government has launched a wide range of development and reconstruction programmes to accentuate the process of development and peace building, with key focus on addressing regional imbalances and equity. The international aid agencies have, further, designed comprehensive sets of development programmes, to expedite and expand the reach of basic services, to a wider cross-section of the populace.

Facilitating development in a conflict-prone setting, like Afghanistan, is always going to be a herculean task. The development process has to operate in a complex situation, and under serious constraints that the country has been facing post 9/11. Nine years on, there has been a lot of criticism on the pace and scale of reconstruction and development efforts, initiated by various development actors, including the State itself. There is a palpable, and an increasingly visible frustration among the US and its Western allies, who do not find their financial contribution commensurate with the pace and scale of reconstruction and development efforts. According to them, it has failed to gather momentum. Serious concerns have been raised on the performance of the federal government and its ability to govern Afghanistan.

There is nothing much to write home on the military front either. After nine years of relentless military operations, it has become increasingly clear that the Taliban is far from vanquished. In fact, as per the US intelligence reports, with every passing day they have grown stronger and more organised. Not only have they consolidated their position in their stronghold, the southern provinces but also managed to extend their sphere of influence to the once peaceful northern provinces, like Kunduz, Baghlan, etc. The Taliban, al-Qaeda nexus is converging faster and even attacking Kabul at will.

Despite a massive injection of international assistance and security personnel, much of international assistance has not been very effective due to endemic corruption, resurgent Taliban and a thriving illicit economy. These have combined to undermine the influence of the national government. Where is the present day Afghanistan heading? Is the dream of a new Afghanistan fading?

There has been concerted effort by the US and other Western allies to hold the local government responsible for this failure in the development and governance process. However, the contention is, when every decision is guided by the policies of the US and other allies, how can the government be held solely responsible for the supposed failure of one decade of development and peace building effort? Without undermining the criticisms of the ongoing development and governance process it is, therefore, imperative to critically analyse and assess the quality and pace of development of the peace building process in Afghanistan. It is also important to study the key policies of the US and its allies that have a direct bearing on them.

There are a number of myths about the development and peace building process in Afghanistan and the bulk of the international community views the development process under this influence. These myths actually guide and further shape international perspective about Afghanistan. For building a new understanding and perspective, these myths need to be analysed and laid bare.

Like many others, I too, subscribed to the dream of a new Afghanistan and joined an international agency as a governance advisor, in 2005. During my professional stint I closely witnessed the development processes across all echelons of society, from rural to urban areas, from north to militant infested south, from governance to the governed and more importantly from the ordinary citizen to the power corridors of Kabul. Having worked in Afghanistan for over six years, as an international advisor on governance, I thought of undertaking an in-depth inquiry on some of the above stated concerns. *In Search of a New Afghanistan* aims to apprise the reader about the ongoing development and peace building processes in Afghanistan, post 9/11. The book also attempts to break many misconceptions, and depict the challenges lying ahead of Afghanistan.

While working as a development professional I also came across various striking facets of the country that usually go unnoticed. Most readers are aware of its delicate geostrategic location, its history of civil wars and invasions and its impoverished state. But beyond that, few have had an opportunity to take a peek into the heart of this country. There are many hues of Afghanistan that remain hidden from the eyes of an outsider, who has seen it only through the lens of strife so far. That Afghanistan can be a fascinating place to live in and even fall in love with, despite the ongoing hurdles, is difficult to comprehend for most. The book intends to unveil several of these fascinating aspects, while elaborating on the thrill and challenges of working in Afghanistan.

In Search of a New Afghanistan is an easy-to-understand tale for all and sundry, who would like to free themselves from the rhetoric of mainstream perceptions and opinion, to understand Afghanistan, post 9/11 and the challenges the country is facing today.

THE BRICKBATS

Development vs Security

'If we keep our beards long, we are suspected, to be either al-Qaeda or the Taliban operatives, by the US military. If we keep our beards short, we are assumed to be agents of international agencies by the Taliban. We do not want to be killed—we want to live.'

—words of a local Afghan

> Do we have the right balance of development and security assistance, towards reconstruction of Afghanistan? Is the strategy behind pushing the military into both combatant and development roles, yielding any dividends in Afghanistan?

The development process of Afghanistan has been on for nearly a decade now. From a humanitarian approach, with the immediate fall of the Taliban, it has gradually shifted to a development and reconstruction mode. Of late, this process has been drawing widespread flak from the international community, for its sluggish pace and dismal quality. The international community opines that much of the assistance has not been very effective due to endemic corruption, resurgent Taliban, and a thriving illicit economy in Afghanistan. It is true, to some extent, that poor governance coupled with deteriorating security situation have derailed the development and reconstruction process in Afghanistan, and seriously undermined the influence of the national government. Every report or news, which emanates from any part of the world, depicting the status of the Afghan development process, mirrors this perception, in some form or the other. This has become, more or less, a stereotypical rhetoric about present day Afghanistan. Those who understand the country well enough, however, would contend the same. There is a dire need to develop a deeper understanding of the ongoing development and reconstruction process, before succumbing to mainstream rhetoric.

First and foremost, let it be clarified, that the quality and the pace of the development and reconstruction process of Afghanistan look very different when understood in the context of the districts and villages, and not from the national capital, Kabul. Real action, one must remember, takes place at the district and village levels. So, to know the pulse of the situation, one has to visit these corridors of changes—a village, or clusters of villages, and the districts.

And herein is the snag! Most of the development and policy experts in Afghanistan suffer from 'Kabul Syndrome'. It is well known that most of the high level policy experts in UN and other bilateral agencies, positioned in Kabul, have not visited even one Afghan village in their entire tenure of posting due to security concerns. These 'experts' barely have had any communication with the community or the primary stakeholders of the development process. Their analyses are entirely based upon mere compilation of secondary data. Unfortunately, international opinion is largely influenced and guided by the analyses of these Kabul-based experts.

During the last couple of years, the international community has become, progressively, worried about the quality and the pace of the development and reconstruction process in Afghanistan. There is a palpable and increasingly visible frustration among the Western countries, especially, among the donor countries, as they do not find their financial contribution in commensurate with the results on ground. In simple development terms, the impact of the process turns out to be abysmally low when compared with the burgeoning amount of financial resources committed for the cause. At least, that is the most popular notion formed by the donor states and their denizens. The inability of the State to deliver results around expected lines of the donor countries has attracted a series of criticism. The credibility of the Afghan government, especially, its ability to shape the development and the governance process, and more importantly the future of the country has repeatedly been under the scanner.

To have reservations, against this popular international opinion, may seem impudent. However, it is a personal belief that the development process has, indeed, yielded moderate dividends in terms of development, if not governance. This can be better understood only when one views the ongoing development and peace building process within the framework of the serious constraints and the complex situation the country is facing today.

There is always scope for further improvement in the scale and quality of development. There is no denying that the development actors, including Afghanistan, could have collectively achieved more than what they have, so far. There has been a concerted effort by the US and other Western interests to hold the government responsible for the supposed failure of the development and governance process. In a context where the bulk of the development services and functions are implemented by the INGOs directly, how can the State be completely responsible for the supposed failure? In a situation, where every development programme and decisions is designed around the policies of US and other Western countries, how can one hold the State responsible for the failure alone? Even if there is a sense of failure, assuming the international assessment to be true, the same should be perceived as a collective failure. The policies of US and other Western actors are equally responsible for this failure.

There are several myths around the development and peace building process in Afghanistan. Bulk of the international community, unfortunately, views the development process under the influence of these myths that further guide and shape the general perception. For creating a new understanding on Afghanistan, these myths and policy blunders need to be analysed and unfolded. Without undermining the criticisms of the ongoing process, it is imperative to critically probe and analyse the reasons behind the sluggish pace and quality of development and reconstruction in the country.

Well, it may appear to the outside world that huge amount of financial resources, running in several billions, have been employed to accentuate the development and state building process. In reality, however, the country is grappling with inadequate financial resource to fast track the development process. The US and its allies have actually committed a bulk of their aid around military support rather than development. In other words, the resources provided by the Western countries, in the name of rebuilding Afghanistan, are largely used by these countries to service their military apparatus. This is either in the form of the US and NATO forces fighting the hardcore Taliban militants in the Afghanistan-Pakistan border, or their Provincial Reconstruction Teams, popularly referred as the PRT, cooling their heels in the provinces.

The PRT is meant to take up the law and order situation in their hands in advent of any exigency, and aid development and good governance, at the provincial level. However, it is a fact that PRTs have never been found in the thick of any action (in terms of law and order), in the five northern provinces (and one southern province), of Afghanistan, which we have been visiting regularly, in the last five years. The pie diagram, explains the consolidated aid flow and expenditure in Afghanistan from 2002-2009.

Figure 1: International Aid, security and military expenditure, 2002-2009

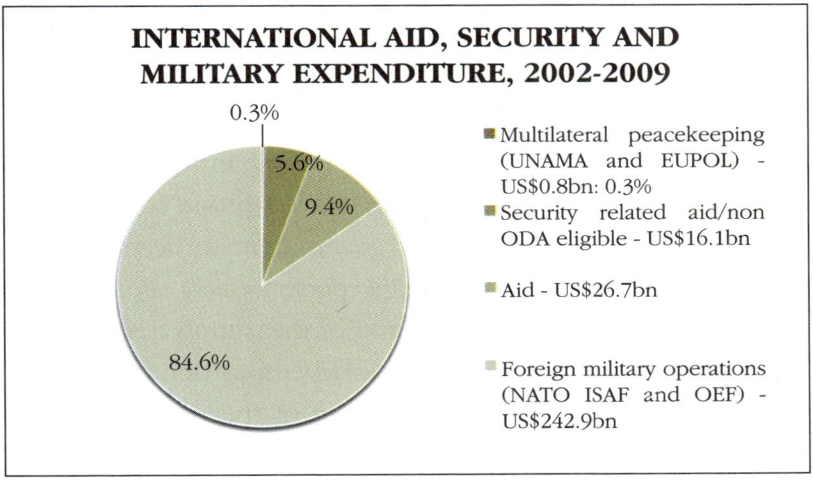

Sources: Development Initiatives based on OECD DAC data; Government of the Islamic Republic of Afghanistan (GIRoA) Donor Assistance Database (DAD); Stockholm International Peace Research Institute (SIPRI) database of Multilateral Peacekeeping Operations; and Development Initiatives research Assistance Database (DAD)

It is evident from the pie above that the consolidated budget spent around military support has been around ten times more than the development aid.[1] The State has received a meagre USD 26.7 billion in the head of development and reconstruction against a whopping USD 242.9 billion for military support.

It is also important to remember that the military budget, of most Western countries, exceeds their civilian budget by volumes. They employ huge resources to capture and drive away the Taliban and al-Qaeda terrorists from Afghanistan through a structured military operation. These countries pack their military budget under the fold of 'rebuilding Afghanistan' grant. These grants may look voluminous, but a closer analysis reveals that a bulk of it is meant for military purposes. A very small fraction of the said grant, actually, goes for development. However, the international community aspires to witness the change in the development scenario on the lines of total volume of the grant committed by them, when in reality only a meagre part of the same is meant for development. Not-so-surprisingly, therefore, a reiterated area under discussion, during my guest lectures across the world on governance in conflict-prone countries has been the failure of the Afghan government to accelerate the development process. The average person easily slips into the mainstream international syndrome of measuring development against the overall grant committed by various donor countries. The international audience is a victim of the popular notions formed due to the inadequate analyses of Western policies and grants meant for Afghanistan.

Some hardcore primary data may be presented to expose this flaw. Oxfam International, in their aid effectiveness study reports that US military incurs a cost of USD 100 million per day, some USD 36 billion a year, to run their military apparatus in Afghanistan. Yet, the average volume of international aid provided by all donors, since 2001, is woefully inadequate, at just USD 7 million per day. According to the Pentagon Budget Release 2010, USD 65 billion has been allocated under war funds for Afghanistan. As Ann Scott Tyson noted in a *Washington Post* article on 8 May 2009, the budget covers the deployment of additional 21,000 US troops to bolster the capability of US military to strike against the Taliban and al-Qaeda militants.

The development aid provided by US to the government of Afghanistan is only a small fraction of the said amount, committed under military support. In 2006, Germany spent Euros 4 million in development and humanitarian efforts but a whopping Euros 475 million towards servicing their military operation.[2]

The buck does not stop here. A bulk of the resources, provided under military grants, are further recycled back to the donor countries in form of salaries to military personnel deployed in Afghanistan, for purchase of modern arms and ammunition for counter-insurgency operations, and for logistics, including transportation of even potable water and wine for military consumption in most of the cases. The logistic supplies are regularly brought by special aircrafts. On any given day, one can find four to five cargo aircrafts standing on the tarmac of the Kabul Airport, over and above the flotilla of other planes carrying logistics for the PRT stationed in provincial headquarters. The local economy does not gain much from the presence of the Western army.

Let us not even tot up the second hand military planes that have been donated, to apparently strengthen the Afghan Air Force, as a part of the international aid programme. A friend, a military aviation expert by profession, once confided that these planes have actually become outdated and redundant, long ago. They are obsolete in their home countries, having outlived their maximum flying hours, stipulated by their stringent military aviation guidelines. The environmentalist fraternity of these highly advanced countries would not even allow the air force to dismantle these planes due to the hazardous waste and related consequences. Some of the donor countries, if not all, find Afghanistan a perfect dumping ground to part with their obsolete military machines, in the name of bilateral grants. Fortunately, Afghanistan is a landlocked country or else donated ships would have exceeded the number of aircrafts. It is good that they do not have a marine force, or else Western countries that find it difficult to dismantle redundant ships in their country due to the organised protest of the powerful environmental lobbies, would have found a perfect dump yard in Afghanistan.

The basic question to be raised here is how much of these resources are, actually, employed for development? And more importantly, even after the massive insurgency operations, spanning a decade, if the Taliban has grown in numbers and become stronger than ever, who should be blamed for this? It is unfair to blame the local government, for all failures in Afghanistan. Even if not averse to these donations, the reality and politics behind the support certainly needs to be explored and exposed.

Military assistance can be further divided into two categories—frontline military operations to capture and drive away the Taliban, and secondary operations to service and assist the frontline operation. A large number of the secondary military operations have been outsourced to Western private security firms. These security companies, consume a considerable portion of military budget of US, and that of other donor states. Large proportion of the money is recycled back to the donor countries through the same channel, as explained above. The presence of these security companies further promotes corruption and nepotism and seriously undermines meritocracy.

In Afghanistan, there are powerful commanders, nestled in every province, with hordes of well-trained gun-toting followers at their disposal. Each commander is from a particular ethnic group and their followers—self decorated soldiers—are mostly from the same ethnic group. The commanders provide status, power and patronage to their followers, for blindly obeying their diktats. Some of these commanders are Mujahideen too. Mujahideens are mostly referred to the Muslim guerrilla warriors who launched jihad (fight against injustice) against the Soviet occupation from 1979 to 1989. Majority of the soldiers have been serving the commanders right from the Mujahideen times since 1979. In few cases, even the second generation has joined the commanders. The allegiance of these soldiers lies with the commander completely, and the nation or state is a non entity for them.

These commanders leave no stones unturned in fixing their loyal soldiers, in the security companies. At the same time, the commanders are routinely paid hefty amounts by the security companies, to consistently enjoy their patronage. The security companies need their blessings for smooth operation, and the commanders milk them no end. Any denial by the security companies would seriously jeopardise their relationship with the local commanders, and put the life of the soldiers, on the payroll of the companies, under serious risk. Hence, for the security companies it is more of a marriage of convenience that gurantees the support of the local powerful commanders, and thwarts the looming life risk they live with.

There is another strange equation here that one is unable to fathom easily. The security companies, enjoying the patronage of the local commander, hardly ever come under the Taliban attacks. This may be purely coincidental, but it certainly raises more eyebrows than one. In Afghanistan there is a wafer thin difference between a commander and a politician, as most of the commanders have graduated to politics. The remaining few, with a large number of followers, have turned into warlords. Hence, the whole nexus of commanders, warlords and politicians gain immensely from these security companies.

The role played by the security companies is far from ideal. Time and again, these companies have overstepped their role and brought disrepute to the ongoing military operation. They have seriously contributed to the widening gap between the Western military and Afghan civilians. The Afghan President vows to drive them away after every misadventure, but soon, after his discussion with Hillary Clinton, present Secretary of State of US, over the special Afghan hotline, he mellows down a bit and talks of a phase-wise exit of the private security companies. He has raised the issue again as recently as the Munich Security Conference, on 6 February 2011.

After military operation, including both frontline and secondary, the next big chunk of the international grant is burned by the PRTs in Afghanistan. These are provincial bases, which combine limited contingents of foreign troops, to establish a deterrent presence, and a small number of civilian aid personnel, to direct reconstruction work, in these areas. The US and NATO powers created PRTs, also, to channel their funds through these teams directly, and get their work going in Afghanistan, after the downfall of the Taliban. Soon, other donor countries adopted the model and PRTs proliferated like wild fire, in almost all the thirty-four provinces of Afghanistan. Western countries adopt one, two or at times three provinces, and commit their military forces to PRT for a certain number of years. This is in addition to the military forces, committed by these governments in the frontline US and NATO forces, fighting with the hardcore Taliban militants. A few countries have limited their military assistance only to PRTs, as this is more or less viewed as a neutral line of support. Since the military personnel do not have to fight out the Taliban, al-Qaeda nexus directly, in the inhospitable and mountainous terrain, such support is considered less risk prone and life threatening.

Besides providing military assistance in maintaining law and order during missions, it is also used to support the government in extending good governance and reconstruction in their respective provinces. As a part of this policy, they focus on construction of roads, clinics, schools, etc. The suggested actions are anticipated to contribute to peace building. Although the basic concept of a PRT may remain same, the individual character and action may differ to a certain extent. Few progressive PRTs, including the Dutch, have worked out 3D strategies to provide a new fillip to PRT initiatives, in the trouble prone provinces like Uruzgan. 3D strategies specify 'Defence', 'Development' and 'Diplomacy' as three core areas of work.

The PRT is often referred as the white elephant of Afghanistan. They are besieged with a plethora of problems, the first and foremost being the need to juggle humanitarian aid with military objectives. This is further aggravated by a lack of any explicit guidance on civilian and military roles of PRTs, backed by the US.[3]

The civilian approach to PRT was best explained by a local NGO worker in Kunduz, 'The PRT outsources their development activities to INGOs, the INGO outsources it to a local NGO, the local NGO to a contractor, the contractor to a sub-contractor, and finally the Afghan community receives nothing.' A large amount of resources employed in the name of development assistance by the PRT, actually, evaporates in form of overhead costs, in the process of changing hands of multiple implementing agencies. The Senate Foreign Relation Committee of Government of Canada, on aid effectiveness in Afghanistan, has cited excessive use and poor oversight of contractors, for promoting civilian cause by the military. Few PRTs, further, prefer to outsource most of their work to INGOs of their own country of origin. The readers are intelligent enough to understand the linkage there after!

The PRTs also suffer from serious intellectual innocence on development issues, as they are not formally trained or educated in dealing with development issues in a conflict-prone setting. A shortage of staff, limited technical and managerial support coupled with inadequate mechanism for project implementation has undermined the effectiveness of the US led PRTs.[4]

Development in a conflict-ridden country is a specialised job, requiring special training and orientation. It is best left for the specialists. A considerable number of international development experts have also expressed their discomfort with the notion of soldiers, donned in military uniforms, sitting over huge cache of arms and ammunition, and facilitating participatory development. While working in Afghanistan one often witnesses PRTs travelling to villages, with a cavalcade of armoured vehicles (some fitted with machine guns on top), to discuss development issues, on a regular basis. It can be termed a development circus, at best, which is only increasing with every passing day in Afghanistan.

This intellectual innocence often affects the quality of development process facilitated by PRTs. This has been noticed by various NGOs, during several presentations on development, to attract financial resources for their respective development agenda. The PRTs hold a big development kitty, but they are least concerned about processes and more interested in the end visibility, that too, in size and numbers. The size of the advertisement board often exceeds the size of the project. This amply depicts their penchant for higher political visibility. In development, however, both processes as well as outcomes are equally important; the former ensuring the sustainability of the latter.

There are countless other examples of how the development process in Afghanistan has suffered due to the intellectual innocence of PRTs. Their understanding of development issues is often found to be rudimentary. Most of their projects are ill conceived because they lack the necessary intellectual rigour and skill to analyse development issues and design appropriate interventions. The PRT conceived projects, are again, not critically assessed against any standard set of outcome indicators, as in professional INGOs. Mostly PRTs go for projects, which are strategic in nature, preferably with greater political quotient, and larger visibility. These are referred as 'quick impact projects'. They do not have much to do with the pressing needs of the community. PRTs are best known for their obsession for infrastructure projects—their thinking mostly beginning and ending with them. Quite often INGOs milk PRT resources to advance their infrastructure agenda in their respective spheres of action. I too, stand accused of exploiting this weakness of PRTs. The community development council (the lowest unit of village government), has often been prompted to identify infrastructural projects and put them as proposals through our teams, across five provinces, to exploit this weakness. Hence, one does not have a right to complain too much about PRTs in this domain, at least. However, what needs to be emphasised is that such quick impact projects cannot be a substitute for long-term sustainable development.

The basic question, however, is that of development principle. When you are exploring solutions for community problems, you cannot go with a basket of infrastructural projects alone. This assumes further significance in a conflict-prone setting. Development should always be viewed from the perspective of the clientele, which in this case is the community. When the development process is donor driven, and not demand driven, questions are naturally raised about the quality of the project.

The intellectual innocence of the PRTs is palpable during development discourses, whenever one gets the opportunity to rub shoulders with the PRT counterparts. In one instance a PRT official, the governance expert for the civilian arm of his PRT, went hammer and tong on how the district governors of Afghanistan should be sent for an immediate exposure visit, to no other place, but China, for improving governance. China and Afghanistan! Are they not, like chalk and cheese, two extreme ends of a spectrum, in every sense? How lessons of a regressive communist regime could fit into a young democracy, still learning its art and practice, was a mystery! He, however, had a right to his opinion, which had to be swallowed, under the circumstances, with a glass of Coke (made in Kabul these days).

Countless reports have exposed that aid projects undertaken by military have shown neither cost effectiveness nor high quality and sustainability.[5] The Institute of Peace suggests that PRT assisted projects suffer from a lack of coordination and oversight. Military involvement in development has brought serious criticism from INGOs too. They claim that PRT involvement in development activities blur the distinction between combatants and development workers, putting the INGOs under high risk. A distinction between humanitarian and military action is integral to the safety of an aid worker in Afghanistan. Anti-government elements often struggle to differentiate the civilian agenda of a PRT with their military agenda, especially in an environment where human rights have repeatedly been violated by military actors. The action of the PRT by default puts the INGOs in the same bracket, making them severely vulnerable to attacks by the Taliban insurgents. International NGOs generally assert their independence from PRTs, and minimise their direct interaction with military forces. Some INGOs even refuse to allow PRT soldiers in their offices only to maintain a safe distance and to avoid unwarranted insurgent attention or attack.

Association with the military has also turned PRT projects, such as schools, into militant targets. Hence, experts feel that PRTs should be engaged in relief activities only when life hangs in balance, and no civilian alternatives exist. PRTs cannot be a substitute for long-term development work. The military has neither the expertise nor the staying power to engage in the development process.[6]

Barring the local Afghans, who are mostly, employed as interpreters, the PRTs remain unpopular among the masses—especially, among the educated and intellectual sections of the Afghan community. They are also referred as 'Purely Relaxing Teams' by a number of local development actors. They see them as a big hole in the development exchequer of Afghanistan. Readers may be warned, at this juncture, to never ask any Afghan about his impression on the PRT, when he is stuck behind the convoy of PRT vehicles, on state highways, especially, the ones connecting the northern provinces with Kabul. One is bound to hear a more radical view about PRTs, during those occasions.

The analysis about the PRT would be incomplete if the views and opinions of a few PRT friends, who want to sincerely contribute to the reconstruction of Afghanistan, are not brought in. The PRTs not only have to deal with poor perception and acceptance in public, but also internally within the system, among its own people. In a candid conversation, during a visit to New Zealand PRT in Bamian, a friend once shared. 'We are stationed here for six months only. The first couple of months pass in understanding the situation in order to promote civilian causes. The third month is a break. Before we can initiate concrete civilian action, we have to prepare for our transition, and succession planning for the last phase of our stipulated stay, in this trouble prone country. We are marred by the faulty policies, and even if we want to do something concrete, the system does not allow us to do so.'

The above criticism may not be applied to all the PRTs engaged in the rebuilding of Afghanistan. There is a handful, who is genuinely trying to make a difference. The larger question is about the rationale behind pushing these PRTs into development and reconstruction. It is hard to fathom how the billions of dollars that go in maintaining a cost intensive giant, like the PRTs, help the development and reconstruction process in Afghanistan. While the PRTs may be struggling to play an enabling developmental role, what is frustrating is to see them even faltering in their usual security function. There was an incident in a northern province, where an irate and violent mob was planning to put the office of a highly reputed international INGO, on fire. The mob was mobilised by the radical forces, to avenge the Guantanamo Bay incident (alleged insult of the Holy Quran). Ironically the word of the mullah is often seen as the last word, especially, during the hour of crisis in Afghanistan. Despite frantic calls and requests by the INGO, the PRT refused to employ their forces to prevent froth approaching crisis—mostly arson and loot. Due to the inaction of the PRT, the office was burnt to ashes, and the INGO suffered a reported loss of USD 2.2 million. The said INGO had to suspend all their development activities, for a considerable period, in order to reorganise themselves.

Apparently, the INGO was told that as per the PRT operating manual, clause 3.2 (remembered vaguely), the PRT cannot step outside their campus after sunset. Incidentally they have a series of operational manuals and directives to guide every step. It is ironic to note that there is a rider for every such clause. Here the rider was that a special permission had to be taken from their political bosses, sitting in the capital of a European country, to trigger action. The INGO managed to get the rider in action, but not before their office turned to ashes. The PRT promised to get into the rescue act the following day to save the lives of expatriate and local staff of the INGOs, holed up in a few private houses of a small town. Fearing there could be a separate PRT clause for a cloudy day, one could only pray, the whole night, for a bright sunny morning, next day. Fortunately, the local police rescued the staff from the irate and unruly mob, before the PRTs could swing into action.

If a PRT, equipped with all modern arms and ammunition and a perfect mandate, fails to take up added responsibility in case of an emergency, imagine the plight and heightened risk of various development actors, working relentlessly, without any security cover in Afghanistan.

The inaction of the PRTs does not stop here. Their campus is a ring fence with tiers of security. The first check point is usually guarded by Afghan forces. One such guard stationed in a PRT outpost confided, on conditions of anonymity, 'We are, actually, the sacrificial lambs for the Taliban insurgents'. They are the first causality of any Taliban driven attack on the PRT camps in Afghanistan. The strategic positioning of Afghan forces at the front gate provides the PRT with additional time and an extra line of resistance, to minimise loss of lives, in the eventuality of a raid by the Taliban militants. A similar situation is also found in some of the US and NATO camps. The larger question to be asked here is whether the PRTs and other foreign military forces, equipped with all ultra modern arms and equipments, are afraid of guarding their frontline check posts, on their own. They see the rudimentary Afghan police forces as their best bet to provide them their much needed extra line of defence.

The world community gets to hear only about the death of international military forces because of their news value and the sensitivities involved therein. They hardly ever come to know about the losses to the Afghan forces trying to protect their Western counterpart. Thousands of Afghan soldiers have died only to shield the Western forces, including the PRTs, after the fall of the Taliban. How can the PRTs, who cannot even protect themselves be expected to protect others, is what most Afghans contend today.

One is also tempted to draw a picture of the surreal opulence enjoyed by the PRTs, in course of their stay in Afghanistan. Some of their soldiers may be living in a container but these containers are fitted with air conditioners powered 24x7 by diesel generators. The interiors and facilities inside are nothing less than those of a plush hotel suite. There are bars, fine dining restaurants, coffee corners and clubs, inside a few PRT campus. The aid workers are often invited by various PRTs for official lunches and dinners. They are perfect hosts. I was moved by their gracious approach towards their guests and I was equally stunned by the diverse display of food and wine. Look out for any international cuisine and you will find it on their table. The wine list at the bar will make any fine upmarket restaurant look modest. This is not to critique their lifestyle, as one would not like to have them staying in tents, either. However, while not being averse to their comfortable living, one is compelled to critically analyse it in the context of their role in the reconstruction process of Afghanistan. Is their contribution to the development process in Afghanistan commensurate with the mammoth expense that goes in maintaining them? For that matter, are they even offering any value to the law and order situation in the province? Those who understand Afghanistan sufficiently would seriously contest their role.

The annual cost of maintaining a PRT personnel is almost equivalent of maintaining fifteen to twenty Afghan soldiers. This has been confirmed by various federal ministers, on and off record, umpteen times. Moreover, the Afghan soldiers do not need a Global Positioning System (GPS) to get into any village within the province. They can travel by the ordinary open back, low cost, green Toyota and also deliberate with the community, more effectively, without a translator. Hence, even if a reserved military force is required at the provincial level, assuming the PRT assessment to be true, a low cost localised model should be explored. The bulky PRT structure should be completely dismantled for a leaner version with the sole objective of preparing a cadre of local forces, with structured training for Afghanistan. This would provide a leeway, to the Western states, to commit more financial resources to accelerate the pace of development. The proposed localisation would, additionally, create close to quarter of a million jobs for the local youth in the coming few years. The trained youths can be further integrated in the civilian police and military forces, down the years.

In all fairness, one is unable to fathom the importance of the PRTs in the development process either. Are they seriously required in the reconstruction and peace building efforts in Afghanistan? Perhaps, the argument here is, 'Can there be a better alternative and a more meaningful way to employ those billions of dollars, to espouse the cause of Afghanistan?' This tentative view will surely resonate with other development practitioners, who have spent sufficient time and effort, beyond Kabul, to witness and understand the development process in Afghanistan.

It is also a matter of speculation, if all the donor countries have committed their PRTs to Afghanistan, in principle and spirit. It is suspected that some of these countries have committed themselves, only, to be on the right side or to be in the good books of the powerful US. There are, unsubstantiated, reports that few countries routinely pay the Taliban to keep their respective PRTs out of the attacking range. These countries have employed a tacit arrangement to save their PRT from any Taliban driven causality. This actually enables them to neutralise the domestic pressure, churned out by the media and the civilian population, against the death of their PRT personnel in Afghanistan. This issue was highly reported, not only in Kabul but also by a section of the Italian media, of a possible nexus of their government with the Taliban. The Italian government, however, vociferously denied any such arrangement, for obvious reasons. One researcher at the George C Marshall, European Centre of Security Studies, found in 2008 that PRTs lead to counterproductive results, such as strengthening of local power brokers and weakening of provincial government. PRT aided development projects are also more prone to Taliban attacks, as already mentioned earlier.

My not-so-popular view on the PRT was corroborated by none other than the Afghan President, Hamid Karzai. The president in his key note address in the Munich Security Conference, (6 February 2011) asked the NATO to stop direct funding to parallel structures in Afghanistan and to do away with the PRT, which has become an impediment in improving regional governance. The Afghan president further said that if his government has to assume full responsibility of its security and governance by 2014, then some of the existing structures, through which Western powers now operate, must be dismantled. These parallel structures were created to help the Afghan government towards aiding security and governance, but the result has been reverse. They have ended up challenging the authority of the regional government. 'The PRT erodes the authority of regional government and impedes our effort towards better governance, and the local populace gets confused in the process,' said Karzai. He has clearly advised the international community to do away with the PRTs, or at least bring them under the fold of Afghan government, for fixing their accountability. How can the president not end up asking for the complete withdrawal of private security companies?

His comment in the Munich security conference stirred quite a debate. The US Under Secretary of Defence, Michèle Flournoy, assured that US was willing to cooperate with the Afghan president on those fresh ideas but there were larger questions about whether the local government was capable of handling it. This is a typical rhetoric used by high level US officials to ward off any suggestion by the government, which is against Western interest and its style and approach of handling Afghanistan.

Assessing development from the quantum of resources flowing into Afghanistan, when in reality vast amount of money is actually being consumed for maintaining military effort, is unfair and inappropriate, to say the least. One has to understand the dynamics and intricacies of the development and reconstruction process in Afghanistan before holding any perception about it, and getting sucked away by popular notions. The immense imbalance between security and civilian aid is partly the reason why the Afghan government continues to remain weak. It is not ones intention to give a clean chit to the State of Afghanistan, by citing paucity of financial resources for not being able to accelerate the process of development and governance, either. There are issues concerning vision, focus and capacities of the State to genuinely facilitate the process of development and good governance. Time and again development experts have raised the commitment of the State to contain big time corruption, consistently reported by mainstream print and electronic media.

However, there is a genuine issue of resource scarcity as well. The issue of resource scarcity is subdued in the backdrop of growing terrorism and poor governance. The reality is that there is very little aid money available for development and reconstruction. At this juncture, the aid money is heavily tilted in favour of military response. This stems from the experience of other post conflict countries, where the expert sees development as a linear process, where you first establish security and then deliver long-term development. While it may have worked in the case of other post conflict countries, it will not work for Afghanistan where we need an integrated and balanced approach to peace building. Afghanistan is still struggling to find that judicious balance of development and military response. Bringing about a change would require reorganising assistance ratio between development and security. The US troops are among the strongest advocates of investing more in schools etc because they can see for themselves how education helps in fighting extremism, far more effectively, than a bomb. Against the cost of one American soldier, over just one year, one can build nearly twenty schools, as noted by Nicholas D Kristof in an article dated 25 December 2010 in the *New York Times.*

The challenge of Afghanistan's instability cannot be overcome by militarily alone. The development response has to be scaled up in order to win the hearts and minds of ordinary people. This would further cut the Taliban forces, right from the root of the Afghan society, where it damages the most.

1. Lydia Poole, Afghanistan: Tracking major resource flow 2002-2009.
2. CBD blog, US Centre on Public Diplomacy at the Annenberg School, University of South California.
3. Provincial reconstruction teams in Afghanistan: An inter agency assessment, USAID Bureau for Policy and Programme Coordination, 2006.
4. Provincial reconstruction teams in Afghanistan: An inter agency assessment, USAID, Bureau for Policy and Programme Coordination, 2006.
5. Lara Olson, Fighting for Humanitarian Space: NGOs in Afghanistan-Journal of Military and Strategic Studies, University of Calgary.
6. Kevin Soreson, A report of the standing committee on foreign affairs and international development.

The Peace Game

'Let me grow old enough either to hold a gun or tie a suicide vest—I will avenge the killing of my parents.'

—a child, who lost his parents in an awry bombing by ISAF

What has turned the US and its allies to apostles of peace, overnight?

Will the peace process work for Afghanistan?

The aftermath of 9/11 attacks witnessed massive military build-up in Afghanistan. The US military forces in communion with its Western allies arrived post 9/11 to weed out the al-Qaeda and the Taliban militants, and irreversibly degrade their capabilities to strike and control Afghanistan again. This was imperative for both regional as well as for global peace and security. The much hyped global war against terror resulted in massive troops rallying with latest military arms and equipments, all across Afghanistan, with a special focus on the hostile southern provinces, the traditional bastion of al-Qaeda and the Taliban. The Predator UAV, armed with drone missiles, was employed in large numbers to target hardcore militants hiding in inhospitable mountainous terrains and the safe sanctuaries of Afghanistan-Pakistan border.

However, after years of relentless military operation, it is becoming increasingly clear that the Taliban is far from vanquished. In fact, as per the US intelligence reports, they have grown stronger and more organised, with every passing day. Not only have they consolidated their position in their traditional stronghold in the southern provinces but also worming their way to once peaceful northern provinces, like Kunduz and Baghlan. The Taliban are massing in the outskirts of Kabul and slowly turning the city into a hot bed of terrorism.

President Obama's much talked about 'military surge' policy has delivered very little to rejoice about, both militarily and politically. Much to the dismay of the Pentagon, it has proven to be totally counter productive. Despite the surge, the Taliban has been able to converge and effectively besiege strategic locations with unfailing regularity. This has only further emboldened the Taliban. According to a Pentagon report, Karzai's government has control over only 29 out of 121 key strategic districts (August 2010).[1] The war against terror is far from over, and this is reflected by the fact that the situation in Afghanistan is getting bad to worse with passage of time.

In recent months, there have been increasing amounts of talk on looking for long-term political solutions for building durable peace in Afghanistan. A brainchild of the US military think tank, 'the peace process' is being zealously pursued by the US and objectively linked with the transit of their army from Afghanistan, post September, 2014. That is why one hears the word 'exit' striking a greater resonance than ever these days, among the international communities, at the behest of US.

What turned the US and its allies to advocates of peace overnight warrants some deep probing, though. There are a number of strategic compulsions tied to this much hyped peace process, which makes interesting research. The US and its Western allies have been getting increasingly tired of the war, and do not see it reaching anywhere near their end goal. The writing is clear on the wall. They are on the brink of a sad realisation that it is beyond their capacity to drive away the Taliban and irreversibly degrade their capabilities. To make a dignified exit, under the pretext of launching a peace process, is the next best and probably the only option. They have managed to receive international backing for it in the Kabul Conference. The international critics, however, see this as an effort to buy peace from the Taliban rather than build peace in Afghanistan.

The US is not going to leave behind a better State, at least, in terms of peace, security and stability. Like Iraq, they will leave Afghanistan, an unfinished, shoddy job. The US may have generated vast amounts of data, in terms of the number of kills, but deep inside they know it has resulted in the resurgence of the Taliban in Afghanistan, spawning in every nook and corner, today. According to international media, the US backed Hamid Karzai government is becoming increasingly weak and slowly losing its control.

One needs to analyse the reasons behind the military and strategic failure of the US in Afghanistan. In recent years, there has been a spate of aerial bombings in civilian areas in the restive south and eastern provinces. This has lead to large scale deaths of civilian population, including women and children. Barring few incidents, the ISAF forces have declined responsibility for those air attacks gone awry. Civilian death is a deeply emotive issue amongst ordinary Afghans, and the US forces have been criticised by President Karzai on numerous occasions for it. Time and again, he has requested the ISAF to exercise caution and restrain from such air raids. Every such awry air raid has turned a major chunk of the civilian populace against the US army and the Afghan government. The image of a puppet government, with strings attached to the White House in Washington has been getting reinforced, with the ordinary people questioning the ability of their government to contain such attacks. On the flip side, this has helped the Taliban to gain position and spread its tentacles beyond their stronghold in the south. The Taliban is using it as a fecund ground to step up its local and international recruitments to bolster their war against the Western forces.

The worst incidents were, of course, when bombs were mistakenly dropped over various marriage parties, over the last few years in Afghanistan, killing umpteen women and children, as reported by various international newspapers and news channels. It was heart breaking to see the children weeping inconsolably in the process of narrating the horrific tale of how they lost their mothers in the attack. In most cases of civilian air bombing, the military argument for the attacks emphasises on the presence of hardcore militants amid civilian populace, while the civilian population pleads complete innocence. There is no point in elaborating on these attacks as they have become routine occurrences in Afghanistan, and despite repeated American apologies and assurances, nothing has changed on ground, so far.

However, it would be certainly interesting to dwell on the aftermath of such an attack. Here, is an instance of an interview of a few victim children whose parents had been killed in an air raid by the ISAF forces. The interview was aired by Al Jazeera TV. The children vowed that they would avenge the killing when they are old enough to either tie a suicide vest or hold an AK 47/56. Even assuming the military version of their attack to be correct, which may flaunt its muscle for killing a handful of militants, an irreparable damage has already taken place; and will take its toll in the future. The forces may have killed a few militants, but they have created hundreds more, in these victim children. Some of them would be the future Baitullah or Hakimullah Mehsud! They will, someday, vent their anger, either against Western interest or against their own State, abetting the process of regional insecurity.

The misadventure of the American army has gone beyond mistargeted air attacks in civilian areas. In a recent development five American soldiers, posted in Kandahar, have been charged for murdering three Afghan civilians, between January and May 2010. These killing were committed for fun or what can be called 'sport' as per military documents, published in various leading international dailies. Though, these cases may seem like instances of individual aberrance rather than a systemic malaise they will only make the job of the US and NATO forces, further difficult and improbable.

There are many other reasons behind this inevitable failure of US forces, in neutralising the Taliban ability to strike and spread unrest in Afghanistan. Time and again, my military friends in Afghanistan have exclaimed how they are chasing 'a lost cause'. According to them, the safe sanctuaries of terrorism are nestled in the tribal belt of Waziristan, on the other side of the Durand Line that separates Afghanistan from Pakistan. It is only its ripple effect that is being addressed in Afghanistan. How can one rely on a strategy that gives free licence to the US and NATO forces to chase the Taliban and go in for the complete kill on the Afghan side of the border, while leaving the, ever doubtful and reluctant, Pakistan army to deal with the Taliban, on the other side? The Taliban, resting in the Pak controlled side of the Durand Line, needs to be dealt with an iron hand, to make any sense of the war against terror.

A large section of the security forces, in informal discussions, candidly hold the flawed and haggard military strategies employed by the US and NATO, responsible for the inevitable failure of the international military in Afghanistan. It is well-known, how a British General lost his job, in 2009, when his personal e-mail leaked such cynicism to the international media. The overall US strategy has been to reverse the momentum of the Taliban, to deny them control over the populated areas, scotch their capabilities, and at the same time build up the Afghan security forces. The operational strategy of 'clear, hold and build' flows out from this core strategy. This implies that the IASF would clear a village infested with Taliban, hold it for a while, and then build their presence before moving to the next village. The operational strategy, however, has simply not been working, especially, in southern Afghanistan. The irony is that the Taliban uses the reverse strategy of 'build, hold and clear' and get away with their nefarious designs. They come in large numbers, build a strong base within a village, hold it for a while and strike to clear the forces from nearby villages. It has given major success to the Taliban, who are getting stronger by the day, while the military strategy of the ISAF seems to be floundering.

The capture of Marja district by the Taliban, in the restive southern province of Helmand, can be seen as a burning example. It has become a tug of war between the resurgent Taliban and the ISAF. Despite all attempts, the forces have not been able to capture this strategic district permanently. Interestingly, the power and control of various districts like Marja, change after sunset in Afghanistan. According to increasing reports by local media, more than hundred such districts are controlled by the Taliban, after nightfall.

Even without being an expert on military matters, what can be surmised is that a combination of all the above reasons may have attributed to the disastrous failure of the US and Western military in bringing peace and stability in Afghanistan.

General Stanley A. McChrystal of the US army raised serious questions with regard to the military strategy adopted by the

US in Afghanistan. He went to the extent of questioning the US leadership over their overall Afghanistan strategy. His comment may have brought embarrassment to the White House but there is a considerable section within the US and NATO forces that subscribe to his philosophy. The courage of the general in acknowledging the ground reality, at the cost of losing his highly prized military job, is quite admirable. He will certainly go down in the history of Afghanistan, as someone who was able to call a spade a spade. In fact, he is already quite a hero among the intellectual class of the country.

At the time of writing this book, General David Petraeus landed in Kandahar, to take charge of the ISAF forces, and to galvanise them to fight the 'Taliban Spring Offence'. This is a common expression denoting frenzied Taliban activities that begin in spring, after lying dormant through inclement winters. General Petraeus is attributed with moderate success in bringing stability in Iraq by the US military forces, during their active years of stay in Iraq. Let us hope that he does a better job in Afghanistan. Let us hope that he is able to reverse the fortunes of the war and save the US strategy from crumbling.

Recently, 90,000 classified reports have been leaked by the whistle blower website, WikiLeaks, based in Sweden. The WikiLeaks reports depict the complicity of ISI role in fomenting Taliban insurgency, in various parts of Afghanistan. It was a foregone conclusion and the Afghan intelligence was well aware of this. The same gets reconfirmed when Waheed Omar, the presidential spokesperson says on record that they had briefed the White House about the heavy handedness of ISI, in aiding and abetting Taliban insurgency in Afghanistan, time and again. But, the Afghanistan-Pakistan policy drivers of the White House had turned a deaf ear, every time.

Historically, Pakistan has supported the Taliban through all possible ways and means. This has given them the necessary strategic depth as well as advantage in Afghanistan. It has enabled them to keep the popular Northern Alliance, seen much as anti-Pakistan alliance, out of power in Kabul. Pakistan would always dither from taking a tough call against Taliban, as that would strategically marginalise them in Afghanistan. It is a secret known to all. Such a briefing was given to me, precisely a fortnight after landing in Kabul, way back in 2005, by none other than my cook, an ethnic Hazara. In subsequent years, analysis along these stated lines, have been shared by umpteen people from various walks of life across all regions. The WikiLeaks exposure has set the stage for more clamour and uproar. One also has to analyse and weigh the strategic option and choices staring at the Obama administration. The US cannot even dream of a stable and secured Afghanistan by isolating Pakistan. They are aware that the actual source of the present day crisis in Afghanistan boils down to Pakistan. Hence, it also has to be part of the solution.

Incidentally, the current logistic supply for the US military comes through Pakistan. The US is heavily dependent on Pakistan for both military and strategic reasons. In case US military severs its ties with Pakistan, the breakaway countries of erstwhile USSR, still heavily under the Russian influence, will not be very accommodating in entertaining any request of logistic bases for the US. Pakistan is not only in a position of strategic advantage due to the proximity of the ISI with the Taliban but also because of its geographical location. The US will keep its dialogue open with Pakistan and engage them, even if the ISI continues to play the spoil sport in Afghanistan. The US policy think tank believes that Pakistan has to be persuaded to be on the right side of the war, with lucrative incentives, like billions of dollars in civilian and military aid, and sharing of latest range of military machines. The mighty US is as vulnerable in Afghanistan, as India is in Kashmir. Whether they like it or not, they have to engage Pakistan. It is no wonder then that US has to turn a blind eye to the misadventure of the ISI in Afghanistan.

The political leadership of Pakistan has little or no control over the high handedness of its army establishment particularly the ISI, on matters concerning India and Afghanistan. The US strategy of making Pakistan a key ally, in the war against terror, may sound cynical but stands politically pragmatic. The murky designs of the ISI in Afghanistan are conveniently ignored by the US, by citing 'the rogue element theory' within the ISI and the Pakistan army. Time and again, the Pentagon has explained that there are certain elements within the Pakistan army and ISI, who owe their allegiance to the Taliban and al-Qaeda. This is more of a face saving explanation for the US, under their Afghanistan-Pakistan policy, to contain the burgeoning pressure of the domestic populace and super effusive American media.

Dwelling on the proposed peace process, the Afghans have learnt an inescapable lesson; that peace, security and prosperity cannot be achieved through war and bloodshed. The ongoing insurgency operation is not going to build a better Afghanistan. Engaging with the moderate Taliban looks like a more rational and pragmatic approach, which can usher in, just and durable peace in the country. The 'moderate Taliban' refers to those, who are ready to denounce violence and terrorism and willing to join the mainstream development and political process. The government of Afghanistan is even contemplating the concept of *afwa* (meaning forgiveness or political amnesty) for the moderate Taliban. The patch-up-terms would include the Taliban laying down their weapon on the terms of Afghan government and abiding by the constitution. It is imperative that President Karzai accommodates some key Taliban leaders in the power structures, to make the peace process work and last, in the interest of Afghanistan. The international policy experts anticipate that the proposed peace process would, eventually, result in a structured power sharing deal between the moderate Taliban and the incumbent government in Afghanistan. A few keys leaders would also be accommodated in the power corridors of Kabul.

A wide range of domestic as well as international concerns are emanating from this aspect of the proposed peace process. The Taliban are notoriously known for curbing and violating women rights. The women right activists are, therefore, expressing their concerns and fears of their constitutional and other rights being eroded, by any such peace deal. They fear they will lose the ground they have gained, over a period of time, and eventually pay a bitter price for peace. A strong political contingent, under the influence of the Northern Alliance, has vociferously expressed their reservation against a power sharing deal with the Taliban.

Peace should be given a chance to prevail in Afghanistan, allaying all such presumptuous fears and concerns. This is the time for some path-breaking and defining steps. It is now or never, the so called 'end game' in military parlance. The international community should not squander the possibility of contributing to the peace process, through a political process in Afghanistan. Also, most of the peace building processes in conflict-ridden countries, fail, as they put up rigid pre-conditions for such dialogue. The State should adopt a flexible and constructive approach to initiate the process of dialogue and place no condition that would even remotely foil negotiation for building sustainable peace. The international strategic contingent is hopeful that the proposed peace process will be able to create a division between the Afghan and the foreign Taliban, which is bound to make the latter weak. This can seriously degrade and reduce the capabilities of the Taliban and set to make the State stronger; extend and expand its authority to safe sanctuaries, located in southern and eastern Afghanistan.

The path to peace is certainly going to be very tumultuous for Afghanistan. There is no homogenous opinion about the proposed peace process, within the international community, either. They are divided among themselves with multiplicity of views and opinions about the proposed peace process. It is again, intrinsically, linked with a diverse set of strategic interests among the neighbouring countries. Each of these countries will make wholehearted effort to influence the Afghan peace process with their larger strategic interests in mind. Navigating a peace process through the complex mire of larger international interests would certainly be a herculean task. One broad consensus that has been arrived at, already, is to engage the moderate Taliban, who is willing to abjure violence and embrace democracy and the Afghan constitution.

Friends in the South Block of the Indian External Affairs Ministry, New Delhi, would brush aside this suggestion saying that there is nothing called a 'moderate' Taliban. According to the Indian Minister of External Affairs, S M Krishna, terrorism cannot be compartmentalised. It is very difficult for India to make a distinction between a 'moderate' and a 'radical' Taliban.[2] It is precisely this stand, taken by the Indian Foreign Ministry in the London Conference (January 2010) that isolated them from the international donor community. The entire Indian Foreign Ministry contingent that went to participate in the Kabul Conference (20 July 2010), was seen by most of political experts as an extension of the London Conference. Much to one's surprise, the stance and approach of the Foreign Ministry did not change much, as they still believed that terrorism could not be categorised. They vociferously opposed any move of the Afghan government to engage with the moderate Taliban, towards buying peace in Afghanistan. Needless to say, they again ended with a thin majority, in a repeat spectacle of the London Conference.

Even if India does not see it, there is a distinction within the Taliban viz radical Taliban and moderate Taliban. The example of the Indian engineer, who was released by the Taliban after months in captivity, will help to explain it more explicitly. It was horrifying to read his tale and it was even more amazing how he managed to win his release, by convincing the Taliban that his actions were not meant to undermine them. The Taliban would not have released a large number of Westerners, after kidnapping them, in the past. In some cases the tacit supply of the green pack may have done the job but it obviously did not influence all the cases. The radical Taliban would not have spared a moment in killing their strategic targets.

During my first visit to Kandahar there was a slight apprehension regarding the additional risk one could attract as an Indian, in the mainland of Taliban. Kandahar is also referred to as the cultural and spiritual laboratory of Taliban—an image created and reinforced by the effusive Indian electronic media. It was naturally believed that more than any other nationals, Indians remained a strategic target of the Taliban in Kandahar. In an informal chat, with one of the security guards stationed in Kandahar Airport, well conversant in Urdu, this longstanding notion about the Taliban underwent a sea change.

He categorised Taliban as 'Afghan-Taliban' and the 'Pak-Taliban'. This was much before Tehrik-i-Taliban, the Pakistan faction, became active in the domain of terrorism and insurgency.

The guard said that there was no risk for Indians from the Afghan-Taliban, but there was an enormous risk from the Pak-Taliban, as they complied with the ISI operation directives for Afghanistan. Brigadier General Jonathan Vance, commander of task force, Kandahar says, every year, thousands of foreign militants enter Afghanistan to join the insurgency (8 July 2010, *Outlook*). It suddenly struck that the Indian media could have, perhaps, been referring to the Pak-Taliban and not the Afghan-Taliban. It was quite evident, as time went by that this was an established fact in urban Kandahar, and most of my Kandhari friends were aware about these intrinsic realities.

The Taliban has been, further, categorised as moderate and radical by various countries, owing to their own political and strategic analysis. The Haqqani network is considered a notoriously radical faction by India. They are infamous in India as they regularly target Indian establishments and interests in Afghanistan. The Indian Embassy remains their hot spot and favourite locale in Kabul. But the same Haqqani network was being viewed, by a few Western countries, as a moderate faction of the Taliban. However, after the weeklong attack of the US Embassy in Kabul (starting from 13 September 2011), that perception changed considerably. The US took a considerable period of time to budge and recognise the Indian request for listing the Haqqani network in the list of international terrorist organisations. The peace process is legitimised, often, by citing examples of factions, like the Haqqani, who are ready to denounce violence should they be accommodated in the political structure of Afghanistan under the peace process. It is reported that an olive branch has already been offered to them through ISI operatives. It needs to be mentioned here that the Haqqani network remains the blue eyed boy of the ISI, and the network receives consistent mentoring, guidance and active support from them. The survival of this faction depends largely on their continual targeting of Indian interests and establishments in Afghanistan. The recent attack on US embassy in Kabul, by the network suggests that they can go to any length to serve the ISI policy of duplicity and deceit; by pretending to be an US ally in the war against terror and simultaneously promoting violent extremism in Afghanistan.

Maulvi Mutwakil is largely considered a moderate, suave face of the new Taliban. It is reported, however, that the same Maulvi, had ensured safe passage to the terrorists, during the hijack of the Indian Airlines flight, in his own vehicle, from Kandahar to Pakistan.

India may see all Taliban as one and the same, but there are divisions and factions within their rank and file. The local populace can enlighten the international strategic experts on this. It is a foregone conclusion and while staying in Afghanistan one can easily make out these factions. The character and approach of these factions of Taliban is influenced by geographical boundaries, size of their followers, proximity with ISI, and their penchant towards radicalisation of Islam. Various Taliban factions may be unified in their dissent, but the degree of dissent varies around the above stated lines. Any opportunity to engage the moderate Taliban in the folds of peace and integration should not be lost. This will, predictably, create a divide within the Taliban, and make them weaker—if only, it is pursued in the right spirit and a greater political will.

For the betterment of Afghanistan the peace process has to move ahead, at any cost. But, as mentioned earlier, the peace process has not only to cross domestic hurdles but also strategic obstacles of the international community—especially, the neighbouring countries—as they would attempt to influence the peace process, suiting their long-term strategic goals and interests in Afghanistan.

Russia and its breakaway countries, from the erstwhile Soviet Union, have an inherent resistance towards engaging with the moderate Taliban. Their resistance stems from the fact that bulk of the Taliban, with their ex-Mujahideen credentials, is anti-Russian. Even though seriously uncomfortable with the idea of power sharing with them, they are not intending to impede the peace process launched under the aegis of the US. Having already ruffled the feathers of the US over the clandestine nuclear programme in Iran, Russia and company want to keep their Afghan cards close to their chest, and play according to the evolving situation.

Iran also has a major strategic stake in Afghanistan, and desperately wants to be part of the peace process. Iran enjoys very close socio-cultural ties with Afghanistan, Persian being the common language spoken in both the countries. It also enjoys a greater degree of acceptance and goodwill than Pakistan, among the masses—a large number of migrant workers from Afghanistan being employed in Iran. The existing bonhomie, coupled with their historic ties, make them natural allies. Over the years, Iran has managed to groom some key Afghan leaders, within local political circles, to pursue their strategic interest in the country. Gulbuddin Hekmatyar is largely seen as one of Iran's protégés. Even though he has been pushed to the sidelines by the present government, he is expected to make a strong comeback. He is also known for switching loyalty and changing camps. Apparently, ISI is attempting to woo him, to secure their strategic grip on Afghanistan. Of late, Iran has also built up a decent rapport, directly, with the president's office in Kabul. The issue of backdoor funding, by Iran to the president's office was also highlighted by the international media.

Iran is, however, currently not in a position to directly drive the peace process in Afghanistan. Having ruffled the US and the West over its clandestine nuclear programme, it stands completely isolated in contemporary international politics without a strategic bearing to influence matters concerning Afghanistan. It is therefore, pinning all its hope on its political protégés, in the power corridors of Kabul, to advance its strategic interests. A promising trade tie with Afghanistan is one of them. With the UN imposing sanctions over its clandestine nuclear programme, Iran is desperately looking for ways and means to bolster its dwindling economy. The newly constructed Zerang-Delaram road project, which is India's plan to provide Afghanistan a shorter route to the sea via the Iranian port of Chabar, is likely to emerge as the game changer for Iran, and unlock potential to promote new trade and commerce between Afghanistan and Iran. The strategic importance of this route was to make Afghanistan's current access to the sea coast, through Pakistan, meaningless and irrelevant. This would create a big dent in the Pak economy, which is dependent on Afghanistan, to an extent. A considerable pie of Pakistan's gross domestic product comes from their export of consumption durables, right from match-boxes to medicines, to Afghanistan.

The highway constructed by the government of India, is for reasons more than bonhomie, for certain. Pakistan had anticipated the looming economic threat it posed in advance, and been desperately trying to derail the project, from the time of its inception. The ISI did everything in collusion with the Taliban to bring it to a standstill. But, the political grit and the determination of the Indian government ensured that the highway project was completed within its scheduled time frame even at the cost of losing several staff and workers in the process. Currently a huge contingent of the Taliban is employed to inconvinence and halt the traffic, in the newly constructed highway.[3]

Iran is eyeing this road as their lifeline, which will eventually provide the much required fillip to its sliding economy through increased trade with Afghanistan. It hosted a special conference in October 2010, and deliberated on the future of Afghanistan. This late kick-in of bonhomie has little to do with the peace process, as such. It is a desperate bid to get into the 'super concerned friends club of Afghanistan,' essentially to win sympathisers in the power circle of Kabul, beyond their existing political protégé. Iran knows that they are walking on a tight rope and Afghanistan provides them with a semblance of hope to reverse their misery. With the peace process on, it is action time for Iran.

China, another regional super power, has not yet expressed any overt strategic interest but is certainly eyeing the vast unexplored, and highly lucrative mineral reserves in Afghanistan. These reserves are, conservatively, estimated to be worth USD 3 trillion. It is naïve to expect China, which badly needs resources to sustain its growing economy, to be a mute spectator in this great peace game. By acquiring copper mines worth USD 2.87 billion, China has in fact laid its road map for future in Afghanistan.[4] But, its best chance lies in strengthening Pakistan to deal with Afghanistan. China knows that they have the perfect strategic partner in Pakistan to promote and advance their economic interests in Afghanistan. If Pakistan wins, so does China. It has, therefore, preferred to play a covert waiting game, patiently working in the backdrop. It is, indirectly, strengthening Pakistan and enabling it to muscle in the peace process, which will ultimately work in China's favour.

India and Pakistan, too, have large strategic stakes in Afghanistan and they are going to influence the peace process, according to their long-term strategic goals. India in particular has vociferously expressed its fear and strategic concerns about the ongoing peace process. It fears that, in the name of engaging with moderate Taliban, the pro-Pakistan Taliban hardliner would be accommodated in the power corridors of Kabul. This would provide them the political leeway to advance the Pakistan agenda, and edge India out from thick of things in Afghanistan. Their concern is genuine and based on past experiences of how the Taliban used to be operated from the ISI headquarters, based in Islamabad. India is, therefore, seriously uncomfortable with any engagement with the moderate Taliban, let alone their political accommodation in the power structure of Afghanistan. Pakistan, on the other hand, will go to any length to justify that the peace process will not last, unless and until, the incumbent government of Afghanistan accommodates key moderate Taliban leaders in the power structure of Kabul. In the garb of peace process, Pakistan would fix up the pro-Pakistan Taliban leaders in the power structure of Kabul. There seems to be a palpable consensus developing within the international community on this, which is not official though.

India, however, has to come up with a more pragmatic approach to deal with the current peace process. It has to realise that the mandate of engaging with moderate Taliban was given to the government of Afghanistan, both by the parliament as well as the peace *jirga* (traditional association of elders). This popular perception, emanating from democratic structures, cannot be suppressed and undermined in Afghanistan today. Before the rigid stand, taken by Indian policy contingent on Afghanistan, isolates them within the international donor club, it is high time South Block reviews its policy and takes a more realistic approach.

Historically, India has suffered due to lack of a strategic and visionary policy for effectively engaging with Afghanistan. A large number of Afghan policy experts, within India, have flayed the Indian approach in Afghanistan. *The March of Follies* by the former Indian ambassador for Afghanistan, Jagat S Mehta, an IFS officer of international repute, in fact, clearly points out many a policy blunder committed by neighbouring countries on matters concerning Afghanistan.

Pakistan and India have locked horns, for gaining more strategic depth in Afghanistan. In a way, Pakistan is fighting a proxy war with India for greater influence and authority in Afghanistan. It wants to render India toothless, on policy matters. India was kept out of the conference in Sochi, Russia (18 August 2010), at the insistence of Pakistan. The said conference was attended by Pakistan, Tajikistan, Russia and Afghanistan. Iran hosted another regional meeting on Afghanistan, but without India. Turkey organised the second round of economic conference on Afghanistan, in September 2010 as an objective follow up to the January 2010 conference. India was kept out of this conference, as well. After realising the growing power of India, it has planned to bring it in, for the forthcoming conference. This is more of a token of goodwill and a diplomatic gesture, rather than a wholehearted attempt to engage India on matters concerning Afghanistan. India is clear that while the world may persuade Pakistan to stay away from terrorism, they will equally submit to Pakistan's 'no India access' conditions, on regional consultation of policy matters related to Afghanistan. Pakistan will continue with their dual strategy; ally with the war against terror, at the same time allow ISI in aiding and abetting Taliban insurgency. This provides them with the required strategic depth, and makes them an almost inseparable player, on any matters concerning Afghanistan.

Meanwhile, India has employed a development kitty of almost USD 1.6 billion, a huge grant even by international standards.

India is the largest civilian donor in Afghanistan, after US and Japan. In addition to the existing historic and cultural ties, India's development forays in Afghanistan have generated tremendous popular and political goodwill (for India), in the country. In fact, India, Germany and Japan are the three most popular countries, in Afghanistan, according to people's choice. India has, further, set up four consulates, in the cities of Jalalabad, Kandahar, Herat and Mazar-e-Sharif. This has given them the strategic leeway, to ensure its long-term strategic policy interest around Afghanistan is very much intact, much to the dismay of Pakistan. India will use its newly developed political goodwill, to block Pakistan from milking the peace process initiated by the Afghan government.

Pakistan fears that with the growing popularity and influence of India in Afghanistan, India will play the Baluchistan card better, much to their discomfort. Perhaps, it needs to be mentioned here that Baluchistan is witnessing a political unrest and upsurge in terrorist activities and has aspirations to have a separate country for the Balouchs, with greater autonomy and identity. Pakistan blames India for fanning the Baluchistan unrest and this hidden passion of the local leaders. However, as of today, Pakistan has failed to provide even a shred of evidence to this end. The said statement was issued by External Affairs Minister S M Krishna in presence of his Pakistan counterpart, in a media briefing, after the much hyped Indo-Pak talks failed on 15 July 2010, at Islamabad. Additionally, the Indian presence and influence in Afghanistan will effectively seal the infamous breeding ground of terrorists for ISI and render Pakistan toothless. This would strategically marginalise the ISI vis-à-vis the Pak Army. This would, further, dent their Kashmir prospects, as they would be rendered powerless to produce, the so called *jihadis* (freedom fighters) for Kashmir struggle.

But, let it not be forgotten that Pakistan has a strategic asset in the disgruntled Taliban. They can be used against India, and Pakistan will leave no stones unturned to that end. A stable and neutral Afghanistan is largely in Indian interest, as it is for other countries. India has already invested too much to back off from Afghanistan, at this juncture, and should use every possible means to safeguard its interests. It should not compromise on this issue. The lesson that needs to be learnt fast is that the best way to get there is to be in collusion with the Western countries and not by standing against them as India would achieve nothing by going against the international mainstream opinion of engaging with the moderate Taliban.

The US is getting increasingly weary of the ongoing war and desperately wants to give it an administrative end, to deal with the burgeoning domestic pressure, and increasingly disappearing Western allies. The Dutch left with their 1,950 soldiers in July 2010 and the UK and Canada have been following their announcement of leaving Afghanistan, from beginning of 2011. The US has fears that they would end up as minority in Afghanistan and that can subject their military to larger casualty. President Obama would not be very happy dealing with such a situation back home, before putting his candidature for the second term in the White House. The US is desperately looking for an honourable exit. More than the government of Afghanistan, it is the US, which is interested in offering the olive branch to the Taliban. The meeting of General Petraeus with Mullah Abdul Salam Zaeef, the former Taliban ambassador to Pakistan, on 16 August 2010, as reported by the local media, depicts the eagerness of the US, to make an exit from Afghanistan. Pakistan can be a strategic asset of the US in putting the peace process on fast track. It would leave no stones unturned to make the most of the troubled waters.

Pakistan desperately wants the trophy of Afghanistan, as a reward, for allying with the US in the so called 'war against terror'. This would be an arrangement for mutual convenience as the US wants a desperate exit from Afghanistan. But, the US would weigh their strategic choices and options, before deciding the same. As of now, the US would keep Pakistan preoccupied and excited with the prospect of post September 2014 scenario (after complete US exit). They may even decide to give the charge of Afghanistan to Pakistan. The strategy of making the problem a part of the solution has often worked in international politics.

But, should it happen, there are larger ramifications for India. Getting the trophy of Afghanistan would enable Pakistan to fix up the Haqqani and the other factions in the power corridors of Kabul and use these elements against India. The Haqqani network of Taliban, led by Mawlawi Jalaluddin Haqqani, has been a constant rabble-rouser against India. The Haqqanis have made massive forays into the eastern provinces of Paktia, Paktika, Khowst, Logar Ghazni and have a strong force of about 3,000-5,000 heavily armed fighters. Should they find a political space in the power corridors of Kabul, India has every reason to worry.

At this juncture, the balance is evenly poised. However, there is a distinct possibility that Pakistan may run away with their module of peace process in Afghanistan. Should it happen, it would be considered a strategic victory of Pakistan and diplomatic defeat of India.

Apart from the international concerns, there are some serious domestic concerns that can derail the Afghan peace process. At the centre of this is the, once strong, Northern Alliance. Once led by the late 'Lion of Panjsher', Ahmad Shah Massoud, the alliance is in a state of chaos. Their continual marginalisation by the incumbent government has made it nothing more than a defunct loose network today. It does not have the political teeth and vigour to alarm the incumbent government. The sacking of Amrullah Saleh, a Mujahideen protégé of Ahmad Shah Masooud, by Hamid Karzai is seen as another effort to further marginalise the Alliance. It is also reported that his firing was done at the behest of the US, to pacify the Pak Army, for lending their support to the war against terror. Amrullah Saleh was known for dealing with the Taliban with an iron hand.

The frustration of Northern Alliance also comes from the inability of Abdullah Abdullah to win the much controversial presidential election in 2009. Actually, after Ahmad Shah Massoud, there has been a leadership crisis within the Northern Alliance, which is struggling to get a leader with a mass base. Currently, a shadow of its proud past and glory, Northern Alliance is seriously unhappy with the incumbent government and more with their idea of engaging with the moderate Taliban. They have always viewed the Taliban as their main enemy, in Afghanistan. They have expressed their agony and anger against any political accommodation of the moderate Taliban, in the power structure of Afghanistan. They are desperate to rediscover their lost political glory and waning popularity. The present government may end up giving the perfect impetus to the Northern Alliance, to reorganise by accommodating the moderate Taliban, under a power sharing deal to buy peace. It will not be surprising if the Alliance reverts to their traditional approach of fighting the Taliban to their last breath in advent of any such developments. This may, further, aid instability in Afghanistan.

Should Russia and Iran find the post peace political set up in Afghanistan uncomfortable to deal with, they may resort to strengthening the Northern Alliance. They will also make an effort to persuade few other neighbouring countries, including India, to join the bandwagon. This would serve as a perfect platform for the Northern Alliance to make a comeback and regain its lost political stature. In fact, this is one of the biggest fears of Pakistan. Any political elevation of Northern Alliance may seriously jeopardise Pakistan's interest in Afghanistan. Historically, the Alliance has vehemently opposed Pakistan and in particular their Afghan agenda. Hence, Pakistan would always employ their time tested, dividend yielding strategy of supporting the Taliban, to the last. This not only gives them more strategic depth but also blocks Northern Alliance from gaining any prominence and political stature in Afghanistan.

The proposed peace process in Afghanistan has to cross many hurdles. The first, of course, is Pakistan, as it not only wants to dominate the peace process but also lead the same, for reason better explained in the previous section of this chapter. The common people of Afghanistan hold Pakistan responsible for their present day misery. Each and every problem of Afghanistan begins and ends with Pakistan. The irony is that Pakistan thinks the same about Afghanistan. They squarely blame Afghanistan for the spread of Tehrik-i-Taliban. The pressure applied by the US on both Pakistan and Afghanistan is resulting in token efforts to mend fences. The recently issued statement by President Hamid Karzai, in one of his tours to Pakistan, that India is a friend and Pakistan is a brother, can be seen in this light. It raised quite a few eyebrows in the South Block, New Delhi. The newly discovered bonhomie however, faded away like a passing cloud, when the National Security Advisor of Afghanistan, Rangin Dadfar Spanta, in a hard hitting article in the *Washington Post*, published in the third week of August 2010, squarely blamed Pakistan for fanning terrorism in Afghanistan. He went to the extent of blaming Pakistan for the recent upsurge in terrorist activities. The common Afghan thinks that their relation with Pakistan is beyond repair.

Pakistan has lost the authority and influence it enjoyed over Afghanistan in the past. Various factions of Taliban are the only strategic assets, at the disposal of Pakistan, to re-exert their authority and command. Pakistan would try to churn out most from the peace process, by employing their strategic assets left in the Taliban.

In a daring act, crossing the US established authority on peace, Pakistan had arrested Mullah Baradar and some other top Taliban leaders, in August 2010, as reported by the *New York Times.* This was primarily to shut down the clandestine peace process initiated by the government of Afghanistan with these Taliban leaders. Though the Pakistan government has officially denied the arrest, but the same is an open truth with its military establishment. The Pakistani security officials were quoted, brazenly saying, 'We have picked up these leaders as they were trying to work out a peace deal with the government of Afghanistan without the involvement of Pakistan'. It is suspected that the clandestine peace dialogue between Mullah Baradar and Afghan government had the tacit backing of the US and UK. Learning about the peace overtures, the Pakistan army was unnerved, as it would have reduced their influence and strategic relevance by volumes. This alarm led to the arrest of the top Taliban leaders. By arresting Mullah Baradar and company, the Pak Army sent one more signal to all factions of Taliban leaders, against any freelance peace deal without the knowledge and control of the ISI. The latest disclosures, coming after the WikiLeaks exposé, that painted Pakistan as a patron of terrorism, were accompanied by a scathing op-ed by Afghanistan's National Security Advisor, Rangin Dadfar Spanta, where he virtually called

Pakistan the saboteur of peace in Afghanistan. Though honest, the vitriolic article has damaged the fragile Afghanistan-Pakistan relationship. It has, further, vitiated the milieu of the peace process. Pakistan is bound to hit back and put a spanner in the peace process, if they are unable to lead the same.

Before the nascent peace process is irreversibly damaged, the US, India and the rest of the world should ensure that it is brokered by the State of Afghanistan, and not Pakistan, or in other words, the ISI. The peace process has to be led and owned by the Afghan government. In a rare assertion of authority, President Hamid Karzai, has proposed a high powered peace council, comprising all segments of the Afghan society, to take forward the peace process.[5] The effort of the president, to bring in nine women representatives in the said committee, needs to be appreciated, as the said arrangement will ensure that the interest and aspiration of women will not be compromised in the proposed peace process.

In pursuit for peace, Afghanistan has to tread cautiously, amid the diverse range of strategic interests of the international community, and its immediate neighbours. Accepting suggestions, only to the extent that influence the peace process, in a positive meaningful way is fine but it should not impinge upon the peace process. It is for the incumbent government now, to resist submission to the larger strategic interests of its neighbours, and other international allies that do not, in any way, benefit this war-torn nation and its worn out people, who are eagerly waiting for some peace, stability and prosperity in their lives.

Writing this chapter, in the rapidly changing context of Afghanistan, was a herculean task. General Petraeus was pulled out of Afghanistan on 28 July 2011 and made the chief of CIA. Apropos to the initial apprehension, General Petraeus has left a much weaker Afghanistan. He hardly made any difference in the context, after taking the reins of Afghanistan, in June 2010.

The diplomatic row between the US and the Pakistan government has entered its lowest ebb, triggered by the arrest of Raymond Davis, on 27 January 2011, and continues to slide further. Mike Mullen, virtually, accused Pakistan with fanning terrorism, in the third week of April 2011, a charge later compounded by the WikiLeaks cables, showing Washington's profound distrust of Islamabad.

The government of Pakistan, flanked by its military chiefs has made an audacious pitch to the beleaguered president of Afghanistan to ditch US and switch sides with China. The development, first reported by the *Wall Street Journal*, has stunned Washington. This is at a time, when US appears confused and vulnerable on the geopolitical and domestic fronts, with big personnel changes in the Obama administration, struggling economy and the president seeking re-election. Even though, the president of Afghanistan will be non committal to any such geo-political advancement, such developments will have a massive effect on the ongoing peace process.

The most recent discovery and elimination of al-Qaeda chief Osama-bin-Laden, in Abottabad, by the special US Navy SEALS, in a clinical operation, only depicts the lethal nexus of the ISI with the terror outfits, spelling havoc in Afghanistan. This has irreversibly damaged the Pak-US relationship. Pakistan is slowly slipping from the grip of US. The recent attack of US embassy in Kabul by the ISI backed Haqqani network, followed by the explicit accusation of the outgoing American Chairman of the Joint Chiefs of Staffs, that Pakistan's ISI was behind the audacious attack only depict the inability of US to contain Pakistan, anymore.

Things are so bad that the *New York Times*, which is essentially the voice of the US establishment and therefore generally supportive of Pakistan, has seen it fit to thunder in an editorial titled 'The Latest Ugly Truth about Pakistan', that something, must be done. They stopped short of specifying what 'that something' might be. An uncontrollable Pakistan will only move things from bad to worse in Afghanistan.

The murder of the ex-president and peace council chair, Burhanuddin Rabbani by a Taliban peace messenger, through his turban bomb, on 20 September 2011, has brought the tumultuous peace process to a grinding halt. As mentioned, the peace process will have to clear a series of hurdles, Pakistan being the first and foremost.

---

1. William Dalrymple, "Souter takes the Call," *Outlook*, 30 August 2010.
2. Statement made at Kabul conference, www.mfa.gov.af, 20 July 2010.
3. Taliban Press Release. 15 January 2011.
4. Three Chinese firms to develop Afghan copper mines, www.china.org.ca, 23 November 2007, Zhang Ming'ai.
5. Karzai set up bodies for peace talks, English Aljazeera.net, 28 September 2010.

The Illicit Poppy Economy

'It is better to grow poppy than apples in Afghanistan.'
—an orchard farmer from Badakashan province

Opium-profits fuel insurgency, but so does destroying poppy crops of the farmers. Why did the billion dollar poppy eradication strategy fall apart in Afghanistan?

Any deliberation on Afghanistan will be incomplete if the poppy driven illicit economy is not dwelt upon and analysed. Poppy is integral to politics, economy and the present turmoil of this war-torn nation. It accounts for one third of the country's Gross Domestic Product, as per UN, and fuels the engine of insurgency with the Taliban, reportedly making USD 70-100 million every year out of poppy. The lure of easy and lucrative bucks, which revolves around this crop, corrupts both the government apparatus and the law-makers. International policy experts on Afghanistan believe that poppy is the root cause of majority of the problems associated with the country. Poppy can be seen as the 'axis of all evil' in Afghanistan.

The history of poppy goes back to pre-Soviet occupation times. Before 1979, poppy was produced in limited scale in Afghanistan. After the Soviet invasion, the civil war deteriorated the political environment in the country and created a structural vacuum. As the Afghan government began to lose control of their provinces, from 1979 onwards, the warlords and the regional commanders started looking for ways and means to generate cash for mobilising the Mujahideen (Afghan resistance against Soviet occupation) and to finance war logistics, including purchase of arms and ammunition. They resorted to poppy, as they found that it can fund their war against Soviet occupation quite easily. Poppy cultivation received a major fillip during that period. In this war, the Mujahideen had a tacit supporter in the US. The intelligence wing of Pakistan Army, ISI, heavily under the influence of CIA, was overtly backing the Mujahideen in their war against Soviet occupation. The American strategy was to indirectly support the Mujahideen, to cripple Soviet might and slowly force a withdrawal through attrition rather than affect a quick and decisive overthrow. Poppy became a dominant praxis in the midst of this intricate power play in Afghanistan.

A power vacuum was created when the Soviet Army was forced to withdraw in 1989. Amid the pervasive environment of lawlessness two things grew steadily—struggle for power and poppy. Various factions of the Mujahideen were jostling for power and political space. In absence of the State and their urge for more power, they resorted to increase poppy cultivation to finance their military existence, for protecting their existing bastions, as well as for capturing new territories. The regional commanders also relied on poppy money to build their regional armies, in their bid to overthrow Central regimes, and to ride their larger political desires. Successive regimes, thereafter, used poppy, as a tool, to generate revenues for financing their political ambitions. Prolonged absence of any legitimate and strong federal government at Kabul created a political vacuum and perpetuated the illicit nexus of power, politics and poppy. It further provided a fecund ground for enhanced poppy cultivation in Afghanistan.

The Taliban had no different a design. The diabolic intentions of the Taliban found a perfect solution in poppy. They started looking towards poppy to consolidate their position and finance their obnoxious design for Afghanistan. Initially, the Taliban had employed poppy, as a tool, to mobilise farmers, in their bid to legitimise their illegitimate occupation of the nation. Poppy production shot up to a record high of 4,500 metric ton during the period of the Taliban in the year 1999. However, during their last year of power in 2001, the same Taliban enforced a poppy purging mission for strategic reasons.

Opium was not a crop of choice for most Afghan farmers. However, they were not in a position to resist growing it either. Like other countries, the farmers of Afghanistan, too, look for a lucrative return from their meagre land holdings, to reverse their economic misery. It is natural for them to lean towards any crop that holds promises of better economic returns.

Agriculture, in conjunction with livestock, remains the mainstay of rural economy in Afghanistan. The agriculture sector is mainly snow and rain fed and plagued with a plethora of problems. The farm sector of Afghanistan remains largely unorganised. The farmers have to consistently grapple with poor agriculture infrastructures and lack of marketing facilities to enhance agricultural production vis-à-vis their income.

Continual fragmentation of arable land, due to rapid and steep population growth, has caused stagnation in agriculture production, and generated large scale unemployment and under-employment. Recurrent phases of drought and flash floods have damaged their crops, keeping farmers entrenched in a vicious cycle of poverty—all of which have aggravated their economic misery, over a period of time.

Growing alternative crops amid poor irrigation, storage, transportation, etc is not only less profitable but also very gruelling. While the rich and organised farmers are still able to cope with the situation, to an extent, the poor farmers find no respite. They are subjected to a series of suffering, owing to their 'have-not' background.

Unlike other neighbouring countries Afghanistan does not have a state procurement system in place, which acquires agriculture produce from the farmers directly and pays them Minimum Support Prices (MSP). Such an arrangement not only protects the interest of farmers, but also prohibits the ruthless private sector from exploiting them. The MSP ensures that the private players operate around the remunerative prices set by the State. As a system, it has worked wonders in the neighbouring countries, to protect and advance the interest of farmers, especially, the small and marginal ones. Farmers receive security and confidence from the State that they would get fair prices for their produce. Besides, the said arrangement ensures food security, as the State piles enough reserve food grains to meet any exigency, in advent of any natural calamity, or war situations.

The Ministry of Agriculture Irrigation and Livestock (MAIL), Afghanistan, launched a procurement scheme in 2009, to acquire a strategic reserve of wheat. But, the pilot effort was pitched far below the existing needs of the farmers. Introduced merely to compensate the farmer for their losses during drought in the preceding year, it was more of a 'fire-fighting mission' than a long-term strategy.

In the absence of an institutionalised MSP, the sale of farm produce is purely left to the struggles of the farmers alone. Farmers go through a lot of struggle to sell their farm produce, with the private sector ruthlessly calling the shot and setting the rules of the game. A chain of middle men siphon away a large portion of the profit leaving the farmers short-changed. The farmers not only end up selling their farm produce at a marginal rate but also suffer from irreparable economic losses. The small and marginal farmers bear the major brunt of the problem in the process.

Let us understand the impact of the above, and the precise game played by the private sector through some cases. The apples grown by the farmers in the northern provinces of Afghanistan, for instance, are purchased by the private merchants of Pakistan, from the orchard directly, by paying almost 1/4th of a USD, for every kilogram, during the peak of harvesting season. Since, there are no cold storages and the farmers cannot afford to keep the fruit for a late sale, the private merchants gain from the deal. They send them to cold storages in Peshawar, pumping them back to Afghanistan during April/May only to sell them at a steep price, of almost USD 3 per kilogram—almost twelve times higher than the buying rate.

'How am I, my people and more importantly my country benefitting from growing apples in my orchard when the private sector, and especially, strangers are reaping all the benefit?' Not a tale of sour apples! This genuine concern was aired by an orchard owner in the district of Baharak, in the province of Badakashan, during an informal chat in his orchard.

The merchants of Uzbekistan play the same game with the potato growing farmers of Bamian, popularly known to the outside world as the land of broken Buddha. The potatoes grown in Bamian are among the best varieties in the world. But a disgruntled potato farmer, in one of the roadside farms, once shared his feelings. 'It is better that I grow poppy, at least I will get a decent income.' One could easily make out the extent of his bitterness and resentment with the existing system, from what he said.

More or less, every farm produce in Afghanistan goes through the same cycle, with the farmers being economically exploited. They are the end sufferers. The above segment can very well work as a manual for the global retail food giants on how to source farm produce cheaply from Afghanistan through vendors, to increase their profit margins. If one digresses to the world of beautiful Afghan carpets one will see that it is not just farmers but that the weavers too are suffering alike. This is a non-farm product, which is in as much peril. Tradesmen from Pakistan and Afghanistan utilise the expertise and skill of these master-weavers to produce gorgeous carpets, at paltry rates, only to be transported and sold abroad, where they fetch astronomical profits. One has to write a separate book to highlight the exploitation of the weavers in Afghanistan. A brief case study will not do.

The above cases speak volumes on how farmers suffer from a wide array of problems. This, however, is the tip of the iceberg. Recurrent phases of war and insecurity have irreversibly damaged the confidence of farmers who are steadily losing grip of their livelihood. They want to make most of their meagre holding. They cannot wait any longer! Their ongoing plight, coupled with lack of security, has gradually turned large number of farmers towards poppy cultivation. They naturally assume that poppy will give them money, security and more importantly an opportunity to better their lives. Poppy is estimated to earn approximately eight times more income, per hectare, than wheat, using less water and other resources. There are no other attractive alternatives at present that can give them a return comparable to poppy. For poor farmers, poppy is the only hope to break the poverty cycle, once and forever. Opium is an insurance against hunger. It operates like a spot and future market, with traders providing credit for future production. It also serves as a means of savings and as collateral for instant credit. Opium, as a commodity, can further be a source of liquidity and a means of exchange.[1]

Poppy can be easily smuggled through Herat, Badakashan and Kandahar to the neighbouring countries of China, Pakistan, Iran and Tajikistan en-route to Europe, erstwhile USSR and other regions. Over three quarter of the heroin sold in Europe, and virtually all in Russia originates from Afghanistan. Few corrupt state officials with appropriate political backing are more than accommodating to ensure safe passage. Traditionally, most of the processing used to take place outside Afghanistan. However, with passage of time local drug lords, in search of more profit, have stepped up heroin processing, in key strategic locations within Afghanistan. It is worth mentioning the value chain of poppy here—Poppy is being harvested, made into opium, and later, also, being refined into heroin.

The Taliban ruthlessly exploited the known weakness of the farmers, especially, the marginal farmers. They started fanning the hidden frustration and ambition, cajoling them to break out from the poverty cycle. They provided open and overt political backing to poppy cultivation, often referring to it as a major cash crop of Afghanistan and also legitimised its cultivation in the country, with the premise that their consumers lie in the Western societies. They maintained since poppy is not grown for its own domestic consumption, denizens of Afghanistan are guarded against the ill-effects of the crop. It is a fact that while Afghanistan produces 80 per cent of the world's total poppy production, the opium consumption rate is not very high here, as compared to other countries across the globe.

The pro-Taliban supporters (with ideological leanings to the Taliban) boldly announce that if the Western countries stop buying poppy, Afghanistan would stop growing it. 'The Westerns are purchasing, hence, Afghanistan is growing' is a quote popularly used by the second rung leaders of the Taliban. The consumer countries should get serious about this aspect and curb drug addictions in their countries.

Part of the logic provided by them cannot be simply brushed aside, even if we have to accept the same with a pinch of salt. The problem boils down to a cause and effect equation. However, the established principle of attacking the cause to root out the effect does not work every time. This statement will attract a certain amount of criticism, but experience shows that the reverse has worked pretty well in weeding out complex and deep rooted evils from a society, as well. In case of poppy, it is a matter of personal belief that it can be eliminated from Afghanistan by attacking both the causes and effects, at one go.

In a milieu, where poppy has received State backing through successive regimes—and given the pitiable conditions of the farmers, who are bent upon making the most from their arable land—we should not be shocked to see their penchant for poppy. It is the complexity of the situation and not just the market demand that has fuelled poppy production in Afghanistan. The local drug lords also frequently compel the resisting farmers, of their region, to grow poppy either by their extraordinary persuasive skills or through their gun-toting followers. It is the drug lords who make fortunes from poppy, and not the ordinary farmers. According to conservative estimates, only 20 per cent of the poppy prices in the international markets flow to the famers. Despite the paltry percentage of economic returns, it is still much better than growing cereal crops or even potato.

During the Taliban regime, the drug lords passed on part of their profits to the Taliban which kept on accommodating the drug lords in the power structures against these financial gratifications. This lethal nexus grew to the extent where the line between the Taliban and drug lords started blurring completely. The drug lords were co-opted into the political and power structures and the revenue from poppy kept funding the nefarious designs of the Taliban and their continual misadventure in Afghanistan. The Taliban now threatened to cross beyond Afghanistan. Around this time, the hardcore al-Qaeda militants were desperately looking for ideal and safe sanctuaries to strike against Western interest, and they realised that there could not be a better host than the Taliban, at that juncture. This was not because of the mouth-watering kebabs one gets to find, in every nook and corner of Afghanistan, but more because of ideological moorings and a complicity of their purpose and design. A bulk of the al-Qaeda militants along with its chief was further familiar with the mountainous terrain of this landlocked country. They had fought the Soviet occupation in Afghanistan. The logistic was perfectly set for planning and executing global designs of the deadly Taliban-al-Qaeda nexus.

A certain transformation was silently taking place in the backdrop of this political subterfuge in Afghanistan. The legitimacy of the Taliban was getting established and the farmers were not complaining anymore. The poppy lobby was getting stronger than ever. They eventually started flaunting their political muscle, and took the farmers at their complete command. This catapulted a situation whereby majority of the farmers started growing poppy instead of food crops. The orchards gradually transformed into poppy fields. The arable lands of northern and eastern provinces slowly gave way to poppy fields and it started dominating the lives and the livelihoods of the Afghan community in a big away. This was as it is a big source of revenue for the Taliban, which kept funding their misadventure in Afghanistan like never before. Soon, it started shaping their policies too.

Poppy had once enabled the Taliban to fix their grip and legitimacy in Afghanistan. But soon, poppy was not required to tighten their stronghold, anymore. There was a change in the tactics. The same Taliban, in 2001, vowed to eradicate poppy completely from Afghanistan. It went to the extent of declaring poppy cultivation un-Islamic. After nearly six years of consistent and overt support to poppy cultivation this was an unbelievable volte-face. But, the Taliban proved it to be more than a blank promise by launching an organised campaign. This resulted in one of the most successful campaigns in poppy eradications, which reduced its production by 91 per cent.[2]

The campaign was so effective that the restive province of Helmand, the traditional belt of poppy of Afghanistan, witnessed almost no poppy cultivation, in 2001.[3] Even the UN approves the figures and grades the campaign as one of the most successful ever, in the history of Afghanistan. The Taliban insistence on a complete ban on production alone and not over trade, however, spiked the prices and revalued the old stock lying with the traders by almost ten times. This created massive liquidity at the disposal of the opium traders to induce further incentive for poppy cultivation.[4]

The strategic analysts, however, viewed the move of Taliban as a part of their larger strategy to get into the good books of the Western states so that their nefarious design on global terror remained unnoticed. Few saw this as a part of their effort to bolster their international image and acceptance to earn a seat in the UN. Little did the world know that 9/11 was in the offing!

After the downfall of the Taliban, the international community led by the US decided to eradicate poppy from Afghanistan. The international community felt that it was imperative to root out poppy to make the dream of a new Afghanistan, a reality. Special anti-narcotic forces were constituted and deployed across all provinces to arrest poppy cultivation. The international policy experts opined that eradication of poppy would not only damage the backbone of the powerful drug lords as well as remnants of the Taliban, but also drive the country towards a legitimate economy. This would cut bulk of the traditional sources of funding, for Taliban, to spread unrest and terrorism. Through such a strategy, the Taliban could also be damaged irreversibly and forever. Little did they know that they would end up fuelling poppy production and simultaneously the Taliban, in Afghanistan after nine years of operation!

The United National Organization for Drug and Crime (UNODC) was given an express mandate to track and monitor poppy cultivation vis-à-vis eradication in Afghanistan. A large number of countries pooled their resources in the specially constituted anti-narcotic funds to accelerate the process of poppy eradication. A special anti-narcotic force was created by the government of Afghanistan under the guidance of UK.

A multipronged counter-narcotic strategy was worked out by the policy experts to eradicate poppy completely. The core element of the strategy was:

a) mobilising farmer's opinion against poppy cultivation,
b) providing them with alternative livelihoods skills, and
c) damaging standing poppy crops directly by employing anti-narcotic forces against paltry compensation.

However, with passage of time the proposed strategy started relying heavily on the third component—the use of brute force to destroy standing poppy crops. The other strategies were pushed to the back burner.

This is precisely what happens when you push military beyond their limit. Be it in Afghanistan or elsewhere, one is a little apprehensive about the military foraying into core developmental areas. They are best left for counter insurgency operations, which they are equipped to handle and are accustomed to do. Poppy eradication is a complex and deep rooted development challenge, best left to specialised development professionals.

As a development professional, it is very difficult for anyone to accept the third component of the strategy, as a viable option. How can you use armed forces against your own farmers, for destroying poppy—this, despite the fact that the compensation is also grossly inadequate. Ruthlessly destroying standing poppy is a quick fix approach to a problem that needs protracted attention. The farmers went for poppy because of their existential situation and the overt support of the previous regimes including that of the Taliban. Should they not have been given, at least, a brief recovery time, to shift from poppy to wheat? Would not such a harsh act, of damaging their field, turn the farmers against the State? Overall, did the compensation even remotely match the degree of the actual loss? These were a few questions that rankled the development actors for quite sometime. One has learnt to believe that community awareness and social mobilisation are the most effective strategies in eliminating deep rooted evil. A more patient approach was required to eliminate poppy from both the mind as well as the fields of the farmers. The policy experts should have topped the social mobilisation with an appropriate initial incentive structure for the farmers to make them say 'no' to poppy. Rather than destroying standing crop and providing compensation later, it would have been prudent, to provide proactive incentives before.

Some Western countries provide financial incentives to their farmers to influence certain farming decisions and for economic reasons. Why could Afghanistan not use the same for a noble cause like eradicating poppy? A few international experts ventured in this direction but they failed to cross beyond the distribution of free wheat seeds. One needs to think bigger when one is talking about exterminating a deep rooted and inherent evil, like poppy.

It might also have been a good idea if the anti-narcotics fund was used to provide incentives to the farmers. The usage of anti-narcotic funds in Afghanistan is another area of concern. The fund is largely employed for construction of community infrastructures, like roads, bridges, etc. Without undermining the importance of infrastructure, one fails to understand how the same can eradicate poppy. The fund should have been specially used for the intended purpose. Infrastructure is a different issue, and should not have been seen in conjunction with poppy. If at all, infrastructural projects, like irrigation, or agricultural infrastructure that provide respite to the farmers and allow them to boost their agricultural produce or cut down their farming expenses, should have been implemented.

In Afghanistan, you have to learn to live with your professional differences to do your job well. Alternatively, you tend to get frustrated and slip into the great pessimistic club of Afghanistan, which currently out numbers the optimists.

The forces went from village to village in every district, of each province, in their bid to destroy standing poppy crops. The act of the counter-narcotic force was the predominant talk of the town, with the electronic media going rife with footages of these ruthless actions.

The force experienced stiff resistance from the organised farmers, especially, those belonging to the southern provinces, like Kandahar, Helmand, Uruzgan etc, equipped with latest arms and ammunition. These farmers are well trained, some having donned the cap of a proud Mujahideen during the Soviet times. It was a 'back to basics' ritual for them, retaliating against the State, with all their might. Needless to say, the counter-narcotic forces faced a dismal defeat in a large number of these districts. Many feel the anti-narcotic strategy had serious flaws in its design and was poorly conceived and executed.[5]

They even had to run for cover, especially, in the restive province of Helmand, Uruzgan and Kandahar. Loss of property and life was reported from both sides. However, the biggest sufferers of this state led attack against poppy were the farmer of Afghanistan—especially, small and marginal farmers. Their livelihoods were broken irreversibly by this ill-conceived approach of the anti-narcotic forces. Though an inadequate compensation package was designed for the victim farmers, the benefit hardly reached the farmers due to variety of reasons—the predominant being the presence of some corrupt local government officials.

Opium cultivation area rose to a record high of 193,000 Ha in 2007, only marginally falling to 123,000 Ha in 2009.[6] Nine years on, the anti-narcotic strategy has hardly paid any sound dividends in terms of eradicating poppy. Poppy is still driving the illicit economy in Afghanistan and according to the latest report the drug lords have become stronger than ever. Poppy continues to fund the nefarious designs of the Taliban. The State of Afghanistan, however, achieved moderate success in the stable northern provinces.

The poppy eradication programme can be considered the single most ineffective programme, of American foreign policy in Afghanistan. Late Richard Holbrooke, the administration's coordinator of Afghanistan policy, by his own admission, said that the strategy was ineffective and wasteful. This in fact has proven to be counterproductive as the poppy farmers have turned towards the Taliban, in big numbers, for succour. The Taliban is anyway, contemplating an all out attempt to oust the US and the NATO forces, to respond to the military surge strategy of President Obama. The turnout of poppy farmers, in big numbers, towards the Taliban, could not have come at a more opportune time, than this. The Taliban, in fact, cannot stop rejoicing!!! This is another international blunder that has fuelled the insurgency in restive poppy belts of Afghanistan. In a way, the poppy farmers were mobilised for the Taliban, by the poppy eradicating strategy of US, and other Western countries. The Taliban is again in an advantageous position to strongly employ poppy as a tool to woo the farmers, especially, those from south. The same Taliban, which discouraged farmers to grow poppy, back in 2001, will lend more than a shoulder and patient audience to them, now.

A whopping, USD one billion was employed under the poppy eradication programme of the US. This excludes other grants pledged to the anti-narcotic fund, established by the State of Afghanistan. Would not distributing that money, among four million odd farmers of Afghanistan, for mobilising them against poppy, yield better results? Considering only 15-20 per cent of the total four million farmers, actually grow poppy, it would have been a modest kitty for them to get the farmers started on cereal crops. May I be forgiven, for sharing the crudest strategy of one's professional career!

Who should be blamed for this failure? Why has the billion dollar strategy backfired and failed to yield the desired results? There are three primary reasons suggested by the international brigade of anti-narcotics policy advisors behind the failure.

a) Failure of the State to establish its authority and render succour to its desperate citizens.
b) Growing influence of the Taliban.
c) Growing insecurity and lawlessness.

It is appalling how you can literally bury, anything and everything, under the above three justifications in Afghanistan. Those who are gunning to bring the State of Afghanistan under the fold of accountability framework should also demand the same for these policy advisors and the international poppy eradication strategists. It is further baffling to see these anti-narcotics advisors, including United Nation Office for Drug and Crime (UNODC), appear in the international media to lecture on increased production of poppy in Afghanistan, without an iota of remorse.

It is, however, imperative to analyse the spurt in poppy production beyond the US policies to develop a broader understanding of the same. Various UN and other military reports have alleged the hands of a few powerful politicians, and kith and kin of various law-makers, in the increased production of poppy. The UN and other bilateral agencies have often condemned the incumbent government for their lackadaisical approach to contain poppy production and for their lack of political will and drive to eradicate poppy from Afghanistan. Various US officials, including the former US State Assistant Secretary for the Bureau of International Narcotics and Law Enforcement Affairs, Tom Schweich, has on record said that opium production is protected by the government of Hamid Karzai, as it hugely benefits from its production. Certain tough decisions are required before it gets too late. But the irony is that nobody is willing to take such decisions in the power corridors of Kabul, including its head.

Every failure comes with a lesson. It is interesting to note that the overall poppy production may have increased in Afghanistan but it is almost on the verge of extinction in northern and some of the eastern provinces. This may sound contradictory, but the reality is that poppy has been largely confined within the peripheries of trouble prone south and few eastern provinces. This is not reflected in the larger picture (consolidated poppy production) of Afghanistan, as the gains in northern provinces are negated by the increased production in southern provinces. The very fact, that few northern provinces are receiving the presidential award for not growing poppy, consistently, over the last couple of years, stands testimony to it. This silent change has a few lessons in it.

There is no better district than Jurm, a valley located in the windswept mountainous province of Badakashan, as an invaluable case study. Jurm is one of those picturesque districts where the entire habitat is settled over long stretches of unending valleys. A predominantly poppy growing district, till the beginning of 2005, it has emerged completely poppy free, today.

A combination of reasons has led to this change in the valley. But two key players, namely, the INGOs and Community Development Councils (CDCs) must be credited for this telling change. Perhaps, it needs to be mentioned here that the CDCs are democratically elected village level structures, constituted under the flagship programme—the National Solidarity Programme (NSP), under the aegis of Ministry of Rural Reconstruction and Development (MRRD).

The INGOs suggested a series of new crops, and introduced horticulture and modern techniques to farmers, to make their farm income grow fast. Alternative livelihood skills were also initiated to supplement their farm income. The strategies worked in most of the cases, as they presented a viable and licit livelihood model for farmers. The initiatives of a few frontline INGOs, through the CDCs, to mobilise the farmers against poppy production, further, complemented the efforts. The counter-narcotic department should have taken a cue from this moderate success and revised their strategy. Engagement of the CDCs and the community, is a must, in eliminating poppy from Afghanistan. The whole process has to be community led and community driven. I have witnessed umpteen CDCs taking up extra initiatives, in their respective villages, to mobilise farmers against poppy cultivation. Such initiatives are obviously not automatic. The CDCs have been mobilised to curb poppy production with induced, structured capacity building interventions. Such effort should be incorporated as a cardinal and a non-negotiable part of the national poppy eradication strategy.

Coming down to south, where the counter-narcotic strategy has collapsed altogether, one has to go beyond various data of poppy cultivation, to derive learning insight, and understand various dynamics of poppy cultivation. The year 2009, was a big lesson for the development actors in south, to understand the reasons behind consistent growth in production of poppy. Ask any international anti-narcotic expert and they would immediately highlight lawlessness and growing influence of the Taliban, in volatile and insecure southern provinces, as reasons behind increased poppy cultination. But the reality goes much deeper, and beyond the periphery of insecurity and lawlessness.

As mentioned earlier in this chapter, the farmers of Afghanistan think, behave and act, like farmers of any another country. They would cultivate something for better yield, not only in terms of production, but also for the money it earns. In other words this is called 'farming intelligence'. The market for food grain is rather unorganised in Afghanistan. Poppy, not only gives them better return and a sense of security, but also puts them on the right side of the powerful drug lobby.

In the year 2009, prices of wheat spiralled phenomenally high, in South Asian countries, like India, Pakistan and Afghanistan. This was mainly because of a failed crop, due to prolonged drought (in the preceding year, in 2008), in certain food basket provinces of the South Asian countries, especially, in Pakistan. Afghanistan was also hard hit by the rising costs, as it has to depend on Pakistan for a certain portion of their domestic consumption of wheat. The absence of distribution and storage infrastructures in Afghanistan goes a long way behind this dependence. Price of wheat, which otherwise varies from 30 to 50 cent (of USD) per kilogram, rose to almost USD 1.30 per kilogram, before the sowing season.

Anticipating a good domestic market for wheat, a bulk of the farmers in the three prominent districts of Kandahar viz Arghandab, Dand and Daman, went for wheat production, in the year 2009. Their decision to opt for wheat over poppy had nothing to do with the anti-narcotic strategy, or alternative livelihood strategy of the INGOs, but to make most out of the troubled water. Farmers made a tacit calculation that wheat would be more profitable than poppy that year. This is an example of the farming intelligence one has mentioned earlier. These areas have otherwise been part of the traditional poppy belts, and notoriously known for their lawlessness and hostility of the Taliban. The mass exodus of farmers from traditional poppy to wheat cultivation, in itself, speaks volume about their mindset. They would say no to poppy, when they see a more lucrative livelihood option.

Due to sufficient rainfall and enabling climatic conditions, there was a glut in wheat production, in 2009, in these three districts. The glut was further complemented by a bumper production in the other provinces of Afghanistan, as well as in neighbouring Pakistan. This immediately resulted in a free fall of wheat prices, till it stabilised to the normal range of 30–50 cents (of USD) per kilogram. The farmers of Kandahar failed to reap the dividends due to the fall of the prices triggered by the bumper production. There was no end to the pathetic tales of the farmers. There were no takers of wheat in the local Kandahar market, as the supply of wheat far exceeded the demand. The problem of grain storage, further, hounded the farmers, like never before. Poppy required very little storage space, and was mostly lifted from the farm by traders. Hence, the farmers were ill prepared on the storage front. They helplessly watched their wheat, rotting in open spaces, unable to do anything. The farmers pleaded the governor of Kandahar to assuage their suffering by asking the World Food Programme (WFP) to procure their wheat, and use it for development programmes in the southern provinces. Incidentally, the WFP procures bulk of the wheat from developed countries, transports the same through sea route either to Karachi or Iran and brings them to Afghanistan through road transport. The transport cost of this wheat is, naturally, phenomenally high. The same wheat is used in various development programmes of the WFP in south as well as other provinces of Afghanistan. It was only prudent on the part of the governor to request the WFP, to procure wheat locally and distribute the same locally. A huge transportation cost could have been saved through such an approach. Besides, the local people would have preferred local wheat, grown in their own soil.

One often notices that in Afghanistan common sense is the most uncommon thing. The WFP expressed its inability to entertain the request of the governor in the presence of various international procurement manual and processes followed by the UN organisations. The rejection of the WFP naturally annoyed the farmers and other stakeholders in the province of Kandahar. Towards the beginning of 2010 the WFP launched P4P (Purchase for Progress) to procure part of their wheat requirement from the private sector of Afghanistan. However, till December 2010 not a single grain had been procured from southern provinces of Afghanistan, despite a series of attempts.[7]

The private sector had, apparently, quoted a rate, 20-30 per cent higher than the prevailing market rate, and this went against the international procurement manual vis-à-vis international parity of price policy of the WFP. The UN agencies are notoriously rigid in terms of following their international rules and regulations, even if the local situation merits certain flexibility and freedom. It is tempting to ask whether a context or a situation, like southern Afghanistan, merits a slight bending of the WFP· standard international procurement guidelines or not. The rate quoted by the private merchants may have been 20-30 per cent higher than the WFP (calculated on the basis of international procurement standards) but what about saving the transportation cost involved in bringing the same wheat from a third country by naval and road transport to Afghanistan, or even bringing it from northern to southern provinces? How can one expect the nascent private sector of southern Afghanistan to supply wheat at internationally competitive rates, given the fragile economy of the country? The WFP has a lot of answering to do and one can be almost certain that its policy advisors would come out with a series of clarifications, downplaying this analysis.

There was, further, an agreement developed between the WFP and Ministry of Agriculture, Irrigation and Livestock (MAIL), whereby 20 metric ton of wheat was supposed to be procured by the WFP from MAIL, in the year 2009-2010.[8] The MAIL was supposed to supply the proposed 20 metric ton of wheat from the strategic reserves of wheat, which they were planning to develop, by directly procuring them from the farmers of Afghanistan. The proposed arrangement between the WFP and MAIL failed. The reason being the procurement rate quoted was 18 per cent higher than the prevailing market rates. This explanation was provided by the WFP on their website. Data does not speak for itself. It is we who attach an impression to the data. In this case the cause of the agricultural sector and more importantly the plight of the farmers should have remained supreme, in the context of Afghanistan.

Many a developmental professional firmly believe, that the WFP should have bent its international procurement rule a little, looking into the noble cause in Afghanistan. WFP has finally started procuring wheat from Afghanistan. This step will, not only go a long way in organising the highly unorganised agriculture market, but also provide security and confidence to the farmers to grow cereal crop, rather than poppy.

But in the context of Kandahar, it was one lost opportunity, which could have been used to fuller advantage, and as an effective step towards poppy eradication. The WFP should have gone all out, and procured wheat directly from the farmers. This would have aided the efforts towards arresting poppy cultivation in Kandahar and adjacent provinces. Even the MAIL should have stepped into the occasion, and used this opportunity as a perfect pilot. This could have been a stepping stone, towards establishing a MSP system in the southern parts of Afghanistan, and for providing the necessary confidence to the farmers in the south to grow cereal crops. Moreover, the anti-narcotic fund could have been used for the same purpose. It is often reported in the media that a huge amount of the anti-narcotics fund lies idle, with no real plan for its usage. It is far better to establish a system like MSP, than construct roads and bridges with this money.

The farmers of Kandahar suffered a huge loss, and were upset to the extent that they dared any anti-narcotics officials and government staff (or INGOs) to step in their village, and advise them against growing poppy. The farmers complained that this was a lesson big enough for them to continue with their traditional and secured crop, poppy. The governor of Kandahar was very vocal against the inaction of the WFP, and criticised them openly in a provincial coordination meeting that was also attended by me. Unfortunately, these meetings are thinly attended by senior representatives of the UN and other agencies. While for some, these do not merit their representation, for others the high security risk is always an excuse. The current governor of Kandahar is not known for mincing his words. He went further, and raised the issue at the highest echelons of the UN, and finally managed to get the rider of the WFP in action. Around mid-2010, it was reported that WFP has revised their policy and would start procuring wheat from the private sector of Kandahar, as well. It is a wonder though, if the private sector of Kandahar can comply with the international procurement manual of WFP. Currently the WFP says that the rate quoted by the private sector is 20 to 30 per cent higher, than the available market rates. The prevailing gap would have to reduce for the private sector, to supply wheat to the WFP, eventually. Afghanistan has always learned its lesson the hard way.

However, there are a few compelling questions to be answered. Have we lost an important opportunity to reverse the trend of poppy cultivation in Kandahar? Why should the farmers in Kandahar grow wheat anymore? And, more importantly, is this damage irreparable?

UN reported that poppy production went down, by almost half, in the year 2010.[9] There are various theories regarding it, doing the round in Afghanistan. The UNODC has estimated that more than 11,000 metric tons of poppy is stockpiled in Afghanistan. If opium yields were down in 2010, those stockpiles would gain more value. The experts see the hand of drug lords behind the manipulation of poppy production, as they want to gain more from their stock. However, news of reduction in poppy production is certainly a ray of light, at the end of the tunnel.

Afghanistan has to find a solution against poppy production, irrespective of production graph. The narcotic problem is deeply entrenched; hence, there is no simple and quick fix solution in Afghanistan today. The NATO, and to some extent the ISAF forces have, of late, developed cold shoulder towards poppy eradication. The NATO is, especially, wary about making enemies out of poppy farmers, vis-à-vis drugs lords, by being associated with poppy eradication. It is a Catch-22 situation, today. Opium profits fuel insurgency and so does destroying the poppy crops of the farmers.

The whole counter-narcotics strategy has to be revisited and revamped in the interest of Afghanistan. Sooner the better! The new strategy should emphasise on crop substitution and alternative livelihood, community mobilisation and working out an appropriate incentive system, along with setting up a MSP structure in Afghanistan. This would create more agricultural jobs in the farm sector, and make economic returns from farms more lucrative. Besides, more emphasis should be laid on social mobilisation and CDCs should be pressed into action with appropriate incentive structures.

The neighbours of Afghanistan are either accomplices or victims of opium trade. They need to be part of the solution as well. Russia alone has, a reported, 3.5 million opium addicts. They should work in tandem to improve intelligence sharing and border security, to seize cross border smuggling. Concerted efforts should also be made in the consumer countries, to curb drug addiction. Together, this would go a long way in arresting poppy production in Afghanistan.

Alternatively, the option of legalising poppy cultivation can also be explored. This will not only solve the illicit poppy production in Afghanistan, but also lower the price of prescription drugs worldwide; and make health care more affordable. Perhaps, it needs to be mentioned here that poppy has huge medical value, and various pain killing and anaesthetic drugs are prepared from opium. A licensing system would, further, bring the State in a support relation with the farmers, and strengthen their trust.

Such legalisation was done in Turkey, long ago. Australia, India, France, Spain and Turkey grow poppy, but with better control and regulation. They currently dominate the global prescription medicine market. With a governance structure, like CDC being in place, in every village, legalisation and regulation of poppy in Afghanistan, too, may not be a distant reality. Senlis Council in their report entitled 'Poppy for Medicine' has proposed a technical model for implementation of poppy licensing and the legal control of cultivation and production of Afghan morphine. However, if Afghan poppy starts dominating the international market, it may hit the interest of the established international market players. Hence, one is not sure as to how much of this would be allowed in the present situation, where policy goals are set and determined by the donor countries, in Afghanistan.

1. The opium economy in Afghanistan-An international problem, UNODC, 2003.
2. Annual opium survey report, 2001, UNDCP.
3. Annual opium survey report, 2001, UNDCP.
4. The opium economy in Afghanistan-An international problem, UNODC, 2003.
5. Lt Col John A Glaze, Opium and Afghanistan: Re-assessing US counter narcotic strategy, www.stratgeicstudiesinstitutes.army.mil, United State Army College, 22 October 2007.
6. UNODC predicts stable opium crop in Afghanistan, Afghanistan Opium Survey, 2010, UNODC, 10 February 2010.
7. WFP Annual Report 2010-11.
8. WFP Annual Report 2010-11.
9. Afghanistan Opium Survey 2010, UNODC, September 2010.

The Obsessive Media

'A balanced and rational view of Afghanistan has become a casualty, because the only aim of media has been to provide "breaking news".'

—a development worker in Kabul

Media, in its obsession with war, is portraying an incomplete picture to the international audience. Will the media learn to see Afghanistan beyond the peripheries of terrorism, at times, if not always?

Afghanistan has always been under media glare for all the wrong reasons. Media has been shaping international perception and opinion about the ongoing development and reconstruction process in the country. However, the focus of the international media has been on the war against terrorism, and the expanding influence of the Taliban and al-Qaeda in Afghanistan. The development and reconstruction agenda has been left behind in the process. Growing insecurity coupled with increasingly expanding influence of anti-government forces invariably capture the headlines of the international print and electronic media. The local media, too, follows the same foot print under the influence of the international media.

Media has also failed to play a progressive role in accelerating the reconstruction and peace building process of Afghanistan. Instead of highlighting the real gaps and issues impeding the process of growth and development, media has obstinately focused on war and insurgency instead. Hence, by default, a bulk of the international community has developed a mass hysteria of perceiving Afghanistan from the lens of war and terrorism alone. The media has to be held responsible for the same as this stems from their unstoppable urge to cover war and terrorism only. And again, it is media, which is fuelling the imagination and impression of the Western audience by consistently projecting the country in a pitiable condition. Media has, inadvertently, generated a vicious cycle, whereby they are catering to the appetite of the international audience, something the media itself has consistently stimulated in the first place, and encouraged over the years. Media has created a depressive gloom around Afghanistan.

By continually projecting Afghanistan as a fragile, insecure and unstable country, media has also, inadvertently, played up to the gallery of Western policy makers. It has provided the policy makers a leeway to cover up their Afghan policy blunders without ruffling the domestic populace and the media. It has provided them the license and justification to keep their military for a longer duration.

Even if for our own reference, we must understand, and analyse the premise of the media in projecting Afghanistan only from the perspective of war and terrorism. This can be best exemplified by the increased reporting on the drone attacks these days, attracting more media coverage in the world, than ever. A misdirected drone attack, killing several innocent people, would rotate more eye balls among the Islamic countries, while a directed one would do the same for the Western audience. Hence, in both the cases, the drone attacks pull an increasing number of audience. The media, most of the time, ends up playing the preferred music to their targeted gallery to suit their commercial interest. A balanced and rational view of Afghanistan becomes a casualty when the only aim is to make news more sensational.

One has strong reservations over the way Afghanistan has been portrayed by the media, as if to prove that there is nothing beyond the string of suicide bombing and Improvised Explosive Device (IED) attacks in Afghanistan. The real news about Afghanistan is somewhere lost in this process, and the audience hardly gets to see the actual picture. It is not to say that the issues highlighted by international media are totally incorrect, or grossly exaggerated, or that everything is hunky-dory. However, there is certainly more to Afghanistan than the spate of suicide bombings and gun battles. The country deserves to be known beyond the spread of militancy and growing insecurity.

In the recent years, there has been a spurt of development activities, even amid the high decibel of bombs and F16s, flying all over Afghanistan, to degrade the Taliban might. The development activities have lent momentum to the rebuilding process. However, in the backdrop of sustained terrorism, media and the policy experts are unable to assess these activities in the right perspective. Driven by the popular medieval notion that development cannot happen in the backdrop of terrorism, which is partially true, they are unable to capture the bigger picture. It is not that development begins where terrorism ends, or vice versa. In fact, balanced and all round development can assuage and pacify terrorism. Media needs to understand and view development in isolation to terrorism in order to depict the real picture. It is impossible to subscribe to the opinion of policy experts that terrorism has completely derailed the development process in Afghanistan, as a number of astonishing changes have taken place, despite rise in terrorism.

Media has to learn the art and practice of seeing Afghanistan beyond the peripheries of terrorism sometimes, if not always. Media, along with the international policy experts, has instead blurred the line of terrorism and development. The pessimistic approach and coverage by the media is also not doing any less damage in undermining the influence of the government. In course of my professional assignment there was an opportunity to interract with a journalist, who was especially flown from the US to write an article on the status of governance. The journalist, within minutes of our meeting, discussed the framework of her story. Needless to say, corruption was the central issue. It was plaguing the process of governance and the very fact that the government officers were not literate enough, was making the situation go bad to worse. As a governance professional it was impossible for me to subscribe to this picture, and especially, the fact that illiteracy could in any way block decision making at the village level (governance). It was my suggestion that she witnesses our work to decide about local governance in Afghanistan. She was by far the most professional journalist one had ever met. Even though, initially, she did not agree to my perception on governance, she decided to give it a try. She went to a remote district of Afghanistan, with an independent team, and spent five days probing every detail of our work. And eventually, she came up with a frontline story, in a leading US daily, suggesting what she saw was indeed a model of good governance for Afghanistan. It is my firm belief that media is a powerful body, as it can shape mass impression on issues concerning public good. If media starts looking out for positive things in Afghanistan, the country can slowly get out of this depressive gloom. The role of the media has to be constructive, in the least, if not always positive.

To induce positive thinking and to bring development centre stage in Afghanistan, my organisation introduced a media fellowship programme for local journalists in northern provinces. A selected bunch of development journalists, from the print and electronic media, was provided with fellowship and appropriate training, to mainstream development news in print and electronic media. The journalists were encouraged to write positive development stories. The programme was a huge success, and soon expanded to three other provinces. In a short span of time, 30 per cent of the news coverage in mainstream print and electronic media, turned to affirmative and analytical development stories.

There is no problem if media writes war stories but it is a tad frustrating to see them ignore all affirmative actions and changes in Afghanistan. It is a matter of some concern when media fails to see anything beyond war and terrorism in the country. A few journalist friends, engaged with the international print and electronic media, based in Kabul, accepted, over candid conversations, that there was very little appetite to development news from Afghanistan. Most of the times, such stories were trashed, by the editors who operated from their Western headquarters. While it was possible to launch a fellowship programme to educate the local journalists, one wonders what can be done to change the mindset of the erudite editors.

Obsessive coverage of war, amid loads of positive changes that are taking place in the development front, is only portraying an incomplete picture of Afghanistan. During a recent lecture tour on Afghanistan, to London School of Economics and IDS Sussex, UK, I was miffed and dismayed to find that none of the students had a single question about the development and reconstruction process. All the questions were about the Taliban and terrorism. The international media has made the international community believe that there is nothing else happening beyond war against terror, which is grossly wrong. This is what, one may refer to as, an incomplete portrayal of Afghanistan.

A lack of understanding of key development issues by media can be a severe lacuna, at times. On 29 May 2010, I was watching a documentary, made by a leading international television news channel, on the street children of Kabul. The presenter, of some international repute, and also considered an Afghan expert, claimed that there were about 10,000 street children, toiling around the streets of Kabul to make a living. Having lived in Kabul for more than six years, it was hard to digest such implausible facts and figures. If the presenter could help me find even 1/10th of the said figure, in the streets of Kabul, it would be time to say goodbye and quit the development sector, forever. The presenter was grossly confusing the problem of child labour with street children. Any development worker knows that technically, the two issues are different and so are their causes.

It also disillusions one, no end, to see at times naïve and inept comparisons being established by media. The fabricated linkage between terrorism and child labour, and how the former is influencing the latter, is far from true. Someone needed to remind the presenter that in Delhi alone (which never witnessed a war over a century), the number of child labour exceeded those in Kabul, by manifold. The child labour is an outcome of poverty, unemployment and not war, generally.

At the end of 2008, the international media ran a relentless campaign on shortage of food, due to drought in Central Highland region of Afghanistan. They projected the region, especially, Bamian, as one under serious food risk.[1] They went further, projecting concepts like food-riot and starvation deaths accompanied with numerous secondary data generated by them. Their imagination did not stop at that and went, further, to link it with the growing insecurity and a derailment of the peace process. One has visited scores of villages in Bamian, after the drought, and has never heard of even one incident of starvation death, or the so called 'food-riot'. These concepts are still alien to Afghanistan.

In the past few decades, there has been no dearth of enterprising and industrious journalists drawing linkages and correlations, of literally any problem in Afghanistan, with war and terrorism. In truth, notwithstanding the growing insecurity, Afghanistan has made a decent progress in a few key sectors. In the course of my professional stint, I have travelled extensively and interacted with hundreds of development workers, village leaders and ordinary citizens and I am elated to gauge their hope and optimism about Afghanistan. And this hope is catching the imagination of ordinary men and women, like never before.

Afghanistan has never been represented by media from the perspective of this growing hope and optimism. Even, if some of them are successful in their attempt, they are so far and few in between that they are lost in the blaring hysteria and obsessive preoccupation with terrorism of mainstream media. All the positive and rebuilding work, happening in Afghanistan, gets forcefully cowed in the backdrop of consistent insurgency, insecurity and increased poppy production as reported by the media. It is high time that the international media gets its agenda right. They must start potraying a complete picture of Afghanistan, beyond terrorism and insurgency!

---

1. Will next US president rethink Afghanistan? BBC, 21 October 2008.

The Elusive State

'Election is a matter of relative choice here—You have to choose the one who is least corrupt.'

—a shopkeeper in the province of Kunduz

What is blocking the State from extending good governance and connecting the war-tired citizen into the fabric of a nation? Why is the State still so elusive?

There is an inescapable link between governance deficit and conflict. The established link becomes, further, critical in the context of a conflict-prone country, like Afghanistan. Here, while governance deficit can lead to increased conflict, better governance can assuage the plight and suffering of its citizens, and weave them back into the fabric of a nation. This can go a long way towards building durable peace in a country embattled with three decades of war, and a recent Taliban upsurge. Hence, fixing the governance process of Afghanistan has been a high priority agenda, set up by the international community, and the Afghan government, in the Tokyo and Bonn conferences, after the downfall of the Taliban. After almost nine years of state building, the very state institutions that the Bonn process helped to create, lack the human and institutional capacity to function effectively. There is a palpable governance deficit, which is seriously affecting stability and growth.[1] The institutions of Afghanistan are grappling with poor capacities to pacify the sufferings of the masses, by provisioning services, better regulatory control and pro-poor policies. While the citizen's needs are diverse and acute, the response of the State is still very inadequate. Such a situation is only widening the gap between the State and its citizen. Rampant corruption in the governance system is, further, aggravating the situation, and seriously denting the image and perception of the government. Citizens are getting slowly alienated. The current governance deficit is only strengthening the Taliban. In a way, the government of Afghanistan is inadvertently playing to the gallery of the Taliban. And the Taliban is constantly gaining from this unfolding situation.

The country has witnessed a wide range of state building efforts, from multiple international agencies, along with the UN and other bilateral and multilateral agencies. However, the achievements are not even remotely close to the popular expectations, and can be most humbly stated as sub-standard.

In the last couple of years, the government has constantly attracted criticism from the Western countries, for its inability to govern Afghanistan. Who should be blamed for this failure? It would be unfair to put the blame completely on the Afghan government, as bulk of the international community, including the UN agencies, have all been engaged in state building. A large number of INGOs have also pursued the same agenda. It is considered one of the most glamorous programmes in Afghanistan. In fact the programme portfolio of any INGO seems to be incomplete without a state building/governance component. For the UNDP and USAID, it is simply the buzz word. But while much hype has been created by the UN and USAID about governance and state building, not much has been achieved on ground, actually. The international community, including the USAID and the UN agencies, must accept a considerable part of the blame therefore. In the name of state building they have, actually, created large number of programmes and policies. Even though, some of the policies have been ratified by the government, the same has rarely been translated into action, in true spirit and principle, hardly making any dent in the status quo.

If the nascent state institutions had come up with effective capacity on their own, in this fragile and landlocked country, the international community could have left by now. While toppling a repressive regime, that harboured terrorism and extremism, is easy, we know stabilising the state, in post conflict nations or in complex situations, as in Afghanistan, remains an arduous and a daunting task. This requires short and long-term strategic vision and coordination to ensure that the scarce aid resources are optimally utilised, to gradually create a functional and self reliant nation. In addition, a massive and systematic capacity building investment is required to gear up the new institutions to take up an expanded set of roles, and promote good governance practices. Every foreign aid actor's exit strategy should have been aimed at helping the government institutions stand on their own feet. None of the above has happened, yet. While the democratic process was successfully implemented, the parallel process of building institutions (to enable the government to deliver public services), lagged far behind. Hence, state institutions without the necessary resources and capacity, to deliver on popular expectation, has inevitably created a vacuum, a by-product of which is growing disillusionment with the State.

Why is the State unable to ride on popular Western support, and proactively pacify the suffering of its citizen? Why is the State not being able to deliver good governance? In order to understand the failure of the State to deliver around popular expectations of its citizen and the international community, we need to probe the complex set of constraints, around which Afghanistan is currently operating. There is, further, a need to understand the contextual barriers plaguing the ability of the State, to deliver good governance. The state building process in Afghanistan is marred by a lack of vision, coupled with inherited structural, procedural, contextual and policy issues. The worsening law and order situation and the constant attacks by the Taliban on the rudimentary institutions are, further, putting a spanner in the process of state building. The analysis would be unfair and incomplete if the hollow approach, adopted by the international agencies, including US, UN and few INGOs, focusing on governance, is not mentioned here.

Steering the governance process in the backdrop of the gruelling challenges mentioned above, remains a topsy-turvy task. It tests the strategic vision and technical acumen of the State at the highest level. Let me dwell on the issues confronting the government of Afghanistan in building its rudimentary governance structures and processes.

The first challenge in any state building process remains attracting a brigade of highly competent and committed staff, for running the state machinery. A sizable chunk of the best available human resources in Afghanistan is engaged either with the UN or USAID contractors/INGOs, because of the exorbitant range of salaries they provide to the local Afghans. Perhaps, it needs to be mentioned here that a big chunk of USAID grant is provided to the US based (and registered), private companies, popularly referred to as USAID contractor, in Afghanistan. According to estimates, drawn up by the international human resource firms, based in Kabul, a government staff gets paid, at least, two or three times less salary, than his counterpart working with an international agency in Afghanistan. The salary gap widens further if the salary of local government staff is compared with the Afghan national employed with UN and US agencies, including USAID contractors. The meagre salary paid to the government staff, is often perceived as the key reason behind rampant corruption in bureaucracy.[2] However, that is no justification for corruption by state officials.

The international agencies, further, top up the salary of their staff with a wide range of perks and incentives, including overseas exposure/training visits. This makes jobs with international agencies more lucrative, and attracts a beeline of Afghan candidates, against each vacancy. The international agencies get away with best of talents. Even though, the State provides security of long-term employment, it does not make much sense, in the Afghan context. People here are bent upon making the most in immediate terms, given the recurrent phases of war and insecurity. Such a situation leaves very little choice for the state agencies, in terms of attracting better human resources. It is not to cast any doubt on the quality of human resources available, but the fact remains that there is a need for more competent people for the government jobs. The State is seriously struggling to attract a capable brigade of human resource, under its fold. Even though Afghan Civil Service Commission has been constituted and entrusted with the task of recruiting competent staff in key positions, they have to operate within the above stated constraints. The problem does not end here. There is, further, a constant exodus of competent government officers to lucrative INGO and UN jobs. In a situation where the State is already struggling to draw and retain fine talent to bolster the government department, the Taliban does the most damage. As a part of their south strategy, especially, carried in southern and now even eastern provinces, they systematically target and eliminate the talented, and especially, honest senior officials of Afghan government. One has lost count of how many such targeted murders have been carried out, in the last six years. The murder of Abdul Latif Ashna, the Deputy Governor of Kandahar, on 30 January 2011, is another example of targeted killing by the Taliban, to weaken the State. He was known for his impeccable integrity and was vouched as one of the most competent and honest officers of the Afghan government. These are officers who could have changed the way Afghanistan operates and connects with the masses. They are silenced by the Taliban in their bid to weaken the State and alienate the masses. He was with me in Bangladesh during the last two weeks of December 2010, on an exposure visit organised around meso-level governance. We spent a day together, on 27 December, to discuss how some of the lessons from Bangladesh could be employed in Kandahar. We even discussed some of the chapters of this book. It was like a shell shock to learn about his murder within a month's time. The incident shattered me both personally and professionally. As a professional working on state building it pains one to lose any competent and honest officer. And we have lost so many of them in the last five years. Any such death derails the state building process and brings us to ground zero. These are some of the weaker moments when one tends to lose hope for Afghanistan. It is also extremely frustrating professionally. But, one has to rekindle the hope, as there are still a considerable number of officers who want to give it a try, in the trying and tiring circumstances of Afghanistan. The good work must go on as that would be a perfect tribute to the departed noble souls.

In a situation, where the State is already grappling to draw quality human resources due to poor salary, the targeted killing of Afghan officials by the Taliban, irreversibly damages the state building process. Looking into its higher threat perception, government jobs are certainly not the first choice for the qualified Afghan citizens. And for a majority, it does not even figure in their list. They prefer to work in INGOs and UN agencies, which are relatively safer, more secure and lucrative. Hence, the targeted killing of state officials by the Taliban not only derails the state building process, but also throttles the bid of the Afghan government to draw quality human resources into government jobs. It damages the state building process at multiple levels. Perhaps, like terrorism, Afghanistan has to learn to live with this problem, too.

Unavailability of quality human resources at the disposal of state institutions often makes the path of growth and stability more tedious and slow. It takes a long time for the state institution to stand on its own. An overambitious plan was drawn up to engage civil servants from India to build the rudimentary state institutions by the government of Afghanistan, as a part of a bilateral agreement.[3] However, this has proved to be a token approach, limited to a few ministries. It became nothing more than an exchange programme for promoting cultural ties and bonhomie, among two neighbours striving to become great friends. Though, the concept behind the programme was great, it failed to fire, because it lacked the required scale.

The government of Afghanistan has not only to deal with the scarcity of quality human resources to ignite the governance process, but also grapple with the large scale presence of local/ regional ex-commanders, jostling for more power and authority. It needs to be mentioned here that the term 'ex-commander', is used for high ranking ex-soldiers, who have previously served a regime, or participated in any war in Afghanistan. The ex-commanders are a legacy (and outcome) of the series of war and unrest the country has witnessed in the past. In a bid to accommodate them for balance of power, the State of Afghanistan ends up seriously compromising with the quality of governance. A considerable number of these commanders are proud Mujahids, who fought the Soviet occupation. They have hordes of followers and the wherewithal at their disposal. Once an old man, in a village of Badakashan, told me the number of commanders exceeded normal citizens in this country. This may not be demographically possible, but an intense frustration was hidden in this hyperbole. Perhaps, he meant, the country had more ex-commanders than it could afford to have. Having lived in Afghanistan for some time, his inherent frustration could be well understood. These commanders operate like parallel government structures, in almost all provinces, districts and even villages, at times. The State of Afghanistan may be unorganised in its functioning, but the commanders operate in a very well structured fashion and the bigger commanders nestled in the province/region have their followers in smaller commanders, cooling their heels at the district level. And they have an impeccable chain of command and information sharing system. It is a pleasure to quote their operational style, during my lectures on governance in conflict-prone settings.

The State may be grappling with lack of resources, but these commanders are highly skilled in mobilising resources within their regions. It has been reported, time and again, that some of these commanders also receive money from Western countries and their intelligence agencies, to advance their respective strategic interests. The income generation project of various INGOs may have failed, but these commanders are well conversant with the art of spinning money in a conflict-prone setting. The problem boils down to the fact that they just know the art of building personal wealth and at best wealth for their followers. The other thing, perhaps, they do not know is the vision, art and practice of good governance, especially of inclusive governance. A chain of commanders call the shots and operate like a parallel government in some of the regions/provinces/districts.

Very often, it has been noticed that the higher echelons of bureaucracy take orders from these parallel structures, on issues of wider concerns. The provincial apparatus turns a blind eye to the illegal activities of these commanders. Not all, of course. A broader set of commanders always want to be amid thick of things, politically and otherwise, as they have tasted power after the fall of the communist regime. The popular among them get themselves successfully elected to the parliament and other democratic structures. The ones left behind, or the lesser ones, operate as power centres, in their respective areas of influence. Once, a local political journalist confided that lesser commanders may not win an election, but they can ensure electoral defeat of any candidate, in their respective areas of hold. It is extremely difficult for any candidate to win election without the blessing and patronage of these lesser commanders. They attain the status of almost a demigod, during elections in Afghanistan.

It is easier to deal with the ones elected than the ones left behind. The lesser ones want to be accommodated in plum posts within the bureaucracy, their preferred position being the head of a province/district, either in overall administration, or in law and order. The choice of position and area depends upon the profile and influence of the ex-commanders. The profile and influence is again calculated with a simple Afghan formula, which takes care of three things i.e., past heroics, number of followers at their disposal and their connection to the higher political circles. Once they get into any plum post, their efforts revolve around fixing their followers in the bureaucratic set-up. A governance expert may blame the government for accommodating these commanders, and not following meritocracy in bureaucratic appointment as this seriously compromises the quality of governance, and the ability of the State to contain corruption. However, those who understand Afghanistan internally, especially, how the power structures operate will say the same with a greater degree of caution.

These commanders are less threatening when they are accommodated in the folds of the State, than when left alone to fend for themselves. Some of them may start fanning poppy cultivation, and a few may even cross over to the Taliban. The remaining would destabilise the regional and provincial security. The ex-provincial governor of Helmand province, Sher Mohammed Akundzada, (also a powerful ex-commander) of the Helmand province in restive south, after being sacked, openly advocated switching sides to the Taliban. He explicitly revealed that he had turned thousands of his followers over to the Taliban, after he was sacked from the job under the pressure of British officials. The locals suggest that his action bolstered the Taliban. The British soldiers faced the music, in terms of both high causalities and loss of life, in the province of Helmand. Another provincial governor once confided that a provincial police chief (an ex-commander), posed a serious threat to the law and order situation, after being removed from his position. He apparently, wanted to prove that he was indispensable. There is no end to such cases. It takes very little for bulk of these local commanders to switch their loyalties, and operate with an anti-State agenda. It is almost next to impossible to bring them to book.

In the year 2008, the Attorney General of Afghanistan, issued an arrest warrant against the powerful Uzbek commander, General Abdul Rashid Dostum, (also the ex-Defence Minister of Afghanistan). The area of Sheerpur, where Dostum resided—a posh locality of Kabul, abode of the rich and powerful people —turned into a military fortress overnight. His loyal followers promptly landed up from the northern belt, especially Mazhar-e-Sharif. They thronged Sheerpur area, ring fencing the residence of General Dostum with modern range of sophisticated arms, daring the State to arrest him. After exploring all options the government of Afghanistan negotiated a peace deal with the powerful commander, and lifted his arrest warrant.[4] He was provided safe passage to Turkey, to live in exile. This was one of the most timid surrenders of a state against a private militia, one has ever witnessed. By no means do the regional or district commanders exert such power and influence. Nevertheless, they too, have enough teeth to make the provincial and district administration surrender to their military might.

In another case, the district governor of a northern province failed to exert pressure over the district police chief, to arrest a local youth with Taliban leanings, for attacking an INGO vehicle. The gunfire led to the death of a local Afghan NGO worker, injuring a few others. Apparently, the district police chief (another commander), was reluctant in arresting the youth. The INGO got the attacker arrested only after exerting political pressure from Kabul. The governor of the same district, confided in me, 'If I order the arrest, I would be killed within a day'. He further, complained that the district police head was under the proxy control of one of the most powerful regional commanders. Such instances of proxy control are rampant in nearly all key strategic districts of Afghanistan. The large scale presence of such commanders present a typical Catch-22 situation for the Afghan government—accommodating them undermines meritocracy and dilutes quality of governance, and leaving them behind disturbs the security and stability of the region and leads to greater conflict. That is why, perhaps, in a situation like that of Afghanistan, it is very difficult to fit any existing modules on public administration.

By accommodating them politically, the State of Afghanistan, at least, knows that they have to deal with the Taliban only. But their compulsive accommodation seriously affects the quality of the governance. It again, paralyses the State to implement the rule of law, when it comes to fixing the rich and the powerful, for violating the law of the land. This is one problem which nobody can answer, as of now. Afghanistan continues to grapple with the given constraint. Independent Administrative Reform and Civil Service Commission (IARCSC) is trying to streamline a process to recruit district governors purely on grounds of merit. But the institutions will have their own gestation period to bring about the desired change, if they at all can. Even if they manage to get the district governors appointed on grounds of merit, it is not going to solve the problem entirely. Other high level political appointments, like provincial governors and various federal bodies, etc, will be available for exploitation, by the politicians and commanders, to fix their sympathisers.

Beside scarcity of quality human resources, the State is also grappling with poor capacities of the staff. The dysfunctional state institutions with their severly limited capacity reflect the legacy of the long period of civil war, and consequent instability. Bulk of the government staff lacks appropriate understanding and skills in discharging governance functions within the new framework of systems and processes. Governance, in a conflict-prone setting, is always a tough challenge and requires specialised skills. It not only requires the basic understanding of the principles and spirit of good governance but also a diverse set of skills among the bureaucracy, for getting this through. And above all, it requires strategic vision of the highest order, and astute management skills to deal with parallel power structures, at all levels.

Even though IARCSC has taken up the agenda of staff capacity building, an in-depth analysis of their prescribed course curriculum reveals, it has very little exposure to the art and practice of good governance. As of now, it revolves largely around imparting knowledge in English language and information technology skills, along with some basic modules around management.

The UN agencies, along with a large number of INGOs, have proactively taken up the agenda of capacity building of government structures. But the outcome of their capacity building is not even remotely close to the actual need and scale of the government institutions. As we are talking about poor capacity of government functionaries and institutions, it makes sense to dwell upon the existing capacity building approach and strategy adopted by the INGOs, bilateral and UN agencies. The issues of capacity building of governance structures have been mostly pursued by these agencies with a short-term adhoc approach rather than a long-term process oriented approach. However, there is a handful of agencies that have actually adopted a long-term systematic capacity building approach, to build the capacities of the government institutions. The capacity building models of a bulk of the agencies largely revolve around training, international exposure visits, distribution of computers and in imparting language and information technology skills. This may be termed the 'Afghan model of state building'. The training and exposure visits are again not objectively followed up to see, if they have been able to translate the theoretical understanding into practice. Hence, the knowledge generated from training evaporates, as fast as they accumulate, in government institutions. There are again issues of coordination and collaboration among the INGOs, leading to duplication of resources and effort. Training is certainly one commodity where supply exceeds demand, in this restive country. Training on gender sensitisation and planning tops the chart. Few government officers have undergone three to five rounds of gender training. It is not to belittle the importance of gender training in anyway. Our department has trained over 200 government officers as it is genuinely needed in the present context of Afghanistan. But, directing five trainings to one government officer is clearly an overdose of gender. And how does that help? In fact, after a while, an ex-governor of Badakashan province put a blanket ban on gender training, because of an overdose.

One has often witnessed a rush among most of the INGOs and other agencies, to burn their capacity building budget meant for building state institutions. Conducting relentless training for government officers is one of the effective ways of burning this budget. Once, the Director of Department of Women Affairs (DoWA), Baghlan province, shared, how she had to spare one staff completely, for attending various INGO training sessions (almost a weekly phenomenon), as she could not afford any of her other core staff to be away. Currently, a focal point has been appointed by the government of Afghanistan, to coordinate the capacity building activities at the provincial level, in order to avoid duplication of programmes. The capacity building events are getting organised, slowly. However, the question of long-term vision and an approach for building capacities of the state institutions still remain unaddressed.

In the case of exposure visits, the capacity building efforts often get a little too adventurous. Once, a head of the DoWA, of a southern province, was taken to South Korea, by a bilateral agency, to expose her to women-centric projects. Afghanistan and Korea—it is quite a struggle to find the similarity. However, it was probably more conclusive than the exposure visit to China, as suggested by a PRT friend, once. Anyway, she shared that for the major part of the exposure visit she was left to fend for herself, as she had no knowledge whatsoever, of either English or Korean. Apparently, a translator came to her rescue, only at the fag end of the exposure visit. It was a surprise, and some relief, to learn that there were translators who could actually, translate Korean to Pashtu!

Another popular practice, under capacity building, has been the distribution of computers to government offices. One is not averse to distribution of computers, but it has to be for a definitive purpose. What is the point of distributing a laptop to district governors, in the name of promoting e-governance, when majority of them have neither electricity nor a generator they can afford to run. A large number of the officers are in fact, computer illiterate. There is no end to such misadventures.

While dwelling on computers, here is another interesting incident worth mentioning. In 2009, there was a plan to support DoWA to start a computer training centre for girls, graduating from Kandahar University. The idea was to enable these female students, access better employment opportunity, by formally training them in computer application. A comprehensive budget was presented by the DoWA. The head of DoWA wanted us to purchase nine new computers for the proposed training centre. Having been rather successful in mining out old computers from the storerooms of any Afghan government department, in the past, we soon discovered fifteen old desktop computers gathering dust in the storerooms of DoWA. Apparently, these Pentium III computers had been retired, as they had developed minor technical snags. My analysis is, however, different. The computers were thrown away, because their supply exceeded the demand. My colleague got nine of them repaired from a local computer shop in Kandahar by paying a meagre USD 178. The first batch, of twenty-one girls, has completed their formal six month training from the said computer training centre and many more will complete their training in the coming years.

To cut a long story short, nobody seems to have a comprehensive plan for building long-term capacity of the feeble state institutions. Bulk of them, are hell bent upon burning the budget at their disposal, by aggressively pushing their short-term adhoc plan. Having worked in the sector of governance capacity building, for over fifteen years, it is clear that capacity building of the State produces best results when it is pursued with a comprehensive plan coupled with a long-term approach. Targeting the individuals, like the human resources employed in government departments, as well as the organisation collective, is a must. There are, again, serious questions with regard to measuring results of any state building programme. In the INGO sector, people get far too obsessed with it in the name of promoting good governance, failing to critically question what good governance is set to achieve and produce. This tendency is not necessarily confined to Afghanistan. It is only more acutely visible in conflict-prone countries. We need to continually challenge ourselves to ensure that we are not ensnared into this popular trap. Any state building programme, should not only promote good governance but also enable state institutions to improve, and expand the reach of public services. Such an approach would be immensely useful for the struggling government institutions. It would, not only help the rudimentary government departments to consolidate their operation but also provide need-based services to the masses, to assuage their plight. This will establish a concept of nationhood, in a setting where people are mobilised more around ethnicity and regions. The faith and trust of the citizen, on the government, are decreasing with every passing year. If Afghanistan has to survive and prosper, as a nation, the state institution has to extend good governance and expand the scale and scope of public services. For that they need a comprehensive, long-term, meaningful and sustained capacity building support.

Securing better quality of human resources and training them to take up the designated task are necessary, but not sufficient to improve the process and quality of governance. There are other pertinent issues, too. For effective state building, the State also requires enabling democratic structures at all administrative units. This is to develop plans around the needs and aspirations of the wider community, and deliver those plans, effectively. Such an arrangement provides space and opportunities for the wider communities to articulate their pressing needs, and makes the whole process of development and governance, inclusive. This arrangement facilitates a bottom-up development process and serves the genuine expectations of the wider community. It, further, goes a long way in connecting the citizens of a conflict-ridden country to their government. Beside structures, the state needs enabling policies to guide the structures, to take up development and governance functions, across all levels. This has been the path of state building for the bulk of countries, across Asia and Africa, emerging from a conflict-prone background.

Afghanistan maybe grappling on all accounts of governance, but it has been successful in putting the democratic structures at all echelons—villages, clusters, districts, provinces. However, there is a lack of effective policies to drive these institutions. The State has been able to fix the village level development process very well, with creation of community development councils, and provided them with resources to implement village development plans[5] but they have seriously failed to establish a similar process in the higher echelons, at the cluster, district and even provincial levels. Structures have been created, but there is no concrete vision, or policy, to guide these structures. Due to absence of any policy to guide the cluster and District Level Development Agencies (DDAs), they have become almost defunct institutions. In fact, in one of the districts in Takhar, it was with great difficulty that a list of the members of DDA was generated, as they had never met after their creation, in 2006. The sub-national governance policy has been developed to guide democratic as well as bureaucratic structures, after almost six years of effort, by UNDP and Independent Directorate of Local Governance (IDLG). But the same policy is still, awaiting multilevel approval, before it can be implemented. Process of implementation will again, have its own teething issues, further, delaying the whole process. Policy making is not confined to rural development alone. Enabling policies are required in every aspect of development and public administration. Every institution is looking for policies to guide their operation and functions. Even though some basic policies have been developed, still the country badly needs new guidelines to expedite the process of development and governance. The country is simply suffering from a policy paralysis. Every sector and institution is grappling for policy direction to expand their sphere of action.

For instance, the policy of private disinvestment in state-owned companies is not fully developed. It ran into controversy with the sale of a state-owned Ghori Cement Company, in the province of Baghlan, to Afghan Investment Company (AIC) run by Mahmoud Karza, a brother of the president. The local media of Afghanistan termed the sale a symbol of nepotism and corruption.[6] The finance sector is also crying for an effective banking regulation bill, ever since a massive fraud has been unearthed in the Kabul Bank. Hundreds of millions of US dollars were found missing from the bank—much in undocumented and unsecured loans. Most of these loans were provided to the kith and kin of the political heavy weights without any consideration of the merit of the business loans. The bank had to be bailed out by the Central Bank almost from a point of collapse. There is no end to the list of warranted policies, the country requires. The country is also eagerly waiting for a concrete policy for attracting Foreign Direct Investment (FDI). Recently the sale of a copper ore field, to a Chinese company, ran into controversy. Analysts suggest that the deal was undervalued. US and Canadian companies complained about the secretive process of the bidding, suggesting that the bidding was tilted towards China.

An effective FDI policy will go a long way in extracting its USD three trillion mineral wealth, lying beneath the soil, in collaboration with the private sector. The State neither has the resources nor the technical know-how to extract its vast mineral deposit. Some may argue that no private sector would like to employ their financial resources in a restive country. However, security and stability issues are no longer big determinants for employing resources by the overtly aggressive private sector. The private sector is well aware that due to limited bidding, procuring a license will be easy, and it will also come at a huge discount. In fact, there is a very sleek private sector, which has developed specialised skills, to promote and expand business in conflict-prone settings. They relish their opportunities in such settings. A large number of such companies are aggressively employing their resources in the lucrative locales of a few conflict-prone African countries, like Liberia, Sudan, DRC (Congo), etc. If it can happen in Africa, it can happen in Afghanistan, too.

Afghanistan has already received few such investments by private companies. From one private telecom player, the country has witnessed four private telecom players, after the downfall of the Taliban. Afghanistan can similarly generate billions of dollars annually, by leasing its vast mineral resources. All this money can easily put the development action on fast track. Even though, the country has been able to increase its tax and revenues with every passing year, it is not even, remotely, close to servicing its development operations, and other crying infrastructural needs.

For able and apt policy making the State needs higher-order technical support, legal know-how and astute policy making skills, which is certainly in short supply. It is beyond the capacities of UN agencies and INGOs, to help the government of Afghanistan in the area of policy making. Countries like USA, France, Germany, India and their private sectors, are in a better position to help Afghanistan to develop polices for fostering, and regulating its private sector growth. The State of Afghanistan may even draw the support, from the international private sector, towards evolving its policies.

The State lacks the aggressive approach to devise policies around issues affecting the lives and livelihood of its citizen. There is also a visible lack of coordination, within various federal ministries, over the domain and authority of policy making, leading to slow progress in the policy domain. The prolonged cold war between IDLG and Ministry of Rural Rehabilitation and Development (MRRD), over the sub-national governance policy, is well known to the international community, engaged in the process of development and reconstruction. The State of Afghanistan has to focus more aggressively on policy making to bolster the local economy, which is largely dependent on foreign aid money. A rise in local revenues can, further, facilitate a shift from an overtly dependent aid economy to self dependent local economy.

Resource scarcity is constraining the government institutions to expand their services. In June 2010, while participating in a lecture tour on Afghanistan, in Ottawa, one interview modelled around the highly popular 'Hard Talk' by BBC, enquired about state building—'Why are the state institutions not growing, despite huge financial support of international community, committed for the cause?'—A question that has been reiterated in almost all parleys and deliberations on Afghanistan. It is rather obvious that Canada and other Western countries, that have a huge stake and interest in state building, (and have invested billions of dollars for the same) will ask such questions. But my experiences, with four key provincial departments, across six provinces, including Kandahar, suggest that the ground realities in Afghanistan are quite different. The reality is that the provincial departments are seriously struggling with lack of financial resources to expand their services, vis-à-vis reach out. As explained earlier, the provincial departments will only grow stronger, if they can expand their services and reach to a larger set of community, in their respective provinces. For that to happen, the provincial department needs to have the financial resources, along with appropriate capacity building inputs. In the state building process of Afghanistan, while the former is in extremely short supply, the latter exceeds the demand; but again not in the right direction.

We often received requests from the Department of Women Affairs, for financial support, as meagre as USD 200, for celebrating Women's Day. In an informal deliberation, the head of the DoWA, in Badakashan province said, while it was very easy for her to get training abroad, or a computer from any international agencies, it was extremely difficult to get a support of even USD 5,000, to launch a new programme. Few provincial departments do not even have the financial resources to run a generator and other basic services for running the office. Perhaps, it needs to be mentioned here that most of the provinces in Afghanistan do not have electricity and are run completely on generator. These departments just provide a few basic services, to a very limited number of clientele. They purely survive on meagre grants from their respective federal ministries, and in some cases from progressive INGOs. Due to financial constraints, their services are again, confined largely to the peripheries of the provincial headquarters only. One has to understand that training and infrastructures are required in state building. But, more importantly, the provincial departments must expand and extend their services to the broader community, to deliver their mandate, and win the heart and mind of its citizen. The international INGOs and the UN agencies, have to learn this reality soon, if they are serious about state building. The expectation from the PRTs has been to strengthen the provincial departments with the millions of dollars lying in their kitty. However, instead of taking up a vibrant and robust state building role, in the province, they have ended up as mere spectators in the monthly, provincial level, planning and coordinating meeting. Those who understand governance process in Afghanistan, would agree that even a USD 50 million annual grant would be enough to activate the entire provincial machinery. It can, further, enable all provincial departments to proactively cater to the needs of the masses. The only caution to be exercised in the process is that the money has to be guided with a thoughtful vision, coupled with a robust strategy.

Being in such a financial spot, how can we expect the provincial departments to expand and extend their services to their immediate clientele? The million dollar question that needs to be asked is where the billions of dollars that have been received from bilateral agencies, under state building, being employed? Is it vanishing on its way? Is it fixing wrong priorities, or putting the cart before the horse? Or is it a combination of all?

The financial condition of the provincial departments are rather pathetic and are set to deteriorate, further. There is a clear trust deficit growing between the government of Afghanistan and its Western donor countries, over the prevalence of rampant corruption, in the contemporary Afghan governance system. And the voice and discontent of the Western donors, over corruption is only becoming louder, with every passing day.

The State of Afghanistan may be discounted, slightly, for its inability to fix governance in the backdrop of the constraint they are operating under. However, on matters of corruption they have to be solely blamed. Afghanistan has been graded as the second most corrupt country in the world, after Somalia, by Berlin based Transparency International. Afghanistan shares a berth with Myanmar, with a Corruption Perception Index (CPI) of 1.4, on a scale, which ranges from 0 (perceived as most corrupt) to 10 (perceived as least corrupt). In Afghanistan corruption has doubled since 2007, according to a survey by the Anti Corruption Charity Integrity Watch. Afghans paid nearly USD one billion in bribe, in 2009, with almost a third of those surveyed saying, they had to pay a bribe to obtain public services.

Corruption emanates, largely, from lack of efficient and stringent anti-corruption measures, frameworks and policies along with watchdog institutions. The whole accountability machinery and apparatus is weak, and almost defunct in Afghanistan. Whatever little is left, is largely, influenced by the power corridor of Kabul. Any downward accountability of the state institutions is seriously lacking. Downward accountability is reinforced only during elections, where the citizens enjoy the right to elect or reject their representatives, based on their credential and past performance. But, that is not enough for a country struggling with endemic corruption, and lack of institutional teeth to contain corruption.

The quality of political leadership is often questioned in Afghanistan. A bulk of the Afghan political leadership emerges from the deep ethnic divide. They are unable to rise above their narrow political concerns, and the best interest of their immediate political constituency. They rarely think about the nation as a whole. Election is a relative concept here. It is choosing a candidate, who is least corrupt, among the contesting candidates. This was shared by a shopkeeper in Kunduz, during the controversial parliament election, of 2010. There is a need for a new breed of political leadership. People are tired of archaic, ethnic and Taliban influenced politics. Once, a local journalist travelling with me said, if one takes out ten leaders from the current political system, half the Afghan problems will be solved. He pinpointed certain leaders and said that the priority of the international community should be to neutralise them, in the interest of Afghanistan. These leaders are, largely, active around certain ethnic, as well as geopolitical regions. This was the only way to change politics in Afghanistan, according to him.

Beside policies and institutions, the strong political will of government is a must to contain corruption. The political will of the State to arrest corruption has been questioned, more often than not. The rapid proliferation of corruption is hurting Afghanistan badly. It is alienating the poor from the State on one hand, and providing fecund ground for a Taliban upsurge on the other. The faith of the citizen, over their State, is dwindling at an alarming rate.

The inability of Afghanistan to contain corruption, despite assurances from the premier, in all international forum, is not helping the situation. The IMF struggled a lot to strike an agreement in December 2010, over the process through which future aid money would be channelised to Afghanistan. The Kabul Bank fiasco, has further, reduced the faith, of the international finance institutions and Western donors, over national institutions in Afghanistan.

One fails to understand, as to what stops the president to counter the issue of corruption with an iron hand. After all, the issue of corruption is denting the image and perception of his government badly, both within Afghanistan as well in the international arena. Apart from empty promises on various international platforms, he has done nothing much to contain corruption.

The presence of a vibrant civil society and media is also very important for containing corruption in any conflict-ridden country. They exert appropriate pressure over the government, and work as the perfect watchdog to raise a flag, as and when the government crosses the red line. Together, they provide the perfect check and balance mechanism for containing corruption, and fixing accountability. The super active media of India is an excellent example in this regard. The local media of Afghanistan is slowly becoming active, but they have to go a long way to acquire the range of skills and analytical rigour required to unearth and contain corruption in the country.

The development of civil society in Afghanistan has been impeded by more than three decades of conflict, war, displacement and social disruption. The years of unrest have dismantled the civil setup, completely. With the fall of the Taliban, efforts to rebuild the Afghan civil society have been started with renewed vigour. Since 2001, there has been a sharp increase in both the number and types of Afghan civil society organisations. But the fragile civil society has to travel a long way to counter the State on issues pertaining to corruption in Afghanistan. The presence of a weak media and civil society has given an open licence to the various arms of the State to engage in corruption, and run away with it. The presence of a vibrant media and a civil society can come very handy in guarding corruption across all echelons of the State and its political leadership.

The international community can sympathise and stand with the Afghan government over the spread of militancy. But, on issues of governance, especially corruption, the president has to lead the fight. It is going to be a lone battle which he has to fight for his own country. His governance integrity is precariously hanging over the issue of corruption. The growing trust deficit between Afghanistan and Western donors, over the issue of corruption, may stifle the flow of funds. This would make his task, further, difficult. It seems the country is heading for some torrid times, if the process of governance is not pursed with renewed vigour, and sincerity of purpose.

If the State is dreaming about creating a stable and prosperous Afghanistan, it has to get its act together and fix it up, before it gets too late. In fact sooner the better! It has no other option, but to operate within its constraints. Poor governance remains even a bigger challenge than the Taliban.

1. Written evidence from Britain and Irish Agency: Afghanistan Group Committee Report, www.parliament.UK.
2. Fighting corruption in Afghanistan, A road map for strategy and action, Draft for discussion, 2007, Informal discussion paper by DFID, UK, The World Bank, ADB, UNDP, and UNODC.
3. Reaching out to Afghanistan, India and Afghanistan - A development partnership, www.mea.gov.in.
4. Reforming Afghanistan Broken Judiciary, International Crisis Group, Asia report no. 195, 17 November 2010.
5. Promoting community based development, IDA at Work: Afghanistan, www.worldbank.org, July 2009.
6. Mir Sediq Zalia, "A loss making cash cow," *Afghanistan Today*, 6 July 2011.

THE
DEVELOPMENT BOUQUET

On the Right Track

'I teach English in three schools, even though I am paid for only one. I want the youth to realise the power of language, and connect to the world.'

—a school teacher from Bamian

A glimmer of hope is building up in this mountainous and picturesque set up, embattled with terrorism. And this hope is catching the imagination of ordinary men like never before.

Afghanistan has witnessed almost a decade of development and reconstruction efforts, after the downfall of the Taliban. The international media opines that the country has failed to reap the benefits of the large scale assistance, and make significant stride in development and reconstruction. The perception of the international community mirrors the perception of the media. The reasons behind the failure are, largely, attributed to the growing unrest and expanding influence of the Taliban. The public impression of Afghanistan is, further, exacerbated by poor governance coupled with rampant corruption, in all spheres, of political, social and economic lives, of the wider Afghan communities. This has somehow, created a notion that the country has failed to accentuate the development process even, by riding popular international support, and render succour to its denizens, who have suffered three decades of war and unrest.

Careful analysis of the development process, however, clearly suggests that things are not as grim as painted by the media. To understand the development process in Afghanistan, one needs to see development separately from terrorism, despite their inescapable mutual link. The readers should also free themselves, from the clutches of Gross Domestic Product (GDP) and Per Capita Income (PCI) standards—the mainstream assessment tools of development.

The economists are deeply tilted towards assessing development through key numbers and figures, especially GDP and PCI, to name a few. But, the process of assessing the whole gamut of development, through GDP and PCI alone, in a war-torn country, is often questionable. Afghan economy continues to grow, with real GDP growing at 8.2 per cent, during financial year 2010-11.[1] Even though the GDP per capita is constantly rising in Afghanistan, they do not look too great when compared to global standards.[2] The GDP per capita, along with the grim media reports, colour international perception about the pace and quality of development efforts in Afghanistan. They portray an incomplete and inappropriate picture and make the international community believe or succumb to the mainstream opinion that the development process has been completely derailed.

It is not my intention to belittle the importance of GDP and PCI per capita income, and invite the wrath of economists. This is an attempt to merely point at a vital missing link in the process of assessing development, in a war-ravaged country. My limited argument being, there is much more to the development of a war-torn nation like Afghanistan, than GDP and PCI. There is a well known saying that—it is not the data which says as much as we say about the data. The whole development debate in Afghanistan gets a little skewed in the presence of the primary economic data, which looks dismal, in the context of Afghanistan. The telling changes get brushed under the carpet.

GDP and PCI, alone, cannot assess the development of a post conflict nation. These primary data do not reflect the feeling, grit and determination of common masses to build the country. They remain silent on subtle aspects which are critical in building any war-torn country. The vision, aspiration and role of the citizen are cardinal in the growth of a country, grappling with unending war and gun battles. They should, in my understanding, be some of the key determinants of growth as well, in addition to GDP and PCI, in a conflict-ridden country, like Afghanistan.

Notwithstanding the growing insecurity, the country has made a spectacular progress in certain spheres of development, in recent years. The scale can be debated about, but not the very process of development. There are a number of reasons that obstruct the scale of development. Terrorism, coupled with deteriorating law and order situation, is one of those. Paucity of resources to accelerate development, is another. Hence, one has to understand the context of development, within these constraints, in Afghanistan. This chapter attempts to apprise the audience about the broad positive changes happening here. These changes have been largely triggered by the massive development and reconstruction efforts initiated by the State, in collaboration with the international aid agencies. And these changes hold the potential to shape and guide the future of Afghanistan.

Soon after the downfall of the Taliban the international community assembled at Tokyo and Bonn to draft the agenda of development for the war-torn country. The outcome of these conventions is popularly referred as the Tokyo and Bonn Declaration. Following the declaration, the government, in collaboration with the international community, restarted the development and peace building process in Afghanistan, with renewed vigour. A series of national priority programmes were launched, to address the issue of poverty, equity and regional imbalances.

One of the flagship programmes, the National Solidarity Programme (NSP), launched by the government in 2003, is worth mentioning. NSP remains one of the core programmes of MRRD, aimed at developing the ability of Afghan communities, to identify, plan, manage and control their own development projects. Under NSP, more than 25,000 Community Development Councils, popularly referred as CDCs, were established. These CDCs were directly elected by the community, and entrusted with the task of developing formal projects around the pressing needs of the community, and implementing the same with the resources of MRRD. As of now, more than 55,000 such projects have been identified, and implemented by the CDCs,[3] with the active participation of the community. This covers almost 70 per cent of the rural communities of Afghanistan. The programme has made a marked difference in the lives of these groups, nestled in the remote rough mountains of Afghanistan. It has directed the new nation's reach to the rural communities, and laid the foundation for an inclusive and progressive local governance, in nearly 361 districts, and every province of Afghanistan.

In 2006, there was an opportunity to visit a small village called Nylan, inhabited by seventy odd household—located in a valley, in the district of Dhanegori of Baghlan province, at an altitude of 1,732 ft (528 m). The village, as a beneficiary of the NSP programme had implemented a drinking water project (from a spring), with the resources of MRRD. It took one almost an hour to climb the steep mountain, to reach the valley, testing ones physical rigour and fitness to the last count. Needless to say, it felt nothing less than the first climb to Mount Everest when we reached it. Nylan became a benchmark to challenge peers to test their fitness level, thereafter.

It was most amazing to discover that those remote households of Nylan were receiving safe and sufficient potable water, at their door step. This had reduced the prevalence of water borne diseases and arrested the incidences of cholera death, completely. Domestic drudgery of women had also reduced significantly, as unlike earlier, they did not have to travel miles, to collect potable water. Women were using this extra time at hand, to engage in other productive activities. The enrolment rates in the nearby primary schools had gone up as well, as the children did not need to miss classes anymore, to assist in collecting water. The community had also designed an effective set of systems to manage the project completely on their own. Sustainable and effective development at its best!

It may appear to be a very humble project to an outsider, until one realises the sweeping changes it brought in the lives of poor communities, nestled in these remote and isolated locations. This was the first formal state aid, in the history of the village, spanning over a century, spreading much hope and optimism, in the remote hinterlands of Afghanistan. During my visits to more than fifty such programmes, this stood out to be one of the best, and incredibly impactful. Not only had it addressed the pressing needs of the community, but had also woven together the diverse communities and regions of the fractured State under the fabric of a nation; true to its name—The National Solidarity Programme! Some even refer to it as the National Spine Programme, as it has provided a framework to the nation to build up the development process. There are criticisms and shortcomings, too. But they are too meagre to subdue the positive changes the programme has brought about, in the lives of the rural populace living in inhospitable mountainous terrain. 'You must ask your worst critics to visit a few NSP aided remote villages,' was my suggestion to the versatile Ehsan Zia, then minister of MRRD, to ward off any criticism about NSP. The success of NSP, indeed, looks very different from villages, rather than from Kabul.

In Afghanistan there is, historically, little or no tradition of formalised community participation in political decision making, or developmental planning. In that sense the NSP programme has established a new trend, whereby communities are being empowered to make decisions and control issues affecting their lives and livelihoods. There is a major shift in the development paradigm, too. The conventional and authoritarian, top down decision making process, have gradually transformed into a participatory, bottom up and decentralised decision making process. Historically, the rural political space was always preoccupied with the traditional *shuras*, largely run by elite family lineage. These *shuras* mostly remained active on the domain of conflict resolution. They dispensed rouge justice, and remained silent on issues concerning larger public good. However, they were able to secure peace in the village with their traditional form of non-participatory governance.

The NSP has engineered a silent transfer of power in the rural landscape and the CDCs are slowly neutralising the influence of these traditional *shuras*. The NSP has broken the anarchy of traditional leaders to a large extent, if not completely. It has also created a healthy ecology of new leaders. The democratically elected CDCs are represented by close to quarter of a million (mostly new) leaders, spread across the length and breadth of Afghanistan. This is a welcome change and augurs well for the country, as it surely needs fresh and thinking leadership, for a change. How Afghanistan is going to fare up in future, largely depends on the action and thinking of these leaders. They are the ones who will charter the course and build the spirit of Afghanistan. They are the ones who will define the tenets and character of a modern Afghanistan, in a true sense. A considerable chunk of the traditional leaders have also got themselves elected in the new political space, of the newly formed CDCs. This has only lent greater credibility and legitimacy to the CDCs.

Integrating the burgeoning leadership, in the process of development and political decision making, would be a daunting task. These leaders were new to decision making in the domain of public good. They lack the art and skills of participatory decision making, by engaging the broader community. Hence, there is a massive need to build their capacity. It is with some pride mentioned here that our team was the first to realise this need, as early as in 2005. We launched massive capacity building efforts, to augment the abilities of these budding leaders. In any conflict-prone country, there is lot of catching up to do in a short span of time. Time is always in short supply, and hence its wastage is criminal. A bulk of the development actors in Afghanistan, including the State, has not focused significantly, on building capacities of the new leaders in the first phase of NSP. They held the transient nature of CDCs responsible for their lackadaisical approach towards any capacity building investment. To some extent this is understandable. But there are a few, who would differ from this mainstream analysis and thinking. They believe that new leaders can bring in rapid changes with their fresh thinking, energy and alternative approach, in conflict-prone settings. Hence, any opportunity to contribute to the new leadership in a conflict-prone setting should be grabbed with open arms, and not wasted in anyway.

In 2005, the Director of a Europe based INGO, posed me a question in an open and congenial conversation, 'Given their transient nature, what if the CDCs are dismantled tomorrow? Does all the capacity building effort go in vain, then?' Even if the CDCs were to be dismantled, the leaders with enhanced capacities will remain, and contribute to the cause of Afghanistan, forever, is my understanding. They will, thereafter, compete for new political and development space/structures designed by the State, and other development actors. They will become the messengers of peace, and accelerate the process of development through various means and ways. Even if they were unsuccessful, in their bid to gain access to new political spaces, they will always play a constructive role of a competent opposition. The same INGO approached us, to help them in building capacities of the CDCs, five years later. A 'waste of time' as one can see. However, the international community along with the State of Afghanistan has realised the 'missed opportunity'. The recently announced new phase of NSP (NSP III), aims at emphasising massively on building capacities of the newly elected CDCs.

In course of my professional stint, travelling extensively and interacting with thousands of newly elected village CDC leaders, it has been extremely invigorating to see their hope, and especially, note their efforts to rebuild Afghanistan. These unsung heroes have decided to challenge the status quo of Afghanistan, even at the cost of risking their lives. Tired of war, they are now working tirelessly as ambassadors of peace and development, to rebuild Afghanistan. Their voices are striking a greater resonance with the wider community more rapidly, every day. They have started mobilising a swelling crowd, not only by shouting popular political and religious slogans, but also with their sheer faith, grit and determination to rebuild Afghanistan. They are determined not to squander this last opportunity to restore peace and development. The NSP has ignited this rebuilding process, in the country. The government, especially, MRRD, has launched a series of programme, like the National Area Based Development Program, Afghanistan Rural enterprise Development Program (AREDP), etc., to consolidate the gain made by NSP, and complement the rebuilding process, further.

While on the subject of capacity building of budding Afghan leaders, one must deliberate on education. One cannot emphasise enough on the centrality of its role in the reconstruction and development process, in Afghanistan. Education is a cornerstone and a key prerequisite for durable peace, stability and socio-economic development, in every society—Afghanistan is not an exception. This is one area where any amount of investment, now, would pay manifold, in the long run. If we look at the experiences of South Asian countries, Asian tigers in particular, it is the strategic investment they made in the sector of education, a few decades earlier that are reaping multiple benefits, today. Without an educated and technically equipped work force, the nascent economy can hardly take up the challenge to integrate with the global economic systems, increasingly dominated by globalisation. Hence, an effective human resources development programme should be the key to rebuilding Afghanistan. It should lie at the heart of its national development strategy.

Decades of war, civil unrest, internal conflicts and political instability in Afghanistan have destroyed the basic social service delivery mechanisms of the country—education being the most vulnerable social sector amidst insecurity. In 2002, the newly established government inherited a disabled and defunct education system, with an alarmingly low level of literacy, perhaps, one of the weakest in the world. In 1,200 odd dilapidated old buildings, less than a million students (with almost no girls) were pursuing their education. And 20,000 odd teachers, again with no female participation, were engaged in shaping the country's future. The zero participation of female teachers is quite understandable. Under the Taliban, from 1996 to 2001, female education was banned and women and girls were excluded from all aspects of Afghan educational life, from primary school to university. The government closed all the girls' schools in the country and prevented female teachers from working. Many parents feared that their daughters would grow up illiterate. Some girls were secretly educated in their homes, by parents and teachers; others attended underground schools. The enrolment rate in tertiary education (higher education) had fallen to 7,881. This enrolment rate, in tertiary education, was among the lowest in the world (2 per cent of the population over 25 years of age), after the downfall of Taliban.

Since the fall of the Taliban regime in Afghanistan, the country has witnessed a dramatic turnaround in the sector of education. The ministry of education has made significant foray in the sector of education. The State has brought nearly 7 million children under the fold of education and 37 per cent (or 2.5 million) of them are girls.[7] This is the highest enrolment rate in the country's history. Afghans have affirmed their commitment to the country's future, by sending their children, including their girls, to school, in unprecedented numbers. Education has had a profound effect on girls' and women's ability to claim their rights, and to work towards equal status with men in their society, which is still, largely, patriarchal. Educating girls has demonstrated, to have a significant impact on development outcomes, in the long-term. Investing in the education of girls has a high return—both for individual families and emerging states, resulting in increased earning, empowerment and productivity. In a short span of time over 4,500 school buildings have been constructed, with active community involvement, to provide better and safer learning environments. The country has reported over eight-fold increase in the number of teachers to 170,000 (30 per cent female).

The gain made in the primary and middle education system is, further, complemented by higher education. In 2009, some 62,000 students enrolled for higher education. It is estimated that there will be 6,00,000 high school graduates, by 2014. Engineering and medical education is being pursued by the higher education ministry with renewed vigour. Women have started pursuing medical education in big numbers. Information technology education is spreading like wild fire. These are significant leaps which will augur well for the country's future development.

The human stories of change are far more encouraging than the broad figures. Once I met a rather well informed English teacher in the Surk Valley of Bamian province, during one of my scheduled field visits, in September 2007. An English teacher in a rural set up is a rare commodity in Afghanistan. Surk Valley comprises five schools, and is part of Sheeber district of Bamian. He was imparting English education in middle schools, in the said valley, on a government payroll. Even though he was paid for teaching in one school, he extended his services to two other schools. When enquired about his extended philanthropic display, he was quick to remind how his little contribution will lead to a well educated human workforce. English, as a competitive language, could integrate the Afghan youth with the rest of the world, and benefit them greatly. He, further, reminded me about the spread of the call-centres in India, and how the youth of India were gaining from it. His actions may have been limited to a small school campus, but his thoughts were truly global!

Large number of CDCs are displaying heightened interest in the sector of primary education and mobilising rural communities to bring more children under the fold of primary and middle education. A considerable numbers of mullahs are also pursuing the agenda of female education, during their routine Friday prayers. Hundreds of Afghans today, take pride over the fact that their daughters are studying English. Kandahar, the bastion of Taliban, has witnessed a sudden spurt in English training centres and girls have joined higher studies in the Kandahar University, too.

In the media, you will often hear about Taliban attacks and recurrent incidents of acid being thrown over girls, for attending schools. The international audience has heard these dreadful stories, time and again. Rarely are the positive changes reported by the same media. This portrays an incomplete picture of the ongoing development and reconstruction process of Afghanistan.

However, the task is not complete, and there is no room for complacency yet. The State still has to bring 42 per cent of its remaining school age children and illiterate youth, under the fold of formal education. Even though the State has made significant stride in the sector of education, it still has to completely overcome the main barriers, preventing girls from obtaining a good basic education. The key is, of course, the lack of a supportive environment in schools, the status of women in their own communities, along with the influence of conservative and religious forces preventing girls from attending school. The canvas of higher education has to be extended, further. Quality issues, within all forms of education, have to be proactively addressed. However, negating the achievements of the education sector, in the backdrop of the above problems, is unfair and unwarranted.

There are enormous challenges in setting up the education systems in any war-torn country. Paucity of resource remains one such constant challenge. It chases the State of Afghanistan to no end. The deteriorating law and order situation aggravates the situation, further. Even though there are unconfirmed reports of certain faction of the Taliban, to have decided not to oppose girls' education,[4] things have not really changed at the grassroot level. An educated Afghan society threatens the very existence of the Taliban and their extremist ideology. Hence, the unconfirmed reports are brushed aside by the State, as nothing more than a figment of imagination, of a sleek moderate faction of the Taliban, asserting limited power and authority.

In any conflict-prone setting, a thriving education sector must be supported with a robust private sector. This enables the educated youth to productively engage with the market, in order to make a decent living. This becomes imperative in a mountainous economy, where the dependency over agriculture is very limited. Productive engagement of the youth, not only fires the economy, but also binds them in the process of nation building. This goes a long way in securing durable peace in any conflict-prone country. Unfortunately, the private sector of Afghanistan is not coming up strongly, despite a wide array of steps undertaken by the State and the INGOs. The country is endowed with a trillion dollar natural bounty, in terms of mineral ore and lucrative oil and gas, but the State is struggling to convert the natural bounty into an industrial revolution.

The development sector is the second largest source of employment, after agriculture and allied activities. A bulk of jobs in Afghanistan is created by the development sector. Development actions are bound to shrink with dwindling resources and aid money flow. A significant shortfall of financial aid is expected in Afghanistan due to ongoing Euro zone crisis, followed by the painful and slow recovery of the US economy. Focus would also slowly shift to Middle East and Africa, as a consequence of the Jasmine Revolution, which saw toppling of several repressive regimes. The clinical execution of Osama-bin-Laden in the safe locale in Abottabad, Pakistan, would give another reason to the US to expedite the exit process in Afghanistan. Any reduction in availability of financial resources would seriously curtail the development and reconstruction activities, and severely dent job prospects for educated youth. Hence, Afghanistan must employ all its focus towards creating jobs, through exploration of mineral resources, privatisation and literally every possible ways. Creation of additional jobs for youth, would allow the State to consolidate the gains made by the education sector, and further the process of stability.

Even though, the State is struggling to ignite the private sector, it has done reasonably well in driving the microfinance sector, especially, in rural Afghanistan. In the recent years, microfinance has emerged as a key sector for building rural livelihoods in Afghanistan. A thriving microfinance sector will not only aid the rural economy but also help the rural populace, to diversify their meagre productive assets, and be better prepared to guard against any exigency.

Afghanistan still lacks a formal financial infrastructure for accessing affordable credit and other financial services. In the absence of a formal banking system in rural areas, the rural populace struggles to access loans, to bridge consumption gaps, or invest in productive asset. They finally end up either pawning or liquidating their meagre productive assets. Such a situation only perpetuates poverty in the rural setup. Poor families require small and repetitive loans to meet their credit needs and to invest in productive assets, to combat the vicious cycle of poverty. Availability of microcredit and saving services enable the rural communities to rebuild their livelihoods, after years of civil war, terrorism and drought. There has been a massive effort, by all development actors, to promote and strengthen the sector of microfinance. A large number of agencies, like the Microfinance Investment Support Facility for Afghanistan (MISFA), Bangladesh Rural Advancement Committee (BRAC), First Microfinance Bank (FMB), Foundation for International community assistance (FINCA) etc., are engaged in building the sector of microfinance. The State of Afghanistan is, further, complementing their efforts to expedite the spread of microfinance to the country side. The collective efforts of both the State and microfinance agencies possess the potential to build a microfinance movement in Afghanistan, like India and Bangladesh.

The INGOs, in communion with the local NGOs, are promoting SHGs on large scale to provide affordable saving and credit services to the rural populace. Their efforts are, further, complemented by a wide range of microfinance agencies, like BRAC, FMB, and Microfinance Agency for Development and Rehabilitation of Afghan Communities (MADRAC) etc. These agencies are giving loans to the SHGs, to improve their lending abilities. Besides providing loans to the SHG, these agencies are further, providing loans to low income families, along with small and medium entrepreneur to start/upscale their business. The MISFA, as an apex body is working towards coordinating and supporting the microfinance agencies in Afghanistan. This is fuelling the informal economy in certain rural pockets, especially, in the northern provinces. This multi-actor collaborative endeavour has reached 26 out of the 34 provinces and covering almost 15 per cent of Afghan families in the country side, under its fold. Through various instruments of credit, close to a billion dollar of loans have been allocated to poor families to improve their livelihoods. And it is heartening to find that 50 per cent of these loans have been, actually, allocated to rural women. This intervention has come a long way and possesses the potential to transform the rural economy, if pursued with greater zeal and enthusiasm.

Realising the unfolding opportunities and potential, MMRD launched Afghanistan Rural Enterprise Development Program (AREDP), to consolidate the initial gain by promoting and providing financial linkages, along with business ideas to saving and credit groups. The efforts of MRRD are expected to add further momentum to the sector of microfinance.

The INGOs had great difficulty in initiating a saving and credit intervention in Afghanistan. There was a section of professionals, both expatriates and locals, quite averse to the programme, as it dealt with loan and interest. They were uncomfortable with the idea of charging interest against loans, provided to poor families, which goes against the laid tenets of Islam. However, the INGOs were able to win the argument in favour of the programme, as the interest generated, from the families through loans, went into the welfare of their peers, within their group and the village at large. Every agency grappled with the same set of problems, within their institutions, in the initial phase of their intervention.

A large number of mullahs, too, were averse to the programme. However, they were mobilised through proactive persuasion and clarification. It amazes me no end to report that a considerable section of the mullahs have enrolled themselves, under the fold of the saving and credit programme. There cannot be any religion above humanity. And Islam has the highest respect for humanity. It is only the interpretation of a handful of radical mullahs, which impede the flow of saving and credit programmes. This is a futuristic programme and rural Afghan communities, by enrolling in large numbers, have laid down their goal of growth, development and prosperity. The participation of women, in large numbers, has further, emphasised their growing role, within and outside the peripheries of their household. There are umpteen powerful individual stories of women, on how they have been able to transform their lives with the help of microcredit. The most touching one was of a widow, who equated the group to her self esteem, as it had saved her from bowing to her relatives for credit, to avert a crisis, every now and then.

Like the above sector, there has been sporadic sparkling achievements in the sector of health, infrastructure, energy and drinking water, too. The gains in the above spheres of development may be modest. But, one has to look into the gains within the constraint of resources, and deterioration of law and order situation. The achievement of the State and other development actors, even if modest, has to be lauded as it has set up the process and priority of development.

In 2010, UNDP ranked Afghanistan, 155 out of 169 countries, using a Human Development Index (HDI). Even though Afghanistan has fared very poorly, virtually by every development indicators, like nutrition, Infant Mortality Rate (IMR), life expectancy and literacy, it has made a marked improvement from 2004, when Afghanistan was ranked 173 out of 174 countries in HDI, by UNDP. The country is improving for sure. Along with the State, there are a large number civil society leaders and institutions working tirelessly to build a new Afghanistan, driven by the concept of peace, equity and social justice. All these actions would count and converge, someday, into a peaceful, stable and modern Afghanistan.

A lot of international experts would disagree with me, and will not subscribe to my opinion about an emerging new and modern Afghanistan. A development worker to the core, my basic orientation makes me see hope out of despair, unity in divisions and opportunities in every challenge. If one has the guts and gumption to criticise the State for its inaction on a wide range of issues, especially governance, one should also have the courage to admire its achievements in key sectors. More than sectoral gains, it is particularly exciting to witness the ideas and actions flowing from ordinary people, to rebuild the country. One can witness a glimmer of hope building up, in this mountainous and picturesque set up, embattled with terrorism. And this hope is catching the imagination of the ordinary men, like never before. Not everyone is cynical and despondent about the future. A wider cross-section of the Afghan society is in fact rather hopeful and optimistic about their future. They are not ready to squander their last chance in rebuilding the nation. A foundation for a modern Afghanistan is being laid even in the backdrop of militancy and increased insurgency operations.

---

1. Afghanistan Economic Update, www.worldbank.org.af, June 2011.
2. Afghanistan, data.un.org
3. National Solidarity Programme, www.nspafghanistan.org
4. Afghan Taliban end 'opposition' to educating girls, www.bbc.co.uk, 14 January 2011.

THE AFGHAN DIARY

Kabul Days

Relentless attacks, spanning over three decade, have failed to break the spirit of 'this city', and its ability to move on, amid crisis. It still soaks one in its pulsating charm and vibrant tempo.

I came to know of Afghanistan, through the famous and gripping tale of *Kabuliwala*, by the great Rabindranath Tagore. It was the story of Rehmat, the Afghan Pathan, who had to travel all the way to Calcutta (now Kolkata) in India, to earn a living by selling dry-fruits; a tale of an unfortunate, poor man whose ill-fated imprisonment in an alien land, for fourteen years, estranged him from his little girl, who lived far away in Afghanistan.

Like any other Bengali child, I too, grew up with the story. My father narrated this touching tale, umpteen times—each time deeply moving me, and stoking a certain longing within me for this unseen, far-away country. My eyes would brim with involuntary tears, every time I wondered what might have happened to the daughter of Rehmat. As a little boy, I shuddered to think, how she might have managed her childhood without her father. The very thought that his little child may be lost, or may not recognise him when he returned home, years later, disturbed me greatly.

Not just Bengalis, most Indian children, who grew up in mid seventies, like me, were also familiar with this story. They have been through *Kabuliwala*, time and again, as part of their school text. While Tagore's eloquence created a stirring impression of the remoteness of Afghanistan, it was a 1956 legendary Bengali movie, by Tapan Sinha, based on the story that gave us an idea of what this vast mountainous country looked like. A subsequent Bollywood movie made it even more popular. The story had the power, and emotional vigour to connect India and Afghanistan. This one story carried a legacy that marked the India-Afghan friendship, running over centuries now and *Kabuliwala* was my share of a modern day fairy tale. It aroused in me immense curiosity to know more about this strange land that lay wrapped and lost, in vast swathes of unending desolate tracts, and inaccessible, perilous terrain. It was a much better Afghanistan than what it has turned out to be.

Another vivid memory of Afghanistan from my childhood days was the long-bearded, turban-wearing, tall and strong Mujahideen, fighting Soviet occupation, in the barren mountains of Tora-Bora, in the Kunduz region of Afghanistan. Television was a luxury in our times, especially, in humble small-town families, like ours. I managed to get glimpses of those fighters while watching news at my late uncle's house. Occasionally, we also watched Bollywood movies, shot in the snow-capped mountains of Afghanistan—heroes wooing gorgeous heroines draped in shimmering chiffon, in its milky white terrain. It was a treat for our eyes! Having been to those mountains and experienced its cold waves for real, I wonder now, how those Bollywood beauties could withstand the chill, in their scanty chiffons, and still manage a sweet romantic smile!

While watching those movies on Afghanistan, and witnessing the proud Mujahideen fight Soviet occupation, little did I know, that I would step in the land of the same Kabuliwalah at some point of my life to contribute towards the cause of war-torn Afghanistan.

My Afghanistan foray might have been sudden, but not entirely unplanned. I always believed in taking up daunting tasks, and challenging the status quo of the marginalised and disadvantaged section of the society. These values were reinforced in my mind as a part of my formal education in rural development. Every successive job that I undertook thereafter strengthened this purpose, and made it an integral part of my system. It is more of a DNA issue now. I was looking out for a bigger and more importantly, a high order professional challenge, after completing one decade of structured engagement towards promoting governance and basic rights issues (especially, Dalit Rights Issues), in the Thar Desert region of India.

Working for Dalit Rights Issues was one of the telling phases of my development career; my first test of professional success, though very moderate. The Dalits in western rural Rajasthan are still treated as untouchables, and subjected to series of socio-economic marginalisation. If not completely transform their lives, through our efforts, we were able to generate hope and optimism in the lives of the Dalit community. An opportunity to work with an organisation like UNNATI and other civil society partner institutions, made this possible. The professional space and freedom provided to me at UNNATI, allowed me to audaciously address issues that kept the Dalits entrenched in a vicious cycle of deprivation. While working there, I also came across one of the most impressive leaders of the Indian voluntary sector, Binoy Acharya. I learned a lot while working under him, and he became my mentor in many ways. But, more than anything, I developed a tremendous regard for him and his unflinching commitment to the cause of the marginalised and disadvantaged. His words: 'In development there is no room for 99 per cent!' became my talisman, prompting me to step up my endeavour and give my 100 per cent, every time.

Since I had ventured into the development sector purely by choice, I remained fastidious, not only about the tasks I undertook, but also how I executed them. After leaving UNNATI, the struggle for a more meaningful professional stint kept me preoccupied, for a while. I eventually, approached an international agency with the proposal to replicate the Dalit Human Rights campaign at the national level. However, my initial enthusiasm failed to reach a conclusive end.

During those days, 2003-2004, a few of my friends were travelling abroad to explore new frontiers of development, and take up new professional challenges in conflict-ridden countries. One such friend, Sachin Sachdeva, from the developmental sector, working in Afghanistan, would have an impact over me in the years to come. Afghanistan, to developmental professionals, was a destination as important as the Silicon Valley to the information technology sector. But, not for everyone! Only those daring to challenge Afghanistan's status quo by risking their lives, would go there.

I enjoyed prolonged parleys on Afghanistan with Sachin, whenever he came home on leave; which albeit short, were frequent. How he managed so many breaks at such short intervals, was a wonder. Sachin educated me. These breaks were meant for 'rest and recreation', popularly known as R&R, in Afghanistan. They were specially granted to development professionals to ensure they didn't get sucked into the depressive gloom of war and insurgency in Afghanistan. It was a new and alien term for someone who enjoyed just one annual leave. Even if a little envious, I acknowledged its significance; those dedicated souls deservedly earned them. Wedged amidst an ongoing war and insecurity, living as recluses away from families, they needed a break every now and then, to relax themselves—to recoup and rejoin with fresh vigour. I, however, had a battery of questions for Sachin on each occasion which, regrettably, may have defeated the purpose of his R&R. Sachin never complained or expressed his anguish, even if he got tired of me. On the contrary, he would go to any length to entertain me, because of the long-standing friendship and the professional chemistry we shared.

Working in conflict-ridden countries unravels tremendous set of challenges. It tests the making of a development professional, in every possible way. Afghanistan stood apart, as the most demanding of the lot. It beckoned me, and this passion was finally fanned by Sachin. He started exploring my interests in Afghanistan. After a series of consultations followed by a structured, competitive interview, I was selected for a decent job, with an international agency with global repute. My employer was a visionary and an inspiring leader whose foundation carries out development and philanthropic work, all over the world. Perhaps, it needs to be mentioned, the agency I represent is one of the leading non-governmental organisations in Afghanistan, implementing multisector development programmes, worth over USD 60 million, annually.

Soon, it was my time to step into the land of Kabuliwala. It was time for me to discover what happened to the Mujahideen, and to finally witness for myself the snow-covered, milk-white mountains of the exotic Afghanistan. But, by then my knowledge and understanding about Afghanistan had expanded beyond these early ruminations. The horrific sight of the ex-president of Afghanistan, Najibullah hanging from an electricity pole in Kabul was fresh in my mind. The Taliban was an alarmingly new addition. 9/11 and its aftermath, was a shocking new reality. And the lethal nexus of Taliban-ISI was, for every Indian, a new-fangled cohort, to be wary of. I started dreaming about the challenges lying ahead.

Several questions started cropping up in my mind. Will I be able to make a difference in Afghanistan? Will I be able to add value to the lives of ordinary Afghans? Will I be able to complement the ongoing development and reconstruction efforts? It was also time for me to test my knowledge and skills in the international arena. My professional excitement was at an all time high. Even without knowing the ground realities, my mind was working out developmental strategies. Amid all the excitement and challenges, my mind and spirit were getting ready for a tough, yet one of the most fascinating phases of my life.

Taking up a job in Afghanistan requires great preparation on all fronts. Not only do you have to prepare yourself mentally for a rigorous international assignment, but also convince your immediate family, especially your parents, of its worth. My special 'community mobilisation' skills were put to some serious test, at the domestic front, during this time; I found myself falling appallingly short of enabling tools and techniques that would help me win a license for going and giving it a try at Afghanistan. I even doubted my command over 'community mobilisation', for the first time. Finally my wife, Anindita, came to my rescue. Also from the development sector, it was her support I was counting on the most. My past records of gender sensitiveness, in the family turf, worked in my favour. She became my shield, softening the impact of the diatribe, from all corners. Parental sanction came at last.

I had found it hard to downplay the risk of working in Afghanistan with my father, who has been an avid listener of BBC London. It was even harder to leave behind my one year old son, Ishaan. It was, perhaps, one of the most painful personal decisions of my life. My wife bravely stepped up to the occasion, yet again. Not only did she handle the separation admirably, without any complaints, whatsoever, but she also left no stones unturned to fill the vacuum of a father in a toddler's life. She nurtured him and helped him grow splendidly within this new reality. I am not sure, if my son would question my decision to move to Kabul, when he grows old enough. As of now, he understands that his father is posted in Afghanistan and can visit him only on holidays—the same R&R!

Binoy Acharya used to say that a development worker does not have any caste, creed, religion or nation. Humanity and serving the human cause is the only goal. I had applied this theory singularly in every aspect of my professional and personal life. It became particularly apt in the context of Afghanistan where extremely tricky working conditions make it impossible for anyone to last too long. Even when most of my colleagues moved to greener pastures within two years, I kept extending my contract, finally completing my sixth year in Afghanistan in 2011. Even though domestic pressure did increase, over the years, my advance mobilisation skills always came to my rescue; I managed to renew my license for Afghanistan, every year.

Till date, every terror attack, in Kabul, continues to haunt every kith and kin, who put up additional pressure at home with their overwhelming concern. While a certain amount of anxiety is understandable, excessive fretting tips the balance. Most people fail to realise that working in hostile conditions, requires an advanced set of coping mechanisms for the development professional, and his family. In order to accept the reality of these hard working conditions one not only has to conquer fear but also live in hope. Besides, developmental work like soldiering is a serious commitment that comes with a price tag. Afghanistan is a reality that my family and I have had to learn to live with.

In the early 2005 it was easier to get a visa than an air ticket to Kabul. The normal waiting period of an air ticket to Kabul, during those days, was minimum three weeks. The large wide-bodied aircraft of Ariana Airways, the national carrier of Afghanistan, was the only aircraft that flew to Kabul, bi-weekly, always packed with advisors, staff and contractors. Development and reconstruction process was in full swing, with a large number of bilateral projects with India under way. New Delhi was, further, used as a transit route by the professionals from Asia Pacific and few Western countries, especially, Canada and UK, to reach Afghanistan. There was always a beeline of passengers. As I wanted to get the ticket at a very short notice I was suggested by my Delhi based travel agent to try my luck with the manager of the airlines, and see if I could convince him about the urgent nature of my travel.

The office of the Ariana Airways was located inside the posh Hotel Ashoka in New Delhi. By all means, the manager was the most sought after person in the history of Indian aviation. Trust me, those days it was easier to get an appointment with the Civil Aviation Minister, than the manager of Ariana, in New Delhi. I had to literally camp in Delhi, with a 24x7 follow up, applying all means of communication, consistently for three days, before I finally managed to get my ticket for Kabul.

My first visit to Ariana office was nothing less than a nightmare. The whole office was flooded with water due to some drainage malfunction. I was amazed to see the manager working, quite complacently, in such a gloomy and unhygienic environment. I was compelled to ask myself, 'Is it the bad luck of Afghanistan that follows it everywhere, or does it deserve any better?' This was my first exposure to the new Afghanistan in the making. In a leap of faith, I pulled up my trouser and waded through the water to have an audience with the manager. In a sense this was my first contribution to the new Afghanistan.

Even though I managed to get the ticket, the manager cautioned me that he might have to cancel it, should any VIP board the flight, at the last moment. The caveat ensured that I had sleepless nights, till the penultimate day of my departure to Kabul.

I have never fathomed the premise behind special reservation given to political leaders in the public transportation systems, of India. One of the strangest things in India is that there are special reservation quotas fixed for politicians in every train even when they are least likely to travel by them; they are more likely to block the same train during protests. Similarly even when state run buses are the first casualty during political rallies and strikes, the opposition leaders continue to enjoy special reservation quotas in them. Reservation meant for politicians in aircraft at least stands to some logic, as they travel by plane most of the time. But many a politician, especially the powerful ones, end up delaying the flights, causing inconvenience to the air passengers.

Somehow, I was sure that no politician would turn up, at the eleventh hour, in such life threatening conditions. Kabul was neither a place to display political eloquence nor dispensation; it was not a destination for their enigmatic holidays, either. My naïve political analysis was proven right and I was at last issued the much awaited boarding pass. The manager did not fail to remind me of the 'extraordinary favour' he did to me; I returned a beaming smile and promised to remain grateful, forever. Seven years later, there are five flights available for Kabul. The enviable post of the manager in Ariana has disappeared, as it could not withstand the burgeoning competition from the private aircrafts; lost in the annals of Indian aviation history, almost as rapidly as his meteoric rise. This is what privatisation does to state run carriers!

started skimming over the approach path, I witnessed the carcasses of aircrafts, a reminder of Kabul's horrific past. I also saw the gleaming, new age technology fighter aircrafts—I guess, waiting to tame the Taliban.

It was 5 May 2005. From Delhi, where the mercury was soaring over 45°C, one was landing in Kabul at a soothing temperature of 20°C. This was my first pleasant experience of Kabul, with many more to follow. However, I quickly recalled that the same mercury would dip to -23°C, in the peak of winters, and I was immediately concerned. My first pleasant surprise was short-lived, for sure. Deep inside, I started wondering how I would cope with such extreme cold. It is a big worry for anyone, who is at best equipped to cope with just about 2°C and no less. Remind any South Asian about the freezing winters of Kabul and they will not sound very enthused about their future plans about Afghanistan. It is amazing though how quickly I acclimatised to the harsh and inhospitable winters and even started enjoying them after a while.

The Kabul Airport, I landed the first time, was nothing to write home about. The infrastructure was very minimal, and floor area would not even be 5 per cent of the recently inaugurated swanky Terminal III of Indira Gandhi International Airport. Having travelled through the airports of Atlanta, Cincinnati, Dubai, Cairo, London and other Indian airports, it was quite a letdown for me. As a novice international traveller, I always had the impression that international airports were always big and beautiful. I also found, much to my surprise, that in Kabul both the domestic and international airport operated from that same match-box space. Little did I know of the difficulties of a conflict-prone nation, in putting together a big infrastructure project, like an international airport. However, Japanese benevolence came to their rescue, after couple of years, as the government of Japan assisted in constructing a new international terminal in Kabul. The new international airport premises, though still modest, sports a few duty-free shops. I never forget to enjoy a cup of coffee and do some window shopping, every time, I fly out from Kabul. This is a rare luxury, which I missed during the initial three years of my stay there.

I found the airport chock-a-bloc with the expatriates when I walked in. Even with their limited command over English language, the immigration officials were very friendly and cordial in their conduct. The maxim, 'small is beautiful' made sense for once, as I entered the immigration area; I was cleared within five minutes. This is a great surprise for anyone who has been through the Delhi or Mumbai airports. It takes nothing less than twenty minutes in New Delhi and thirty minutes in Mumbai; one may be even grilled about inane things like salaries on such occasions. Mumbai and Delhi may take a cue and learn a few things about speeding up their immigration systems from Kabul. In my last five years, never have I wasted more than ten minutes at the immigration counter of Kabul Airport.

The happiness of having escaped the immigration queue was, however, short-lived. I was in for a series of hurdles, hereafter. The first thing that went wrong was the luggage belt. It simply stopped working—a very common feature of the old Kabul Airport. On inquiring, I was told that I would have to go through the 4x4 ft window (through which the baggage carousel entered the airport terminal), get out of the terminal building to identify, and get my luggage back through the same window. It was quite a back-breaking task for someone, with a chronic backache. Next was the task of locating a trolley. The ones lying around were either wobbly or broken. The better ones, I realised, were being commandeered by private porters, who seemed, to me, helpful airport attendants at first. It required some skill to grab one, and then bargain with them. To curtail my dependence over them I decided to find a way around; I changed my entire fleet and opted for wheel-fixed luggage from my next trip!

The parking area of Kabul Airport proved to be another battleground. The layout was quite confusing; spread over three zones (A, B, C) with no instructions whatsoever. Parking A, I figured out was meant for UN and diplomatic vehicle with UN and CD number plates only. Parking B was meant for vehicles with special passes issued by the Ministry of Interior. It was understood that for a commoner like me, the vehicle would be waiting in Parking C. My guess was right. I made it a point, hereafter, to give a more detailed brief, of the escape route from the parking maze, to my friends and colleagues visiting Kabul. Actually, much of our thinking system gets frozen the moment the aircraft hits the ground in Kabul. I guess this is largely due to the perceived image of Afghanistan, created by the media. You feel like, 'Alice in the Blunderland'. It is only with passage of time that one discovers the wonder of Afghanistan.

Recently, I met two engineers from Bharat Heavy Engineering Limited, India, at Terminal III of Indira Gandhi International Airport, New Delhi, on their way to Herat, a province of Afghanistan. They were assigned the task of assisting the project team, set up by the Government of India, in fixing up the Salma Dam Hydro Electricity Project, in Herat. They were visibly shaken and pondering ways to avoid a night halt in Kabul, in order to reach Herat. They were afraid, as they have learned from the television news about the high threat perception. However, after much persuasion and exchange of phone numbers, they did agree to stay overnight. Incidentally, I have seen many such first timers to Afghanistan, with the same set of syndromes, in almost all my previous thirty odd trips to Kabul. And I have developed certain mastery in counselling them and allaying their fears and concerns.

As the vehicle inched through the busy traffic, Kabul seemed like a normal bustling city—far less devastated than one imagined and not at all as pathetic as projected by the media. Busy construction sites on the streets were a reminder of the new Kabul in making. The city was soaked in a cloud of dust even on a normal windy day. Some thirty years ago, Kabul used to be different, the driver reminded. The war denuded the green hills of Kabul, bringing down large swathes of sand into the city. Rapid urbanisation and infrastructural development eroded the remaining green cover. There is no escape from dust now; nobody was complaining either. It is the price of war and development, Kabul must pay. The denizens of Kabul have learnt to move on, but not hopelessly. They trust they will rediscover the old Kabul with lush green mountains, someday. It is their indomitable faith in life, and their die hard spirit that keeps Kabul still pulsating.

Through the swerving mass of unruly cars and snarling traffic, I spotted a large number of women without burqas—all nattily dressed in trousers and coats. I was beginning to enjoy the ride through modern Kabul. This is not to say that women without burqas are the only symbol of modernism, in Kabul. Over the years, I have been through many a heated discussion with local Afghan colleagues, cutting across gender lines, in various training sessions, on the same burqa and its relevance, in the context of Afghanistan. The general consensus is that it should be a choice best left to women. The women without burqa, I met while travelling from the airport, are the ones who had made their choices and let their actions speak. But, even today, there are scores of women who have decided to stick to their age old tradition. I surmise, more than a personal choice, it is a diktat of the rigid patriarchy they have been forced to live with.

While travelling, from the airport, I found that every house was fenced with high walled boundaries. The large palatial entrance gates were decorated with copper and brass plates or elaborate artwork. The colour of these gates, their designs and motifs, matched the rest of the building. Whether the choice of the gate influenced the pattern of the building or the décor of the house prompted the final touch on the gate, I never figured that out. It is still an enigma for me, like so many others, which cropped up later during the course of my stay in Afghanistan.

Eventually, when I had the privilege of taking a peek into these formidable castles, it was a surprising revelation. Nestled amidst the officious high walls was a different world altogether. Well tended lawns, trees of pomegranates, vines of grapes and huge, gorgeous roses, adorned the interiors. One is amazed to see the array of roses in Kabul which are of the rarest and the most exquisite variety. Another trademark of every old house in Kabul is tall conifers and large manicured gardens. Kabul has still not caught up with the ghetto culture and its climate is cool and romantic. During winters, with heavy and regular snowfall, it is a picture perfect white city—far better than any stretch of imagination.

Unfortunately, very few of the original occupants of these luxurious houses live in Kabul. They have left for safer and more secure locales in the West, mostly Canada or Germany, leaving their bungalows, under the supervision of their relatives. A hundred odd international NGOs, who have swamped the place, have taken them up on rent and set up picturesque offices and guest houses. This has inflated the real estate to such astronomical heights that Kabul can be compared to any global destination today.

As we meandered along the by-lanes of the posh locality of Wazir Akbar Khan, I was surprised to find no street numbers, house numbers or name plates. I deduced anonymity was a necessary prerequisite for survival here. It helped to reduce visibility, just as much, as the high boundary walls. I was quickly learning the lessons in security, which is a must when you want to make Afghanistan your second home.

I was about to reach my hotel when the security advisor announced that a Burmese professional from UN had been killed by a suicide bomber; he was chatting online with his girlfriend, in a cyber café when the attack took place. This shocking welcome news proved to be quite a damper. All my initial enthusiasm vanished like the morning dew. I felt quite shattered for a while. Kabul witnessed the kidnapping of Italian national Clementina Cantoni, the very next week. She was picked up while she was travelling back home after office hours. This incident intimidated the whole expatriate fraternity in Kabul. I had no idea that I would be subjected to such horrific news, over the years to come, with unfailing regularity. In a way these incidents prepared me for a new way of life in Kabul. I would soon overcome my fear of death, and learn to maintain certain equipoise in the face of the worst disasters. Suicide bombing, or kidnapping stories do not startle me anymore. I do not agonise over the fact that it could be me, tomorrow. I have calmly accepted the reality that is Afghanistan.

India in Kabul

You cannot escape India in Kabul. There is little bit of India in every aspect of Kabul life. I discovered, to my great surprise, that the hotel I had been booked into was called Hotel Jaisalmer. Famous for the splendid golden sand dunes at Sam and Kuri, Jaisalmer is a favourite tourist destination in India. People, from all over the world, come to watch the sunrise and sunset, amidst its golden dunes. It also has a beautiful majestic fort that has been epitomised, by the Oscar winning film maker of India, Satyajit Ray, in a movie called *Sonar Kila* (Fort of Gold). During the course of my work I have been to Jaisalmer, many times. The golden city still remains my favourite locale for family holidays. It was hard to conjure the desert of Jaisalmer, far away in mountainous Kabul. I was therefore, curious to know more about the owner and his decision to name his hotel so.

Before checking in, I asked the manager to explain the premise behind a 'Jaisalmer' in Kabul. I found that he was a second generation entrepreneur from Mumbai. The increasing pace of reconstruction and development efforts in Afghanistan, and a billowing Indian population in Kabul, had assured him a good business. There were estimated 3,500 Indians working in Afghanistan. It was only prudent to think that his restaurant would eventually attract visitors from other countries, as well, who were very eager to try out Indian food. The aroma of the hot Indian curries was spreading faster than the economic crisis in America and European countries. The name 'Jaisalmer' was chosen with care to exude the additional charm of an exotic get-away in the troubled backdrop. I was extremely relieved to know Indian curries will not be far away from me in Kabul either. I soon discovered another Indian owned restaurant in the vicinity called the Delhi Darbar. To maintain a cutting edge, its owner represented eastern India. It served great fish curries, to compete with food from western India, served in Jaisalmer. The visitors were not complaining. They relished every slice of the 'taste of India' in a foreign land. Many may find it hard to believe, but Kabul is a hub of great eateries. A surprising range of Thai, Latin, French, Lebanese, Mexican and Croatian restaurants throng the war-torn capital. The presence of an ever-growing expat population and their gastronomical drive, have ensured a reasonably thriving hospitality industry.

Soon Jaisalmer became a vibrant meeting point of every Indian in Kabul, to celebrate all kind of festivals; Holi (festival of colour), Diwali (festival of light), etc. It was a home-away-from-home for us. I remember an Indian consultant, who came on a short stint once, was very upset with the idea of being holed up in Kabul during Holi. Knowing how wildly people enjoy Holi in northern India, it was easy to sympathise with him. To humour him, I took him to Hotel Jaisalmer where he recovered almost magically. He also proved, to every one's satisfaction that he didn't have two left feet, as he initially claimed. Jaisalmer was the best anti-depressant for us Indians. The reverberating buzz of animated discussions and debates, on all and sundry topics, cut through any gloom and injected a happy, positive energy, almost immediately. Even the most inane conversations were pursued with utmost zeal. The famous French restaurant La Atmosphere was another rallying point for expatriate professionals, yearning for good wine and company. The restaurant was more popular for serving exotic range of wines than food. It was a popular food joint and hang out, especially, for the Westerners. It was also the place where most of the love stories among expatriate professional began in Kabul. The youth particularly found it too irresistible a locale to give it a miss. It was filled with expats during evening hours, engaged in intimate trysts, trying to catch up with their share of joy and happiness in Kabul.

My Friends

If you want to enjoy your professional stint in Afghanistan, you must be blessed with four things—good friends, a good employer, a good boss and an engaging and challenging job. Fortunately, I was blessed with all of these in abundance. My friend circle swelled and took the perfect shape of a South Asian Association for Regional Cooperation (SAARC); Pakistani friends dominated my inner ring; a British friend was the perfect icing on it. We worked hard and played hard; gathering routinely to party during the weekends. Barring me, all the other guys were from the MTV generation and I failed to match their energy levels when it came to dancing and staying up late. Being a teetotaller there was a huge risk of ending up as a party pooper in these semi-wild party circuits. I made an extra effort to take care of my friends, instead. And they gave me ample opportunities to look after them. I was the shoulder they could literally lean on, when they lost their way during these late night parties, in an inebriated foot-loose state! It is a role I have played to perfection, right from my college days.

Another memorable incident was the special Holi party, organised for us Indians, by our Pakistani friends, Asif, Akhtar and Bashi. I was overwhelmed and very moved with this gesture. In a truly Indian style we prepared *bhang* (an intoxicant herbal drink), to add an extra punch on that occasion. *Bhang* is made from dried leaves and flowering shoots of hemp, and is synonymous with the festival of Holi in Indian culture. The news of *bhang* spread all over the office, the next day. It could not be kept a closely guarded secret with our reflexes failing us so badly. My friend Mihir was unable to locate the door of his room, Sanjeev was unable to collect the keys from the floor and I was fumbling with my keyboard. Sensing my sluggish response, my Swiss-German boss, Dr Suter permitted me to take a day off, to rest and recuperate. However, in the same breath he enquired if there was any left-over *bhang*. It was great to see an avid vodka lover, asking for the Indian *bhang*. I still owe him a few glasses.

I have been exposed to a very different Pakistan through my expatriate Pakistani friends in Kabul. I am certain they, too, have changed their views of India after meeting us. I, especially, enjoy their crackling sense of humour which is absolutely infective. We take turns in supporting each others' cricket team, when they play against England and Australia. Our national loyalty drives us apart only when we have an India-Pakistan match. Our analysis cuts across any and every theme from the mundane to the esoteric. We are comfortable discussing anything and everything; from the hottest item girls in Bollywood to the politics of Kashmir. The one thing that continues to amaze me is their in-depth knowledge of Bollywood. How they manage to watch the latest movies even in Kabul, almost as soon as they are released in India, is absolutely intriguing; a closely guarded secret, they never reveal.

Our Pakistani friends never fail to treat us with the sweets of Nirala (a famous sweet shop chain in Pakistan) and the mouth-watering biryani of Karachi. My wife knows each and everyone by their unique idiosyncrasy and taste now, and never forgets to send them gifts on special occasions. Through this unique exposure to Pakistan I have realised the importance of a person-to-person contact for normalisation of Indo-Pak ties, which is not a mere political rhetoric.

We had many good friends from India as well. Among them the one who topped the list was, then Country Manager of Air India, Surinder Khanna; an important name in the who's who list of Kabul, especially among the Indians. He was a very unassuming man, who never flexed his muscle for the powers he enjoyed. He was our one point stop for getting air ticket to addressing any emergency, in the domestic front. More than a ticket, his presence within our close network of friends, gave us a sense of security. In advent of an eventuality we knew we could count on him, to take us back to India.

Time passes at an electrifying speed in Afghanistan. As work got more and more demanding my friend circle started denuding. Asif returned to Islamabad. With his departure, the magic of our nocturnal life, on weekends, started fading slowly. Mihir tried stepping into Asif's shoes to keep our social life afloat and kicking, but he, too, left soon afterwards. In every sense, he was a perfect clone of Asif. A beeline of departure started with the security situation deteriorating alarmingly, thereafter. Another very intense friend, Grace left for greener pastures in Africa. She had provided the perfect gender balance to my friend circle. True to her name she was most gracious in her behaviour and conduct. The night life of Kabul got curtailed to basic minimum. These were a few people who had made my life in Kabul easier. They left a permanent void in my system, with their departure. As old friends disappeared, new friends joined the circle. I discovered an amazing chemistry with Zi—a Bangladeshi born, London educated, Canadian domicile, with a great penchant for hard and quality work. She was not averse to partying either. Our Bengali connection remained a strong bond and the fact that we worked in the same department brought us even closer. Another unforgettable friend-cum-younger brother was Aslam Dhamani from Mumbai; a completely self-made man with an absolute razor edge analysis of the stock market. I would reap benefit from the stock market following his analysis and decision. Surprisingly he never followed up or made any big money himself; he simply enjoyed sharing his valuable inputs with friends. My team is blessed with two Canadian gems Reb and Ang whose penchant for perfection will always put an optimal pressure over me to strive for further professional excellence. Together, we have always ensured that we put the best, as a team.

During 2006, when Taliban made an attempt for a comeback, our mobility got restricted amidst increasing insecurity. Incidents of kidnapping of expatriate professionals were on the rise. Soon, organised local crime groups started kidnapping foreigners, under the garb of the Taliban. There were spates of suicide attacks in the streets of Kabul and the restive southern provinces. In some sense, Kabul was changing and so was Afghanistan. We were learning to adjust to this new way of life in Kabul.

Hotel Jaisalmer closed down during this time; its young entrepreneur's over enthusiastic calculations taking a nosedive in the overall environment of risk that was on rise. The government of Afghanistan through special circular banned serving liquor in public places, hence, La Atmosphere was unable to survive anymore, as their business largely revolved around wine. Delhi Darbar in a smart move curtailed their set up and switched over to serving wine (through backdoor though), with food, to maintain the break even factor; which worked in their favour. Even through plummeting business, its mouth-watering chicken malai tikkas, continued to draw salivating visitors. Soon afterwards, another Indian restaurant, Namaste India opened, trying to fill the huge vacuum left by Hotel Jaisalmer. But, looking at the shrinking clientele, I doubt how long it can survive. This is not because of the quality of food they serve, but, more, due to the heightened security risk of Indian interest from the Haqqani network of Taliban. Indian embassy was attacked twice by the same network in the last couple of years. I make it a point to take every friend, to visit this restaurant to discover the taste of India. During every visit I ruefully miss the stimulating vibrancy of Hotel Jaisalmer, and every other good thing that has become a matter-of-past, with time.

Kabul and Afghanistan have changed a lot over the last half a decade. The threat perception for a development professional has increased manifold, since then. Since kidnapping of development professionals was on rise, their movements have been restricted to the bare minimum. As an Indian you always carry an extra risk, because you may get targeted by the ISI backed Haqqani and other factions of the Taliban. With Laskhar-e-Taiba joining the bandwagon of terrorism in Afghanistan, there is always a heightened risk for Indians. Two rounds of attack over the Indian Embassy in Kabul have dampened the spirit of Indian professionals, engaged in the reconstruction and development of Afghanistan. Every attack is followed by a high level visit of diplomats from India's external affairs department, including the minister for foreign affairs to boost the morale of the Indian work force. However, the ground situation remains unchanged due to a resurgent Taliban in Afghanistan. The group has grown in strength and number and extended their sphere of influence alarmingly to Kabul today.

Despite several risks, looming large, it is a great opportunity to visit Afghanistan. Here one can witness the bounty and benevolence of nature in abundance, like never before. There is so much to explore in Afghanistan. Each day I meet new people and experience a new reality. I have built a strong contingent of Afghan friends with whom I celebrate Eid every year. Afghans have a special affinity towards Indians. You have to just mention you are an Indian, and they will open their doors and their hearts to you. Even after six years of hectic professional engagement, I do not think I have fulfilled my professional passion and ambition for Afghanistan. To be honest, I am obsessed and madly addicted to this beautiful country. This is not a job for me anymore. Afghanistan is my second home and its people are extremely close to my heart. I find it hard to think I may have to leave someday. It should be a personal decision, if at all, as I would not like to be coerced or forced by the Haqqani faction of the Taliban to leave this country, I so love.

The Arduous Professional Challenges

One bad moment separates life from death here. But despite the looming threats, 'this profession' has its own share of thrill, excitement and a sense of fulfilment, too.

Afghanistan can be sublimely scenic and beautiful. Its climatic conditions can be incredibly soothing. The amazing combination of the snow and the mountains may attract you like never before. The wide variety of kebabs can be lusciously mouth-watering, and the denizens of this country can be the warmest hosts in this whole planet. From the point of view of a tourist, Afghanistan can be the most romantic haven. One can get carried away and easily addicted to this country, just as I have been. Every bit of it can be so enthralling, so alluring, so fulfilling!

But working as a development professional, in Afghanistan, is a different ball game altogether. It is a relentless run over burning coal. Not many know about the unsung heroes—the large number of development professionals who have lost their lives in their bid to build a better Afghanistan. There are several others, who have been kidnapped and thereafter tormented to a point of no return in the last one decade. Some, who survived the torture are still trying to break out from the shackles of broken spirit and confidence. They must be questioning their decision to have forayed into its perilous terrain to change the lives of its hapless people. Several others are so frustrated that they are on the verge of giving up.

They are hanging onto thin vestiges of hope—barely coping with the perpetual strain of living precariously on the edge. A handful are persevering and counting days to finish their contract and return home safely. A professional stint in Afghanistan can be the passport for a plum international assignment in their immediate future. However, there is a sizable section of professionals who are dedicatedly and tirelessly working to espouse the cause of Afghanistan, amid alarming risk and life threatening conditions.

Working in Afghanistan is extremely difficult as it throws a wide array of challenges, with unfailing regularity. It puts the development professional through the most gruelling tests that require nerves of steel to survive. Not only do you have to prepare yourself to face the spine-chilling harsh winters of Afghanistan, but also grapple with its fragile security situation, on a daily basis. The popular principle of development science takes a nosedive and the alternative strategies do not yield any dividends here.

Even as a firm believer of participatory development, here every day, due to restricted mobility, one moves farther and farther away from the primary stakeholders. 'People before everything'— the consecrated truth instilled in our hearts, by our alma-mater, gets heavily compromised in Afghanistan. One quickly figures out that it is security and not the people, which form the favoured axis of all developmental programmes here. You are caught in a tourniquet, helplessly watching your thinking system undergo a sea change.

I was told by one of my friends working with a leading UN agency once, that most of the UN agencies keep themselves busy in analysing the security situation of Afghanistan. The security experts keep grading various cities as white city, yellow city, etc., as per the level of threat perception. No matter how much you plan, you cannot completely eliminate the serious risks to life and property, here. The UN agencies, even with their best level of security analysis and precaution, have not been able to avert attacks on their employees. That is primarily what the attack on UN guest houses in Kabul and Mazar-e-Sharif suggest. Many other agencies have been able to do relatively better in preventing life and properties of their respective institution, with lesser analysis than the UN agencies. UN, perhaps over does it! Too much of analysis can often lead to paralysis, as people say in Kabul. It is always good to be cautious in Afghanistan. Being over cautious only allows one to get sucked into the gloomy environment of insecurity and be completely paralysed.

One needs tenacity of the highest order to beat all odds and work in Afghanistan. Besides being mentally tough, one has to be tough emotionally as well. One has to consistently deal with a certain amount of emotional vacuum and turbulences, as staying far away from the near and dear ones does take a toll on the personal life as well. Back home the immediate family; too, goes through the same roller coaster of emotions and trying times. I have seen a number of personal lives crumbling under pressures of staying in the fragile and highly volatile environs of Afghanistan. A strong mind and a sound state of emotion are fundamental prerequisites for surviving in any professional capacity in Afghanistan.

Working in Afghanistan requires several others faculties and a series of preparations, at the personal level. In any country, the importance of the local language in connecting with the larger community and the local government can hardly be undermined. Afghanistan is no different. The additional qualification of having some command over Dari and Pashtu can be an enviable skill, in these parts. It also puts you in a comfortable position and provides better access to the primary stakeholders.

Connecting and communicating with people, directly in their language, has several advantages. Among other things it helps to win their confidence immediately, which may not be the case when you are using a translator. This is not to say without learning the local language, you cannot achieve much. But, I do believe that your command over the local language can help you connect with the hearts and minds of the community—a fundamental prerequisite for development jobs where everything revolves around the people. The local language not only puts you directly in touch with your primary stakeholders but also ensures availability of first hand information, directly at your disposal. It reduces your dependency on the translator and enables you to be on the top of your job. You are directly connected to the pulse of the situation. It enables one to easily gel with the larger community and it gives one the required professional edge.

Learning the local languages is not a very arduous task. I have seen large numbers of peers, from different countries developing a smattering command over the language, to be able to manage their life with ease and comfort in Afghanistan. For an Indian or a Pakistani it is easier as there is a lot of similarity between Urdu, Hindi and Dari. There is also a historic connection as the courts in the Mughal times in India were run in Dari and Persian language. The records and the proceedings were kept in the same language.

I learnt Dari not by attending language classes but through my interactions with the security guard stationed in our guest house, during the initial years. My natural penchant and a trial and error method contributed to the learning process thereafter. Developing an average command over the local language enabled me to interact with the local government officials, civil society institutions and more importantly the community directly and learn their impression and perspective on issues of wider concerns. Being a governance professional it has been imperative for me to be in constant touch with the governance structures at all levels, to get a first hand knowledge of the bottlenecks of the present day governance systems. It can place you in awkward situations at times though. During one training workshop for the district governors, a district governor criticised my module for pro-poor governance and challenged its relevance in the context of Afghanistan. My translator, scared of hurting my sentiments, sugar-coated the governor's feedback to me. Fortunately, I had understood every word uttered by the district governor. Had I not, this incident could have seriously undermined and marred my professional standing. I preferred revising the module rather than cursing myself for understanding Dari. A translator's version might often dilute the seriousness of a matter, and the need to contend a fair challenge. No matter how aggravating or humiliating, any professional would prefer to face such challenging situations head-on, and not have them, inadvertently, or conveniently distorted through translation.

In another incident, I happened to have a very interesting conversation with a mullah once, in one of the villages, located in a district of northern province. He was shocked to know I was, actually, a Hindu, offering namaz, under his guidance, at a masjid. He immediately admonished me saying, 'How can you, as a Hindu, offer namaz in a mosque?' I had to explain to him that Hindus observed high respect and tolerance for all religions. We have never been barred by our elders to enter a mosque, church or any other religious place, for that matter. It cut no ice with him! He soon came back with a bunch of photocopied material, mostly pictures to remind me about the gruesome killings of Muslims in Gujarat. He presented several pictures of Hindu mobs attacking Muslim minorities, as a proof. I was familiar with the pictures as they had been splashed in various Indian magazines during the Gujarat riots of 2002. I countered him with the Shia-Sunni riot and requested him to explain the premise between the same. He said that those riots were the handiwork of a few politicians and a thin population of illiterate, radical Muslims, from both sects. I suggested the same premise behind the Gujarat riots. He was finally convinced and thereafter it took us no time to strike a familiar chord. He was honest enough in admitting that he was trained by certain religious organisations, with strategic leaning from Pakistan, and had been asked to fan hatred against Hindus in Muslim countries. He, further, told me that a considerable number of the mullahs in Afghanistan were also trained by the same agencies, and were encouraged to operate with an anti-Hindu mandate. On enquiring how he managed to access the pictures of the Gujarat riots, he was honest enough to admit that the same had been circulated by a religious agency based in Pakistan. The said mullah had been spreading anti-Hindu sentiment for two years, through his Friday speeches. I eventually requested him to also share with the community that a Hindu had offered namaz in their mosque, for the well being of the village and its inhabitants. I was later told by my local colleagues that the mullah had indeed shared it in his next briefing. By going through this incident I also learned about the deep rooted regional conspiracy to fan hatred against Hindus. I guess such campaigns facilitate the recruitment of jihadis for international terrorist organisations to wage a so called jihad against the Indian part of Kashmir. A certain amount of knowledge of the local language can only help in unravelling the undercurrents of the Afghan society.

A command over the local language also helps one to meet with any exigency more efficiently and negotiate more effectively, than ever. I read the story of an Indian engineer, kidnapped and subsequently released from the province of Herat. He could win his release, as he was able to communicate with the Taliban in their own language. He was able to develop a rapport that convinced them that his action in no way would influence the Taliban. In a conflict-ridden country like Afghanistan, where one has to be prepared for the worst, even a smattering of the local language can be of great advantage in a crisis situation.

On the flip side, I have seen hordes of professionals depending on translators even after staying in Afghanistan for a considerable time. I do not intend to criticise them, as it is purely a matter of personal choice. Neither do I intend to take a tough position on this issue, as translation is the bread and butter of many Afghans. Of the two bulk jobs available in Afghanistan today, one is of a translator and the other is of a security guard. I wonder about their future, when peace and stability return and consequently a large number of expatriates leave.

There is a saying in Afghanistan, which is hugely subscribed by expatriate professionals, 'One bad moment separates life from death, here'. In other words, death is only one bad moment away from you. It is all about being caught up in a wrong place, at a wrong time, on a wrong day, culminating into one bad moment. No one knows and realises this better than me. I survived several such occasions where I could have run headlong into that bad moment. Once, I nearly walked into the jaws of death.

This was a suicide bombing that took place in a police bus just 30 meters away from our vehicle. Splinters of glass and metallic parts of the bus were flying all around us. The impact was so powerful that a thick envelope of smoke had covered the entire area, for a long time. We rushed from the scene, and entered my residence, located in the vicinity. We were well trained to deal with such situations. Our minds work much faster during crisis now.

As a part of our training, we had been told to always keep away, or maintain safe distance from military and police vehicles, while travelling down the streets of Kabul, or the Afghan countryside. Such security tips have helped us immensely to keep the bad moments away.

When I finally garnered the courage to go and see the carcass of the bombed-out bus, it was one of the most gruesome, gory and ghastly scenes of my life. One half of the bus had completely blown away, with scores of bodies, lying in pools of thick, trickling blood. Remnants of the driver's body were hanging over the steering. There was complete mayhem in the street, with security personnel cordoning off the site of the suicide bombing. Ambulances were plying, with screeching sirens, to carry the injured and the dead, from the site. This is a common sight and almost a recurrent phenomenon of Kabul life. One thing that the denizens of Kabul have learned, over the wars and the gun battles spanning over three decades, is to move ahead without getting affected by the travails of the moment. Within a couple of hours of every bombing, roads are cleared and everything is back to normal. Life halts for a while and then returns to normalcy in no time. My security advisor, a British ex-military officer, was annoyed with me for visiting the spot of suicide bombing. His security manual strictly prohibits any such moves. This can be seen as a serious breach of security rules and attract disciplinary action. But I was unable to control my emotions that day. I thought about those policemen, who lost their lives in the suicide attack. What was their fault? Were they not also committed to making Afghanistan a better place like us? Were their stakes not much higher than ours?

If I want to credit anyone for our continued existence, it has to be our security advisor. He had put us through umpteen drills and pre-emptive training in survival, including averting a kidnapping threat. Recognising the good ones from the bad ones from their eye-movement was the first tip. This, of course made us untowardly suspicious and doubtful of all and sundry. But, we enjoyed playing Sherlock Holmes, dodging every 'bad moment'. It is well known in human psychology that our minds get paralysed during a crisis. Modelling imaginary crisis intervention situations to prepare the mind well in advance, was another technique used by him. He was right. It honed our responses and reflex system to work faster during a crisis. In a way it helped us to keep the ever chasing bad moment away, to the extent possible. It is a must, if one wants to work in Afghanistan. Every organisation that works in Afghanistan takes their staff through such systematic orientations to ensure their safety. Those who lost their lives in their bid to make a better Afghanistan were simply unfortunate to have been struck by the bad moment I mentioned earlier, while professionals, like us, were lucky enough to keep it away for a considerable period of time. In the word of one Sufi pir I met at a Dargah, the almighty Allah must have kept us alive to contribute to the cause of Afghanistan.

Another incident, in May 2007, that severely tested my nerves was when I was travelling to a district called Talua-u-Barfak, in Baghlan, located approximately 250 kilometres away from Kabul. It is one of the Taliban influenced districts of that province. I was supposed to facilitate a cluster planning exercise, with the members of Cluster Level Development Committee (CLDC). The larger purpose of the exercise was to demonstrate a cluster planning exercise, with the CLDC. I had to do it in front of my highly competent team members, so that they could learn the art of cluster planning, and replicate the same in the other clusters of the said district. As soon as I landed in the district of

Doshi (adjacent to Talua-u-Barfak), I was warned not to visit the district, as the Taliban had issued a circular to the government and all INGOs, to leave the district, or face the music of the AK 47/56 and the rocket launchers. The state and police officials were the first to leave the district. I had to finish the exercise anyway because I was leaving for Africa the next day. Any delay would have seriously affected the timeline of the project and thrown a spanner in our scheduled plan. I have always had the privilege of working with a very efficient and street smart team, in Afghanistan. My colleagues in consultation with our Talua-u-Barfak district coordinator suggested a model for me, which I accepted, albeit with some reservation. I followed my inner voice and completely banked on the advice of my esteemed colleagues, as I was certain that they loved and respected me like a family member. They would be the last people to allow me to risk my life. I went ahead and was surprised to find that the workshop was to be conducted in an orchard, in the remote sleepy village of Sheranow. This was to lower our visibility and avoid the attention of the Taliban, and the related consequences. This was my first attempt to deceive the Taliban, with many more to follow. It was also my first experience of conducting a workshop in an open orchard, among chirping birds. The wafting aroma of pears and fresh apples did distract my attention for quite sometime, but I managed to remain focused on the workshop. Later at tea break, I was suitably rewarded for my resilience with a fresh bowl of farm-grown fruits, along with green tea.

I was just about enjoying the new and cost effective way of community development when the rain god played spoil sport to our orchard community outing. We rushed to the community hall to complete the exercise. I will, however, always treasure that experience of facilitating a workshop in an orchard.

The professional excitement was short-lived, as the anxiety of returning amidst the Taliban threat, was hounding us. We had two options before us: we could either return to our Doshi office, some 70 kilometres away or stay overnight in our modest Talua-u-Barfak office. Travelling back to Doshi was dangerous as we had to cross Kara-ga-Ghang, a place infamous for theft and murder. Staying back in the Talua-u-Barfak office was equally dangerous as the Taliban could attack it overnight, as warned. The Taliban are known for walking their talk. We decided it was better to deal with the marauders rather than the Taliban, though both were equally life threatening. I understood what it meant to be caught between the devil and the deep sea, more than ever in my life. I have always trusted the intelligence and the decision making power of my local colleagues over my own instinct in such situations; hence, the decision to march to the Doshi office was quite acceptable, even in the given circumstances. There was complete lull inside the vehicle, as we started. A little music may have enlivened the long dreary drive, but we could not indulge ourselves, for the fear of the diktat issued by the Taliban, who do not tolerate music in any form. Indians in fact, have been under dire threat and warned to curb their love for music. Meanwhile, the stoic silence of my colleagues, who were naturally worried about my safety and security, was making the long ride even more foreboding. Even with my limited repertoire of jokes, I tried my best to break the silence, but the trick didn't work. Our initial tension had lifted considerably after we travelled some distance and were nearly through the infamous Kara-ga-Ghang stretch. We could see a spark of relief in each others' eyes, but we hardly realised that the worst was yet to come. Our vehicle suddenly broke down on the dreaded stretch. It was suicidal to say the least. We were sitting ducks waiting for the thieves and brigands to maul and rob us. They do not approach their victims with sticks and knives, but with AK 47s and, also, believed in eliminating all proof before leaving the scene of crime. One of my Afghan friends describes it best: 'In Afghanistan there is no concept of half murder.'

The driver suggested we leave the vehicle immediately and take cover at a safe distance in darkness. This was to avert any risk, in advent of the robbers approaching the vehicle. In our security orientation we had been advised not to walk on unfamiliar territory as unexploded mines beneath the ground were waiting to explode anywhere, off the beaten track. In the advent of any crisis, we had been taught to crawl hugging the ground, to distribute our weight so as not to set off the mines. I was told mines can be set off with minimum weight of 40 kilos. I was following the advice of our security manager verbatim and could have won an award for being the most obedient student. I was also cursing myself for not following my wife's consistent request to exercise more, to reduce the extra kilos I had put on during my sedentary stay in Kabul. A few kilos less would have reduced the risk by several notches now. It was completely dark, and we were lying on the ground. The moon was playing hide and seek with the thick black clouds, occasionally spreading its light. Any other time, the hushed night, soaked in soft moonlight, would have been very romantic, but for us it was frightfully ominous. We cursed the moon for its occasional opulence, as it was making us visible. Our luck was certainly favouring us that particular day, even though we thought otherwise. The thieves had left for a greener pasture that night and obviously something more exciting was keeping them away from their favourite haunt. We could only pray for their continued absence.

Meanwhile, the driver had radioed for help to the Doshi office. Soon we could see a string of headlights approaching from the other side of the road. The driver finally signalled us to come out of hiding, and we bravely emerged from the darkness. The moon started looking romantic in no time. We could feel an immediate rush of relief and comfort in each others' tone and body language. There was a convoy of four vehicles now, with approximately a dozen people. Enough to outdo the marauding burglars we thought, or at least put up a decent fight. After we reached our office in Doshi that night, I vowed never to take such a risk again. I promised to be the same obedient student I used to be, once upon a time. It is important not to forget the basic tenets of safety in a moment's exuberance. It is important to keep away the bad moment and not attract the same through our misadventures. It is important to be alive in order to contribute to the cause of Afghanistan. There was no point in attracting extra risk by hurrying things in the context of Afghanistan.

On 7 August 2010, I learned that a team of medicos, comprising six expatriate doctors (from Germany, US and UK), and their Afghan translators had been killed by the Taliban, in the district of Kuran-wa-Munjan, which falls under the Badakashan province. One of the female doctors, killed in the attack, was in Afghanistan for less than a year. She met her bad moment during the very first year of her stay, while some of us have managed to keep it away. And the irony is that we have visited the same place several times, while she was visiting it for the first time. Worse still was the demise of the Indian tabla player Nawab Khan during the last day (26 February 2010) of his short maiden visit to Kabul. While he was packing in his hotel room, to catch the Delhi bound flight, a bunch of suicide bombers attacked the hotel, supposedly used by the Indian embassy for their visiting guests. This was the bad moment I was talking about, something they failed to keep away, while some of us have managed to escape.

Travelling to the various provinces and regions, in course of your work is another risky, and at times, a painful exercise in Afghanistan. Due to security reasons development professionals prefer to travel by air instead. There are special planes that fly from Kabul to the majority of provinces, including down south, carrying aid workers, and a wide array of other development actors. These aircrafts, however, cannot survive purely on the basis of their load factor, and need considerable subsidies from bilateral donor agencies. PACTEC and UNHAS, are two such companies providing humanitarian air services in Afghanistan. They enjoy vast experience and expertise, in flying light passenger aircrafts in war-torn countries, and see their operations complementing the reconstruction and development efforts. But they need subsidies to keep up their planes flying. There are several opulent Western donor countries supporting this cause, and supplying them with additional resources. These planes are the lifelines of development professionals, who have to travel to remote areas to supervise their programmes. With road services gradually coming to a grinding halt, due to the growing influence of anti-government elements, in the once peaceful northern provinces, these planes serve as their last resort to reach remote provinces within Afghanistan.

Travelling by these planes is certainly not a cakewalk and it tests your patience and nerves at every point. In the month of May 2005, I presented a comprehensive plan for building capacities of local governance structures in Afghanistan to my Swiss-German boss. He made a rather cynical remark, after reviewing the presentation. 'If you achieve even half of what you have presented I think a revolution is waiting for Afghanistan,' he had said. I was taken aback! I had a great plan, and he knew me to be a meticulous advisor. Was he then questioning my commitment? The full purport of his comment dawned on me slowly, over the next few months. During the second month of my stay in Afghanistan, when I was ready to execute my plan, my flight to Faizabad got cancelled. With the slightest drop in visibility the UNHAS flights are cancelled, on grounds of safety, and this happened for three consecutive days on the trot. Every day, I had to report at 6 am at the Kabul Airport and after a painful wait for nearly nine hours, the flight would be cancelled, eventually. On returning to the office I'd listen to the wry advice of my colleagues, 'Go slow! This is Afghanistan'. My flight schedule was quite a topic of discussion, within my friend circle and after a while it became the butt of light hearted jokes. I was very concerned with this. I would have rather made my professional visibility higher by contributing to the cause of the organisation than by being their source of humour. However, I was stuck in a situation, where my botched travel plans were part of everyday amusement. I was simply seething with frustration. I slowly realised that this was an inescapable part of the professional journey in Afghanistan, and so I needed to acclimatise to it at the earliest. Even though, I am not much of a believer, I diligently prayed for the visibility to improve, during those days. The gods, eventually, came to my rescue and, finally, on the fourth day, I took off for Faizabad. This however, wasn't the worst case scenario, as I thought it might be. I encountered several other frustrating moments down the line.

Let me share, it can be a rather unnerving experience to be travelling in a small aircraft in bad weather conditions. On a windy day in mountainous terrain, these aircrafts are tossed about, like a cork, keeping one perpetually breathless. The turbulence can be so nauseating and excruciatingly painful that one may not want to fly ever again. I remember one of my Pakistani friends, Sultan's experiences. After every flight, he would vow never to travel by small airlines again, which he had to promptly break for obvious reasons. Apart from the harrowing and bumpy rides they offered, the routing of these airlines, especially that of UNHAS, added to the travel blues. For flying to Bamian, which typically takes twenty minutes from Kabul, they would fly the plane via Kandahar, Herat and then land in Bamian. While a new traveller might enjoy a free air ride and not complain about stretching the twenty-minute journey to five hours, veterans are usually frustrated to the core. Later, one my friends employed with UNHAS explained this 'aviation commercial intelligence'. 'We are managing three routes with one plane and one set of pilots and cabin attendant'. I asked in the same breath, 'While I understand your intelligence, will anyone understand our frustration?' UNHAS has, apparently, revised the route map, recently, and so a journey to Bamian wouldn't seem like travelling half way across the globe, anymore.

Over the years now, I have lost count of the days that I have returned from various airports, in Afghanistan, due to cancellation of flights. There were several other occasions, wherein the flights took off and were unable to land in their respective destinations, again due to low visibility. However, the worst was when the PACTEC operators made me stand in the open air, in the freezing temperature of -5°C, from 6 am to 3 pm, with the hope of improved visibility for the flight to take off, which they finally had to cancel. I had no option, but to face the freezing winds, as I could not enter their container shaped office, packed with Afghan ladies (fellow passengers). They were visibly uncomfortable in the presence of a male—a typical Afghan syndrome emanating from its culture. I paid for it with a prolonged bout of fever, wherein I was completely bedridden for a while. The irony is that, like my Pakistani friend Sultan, I may vow to stop flying these routes, but

I cannot do so. These planes are the lifelines for professionals like us in Afghanistan. But, these were some of the occasions, where my frustration knew no bounds and I questioned the future of the country.

During those early days, when my spirits nearly broke, I finally comprehended the full significance of my boss's sardonic remark. He was merely cautioning me against drawing up an over-ambitious plan. Such plans would always be subjected to a series of uncertainties owing to the fragile and harsh conditions of Afghanistan. Such context merits moderation of both plans and approach. The 'Go slow. This is Afghanistan.' syndrome would have quickly sucked me in, like most and made me smug, but I thrive amidst challenge. I refused to cut back on my plans. The cancellation of flights prompted me to go whole hog and execute the plan to the fullest. My over ambitious plans were achieved over the next five years. The same programme was also highly raved about by the international media as a frontline model on local governance in Afghanistan, subsequently.

I must digress here to say that it is very important to have a good boss to enjoy your professional stint in Afghanistan. I was particularly blessed in this sense, as I had the honour of working under two great professionals. Together, they would ensure that I had the most meaningful stint of my professional life in Afghanistan. While one of them was known for his tremendous development acumen, the other was by far the best CEO, I ever met. One thing both had in common was a penchant for humour. With their departure, they left a permanent void in the system. The humour quotient in our organisation has visibly dropped, since then.

Over the years, I started relying more on road travel, successfully cutting down my dependence on flights.

Nonetheless, it remained one of the important means for travelling to down south, and occasionally to even the northern provinces—with the road travel getting choked in the recent years, due to the growing influence of the Taliban. I relied more on PACTEC than UNHAS for my travels to various regions. PACTEC has developed the uncanny knack of making it every time, even with drop of visibility. There is a saying in Afghanistan, especially, among the young development professionals, you can blindly trust three things in Afghanistan—a PACTEC flight, a Japanese girl friend and the World Bank funding the government of Afghanistan. Over five years that I have spent in Afghanistan I have realised the veracity of the above saying, especially, in the context of PACTEC. Being married, I never toed the idea of having a Japanese girl friend, but I have heard loads about their loyalty too.

Even though travelling involves a huge risk in Afghanistan, it has its own share of thrill and excitement, as well. One of the striking moments for me in Afghanistan was my first visit to Bamian in July 2005 to witness what remains, a gaping space of its monumental Buddha carvings. These gigantic statutes (121 feet and 180 feet high, each) were carved along the side of a cliff in the Bamian Valley in the sixth century in the Hazarajat region of Central Afghanistan. These were one of the most magnificent remnants of an Indo-Hellenic heritage. Today it is a testimony to its tragic destruction by the Taliban, which shook the world in March 2001.

Enclosed within the high mountains of the Hindukush, in the Central Highlands, the valley of Bamian is very different from any other region in Afghanistan. Both in its terrain and a strange reddish hue of its mountains, Bamian stands apart in certain majesty of its own. Small man-made caves, which once served as homes to Buddhist hermits, who came along the Silk Route, dot the mountainside.

The broken relics of the magnificent Buddhas stand close to the Bamian Airport. They are colossal, cavernous hollows today but awe inspiring all the same. They harboured two exquisitely carved Buddhas once. Its stoic silence reminded me of the horrific torture it underwent at the hands of the Taliban. A young guide, who took me up through the tunnels to have a view from the top, narrated the story of that fateful night when the Buddhas were destroyed. He recalled how the locals saw the Taliban trail in unsuspected at first; how they slowly spread fear among the locals with their strange ruthless behaviour, killing older folks, or burning down homes, if they refused to take their orders; and how Bamian woke up that fateful night with the thundering sound of the blasts that shattered their peace, once and for all. All international appeals to save the Buddhas had turned to deaf ears.

Despite its shocking past the historic remains of the broken Buddhas still exude a certain peace that quickly envelops any sense of misgiving. In the recent years, Japanese benevolence has restored this World Heritage Site, to the extent possible. The Taliban may have broken the Buddhas, but its spirit is still palpable in the ruins of this World Heritage Site.

Travelling across the state highways in a white Land Cruiser is another gripping experience and a real joy, which I look forward to even today. From the speeding vehicle, the picturesque mountains and the rural setting of Afghanistan look mesmerising. Rushing through the small market towns, like Charakar, Pul-e-Kumri, Takhar, Kishim, located along the highway, connecting Kabul and Badakashan, one is taken up by the vibrancy and pulsating life along the roadside. The real Afghanistan is in these local markets. Stalls heaped with fresh fruits and farm vegetables add a dash of colour to the otherwise barren surroundings. There are several good eating corners serving steaming hot kebabs, on the way. One of these is located in the outskirts of the sleepy town of Jubalsaraj just before Salang Pass. The stuff they dish out is simply irresistible. I have never been able to give it a pass, while crossing the Salang Tunnel.

Another common sight along the highways is hordes of donkeys carrying consumer durables and grocery from these markets. These donkeys are always guided by their masters. This particular aspect needs to be noted in Afghanistan. In the recent past, militants have used donkeys to wrap suicide vests and target military or police vehicles. We have therefore been oriented to be extra cautious of any donkey without a master. My donkey-observation exercises, however, have gone beyond the security aspects over the years. I can expertly identify the best donkeys from a distance and know where they come from. The best of them are found in the region of Darwaz in the Badakashan province. They can be easily identified from the size of their ears. I can categorise them not only by the length of their ears but also by their peculiar jaw movements, and other identification marks and crazy habits. I can easily make out the lazy ones from the agile ones. The only cardinal rule to be remembered, though, is not to go anywhere near a donkey that is wandering without its owner. That may spell danger with a capital D.

While travelling through these roads, you will also witness abandoned military tanks and machine guns, which will remind you about the horrific past of Afghanistan. But the Afghans are born entrepreneurs, and every action of theirs speaks volumes of their inherent entrepreneurial abilities. The Public Work Department of Afghanistan has employed the long and wide chains of these abandoned military tanks, for setting up speed breakers on the approach roads connecting the districts with the state highways. Reuse of military resources for civic cause at its best, one would say. In fact, those speed breakers serve the purpose much better than the prevalent metallic ones. These chains with their sharp spiky edge pose a huge risk of getting the tyres damaged beyond repair. No driver, therefore, dares to speed over them. They always come down to a grinding halt.

PRT and ISAF convoys, plying over the state highways are again a common sight. But you can cross them only when they permit you to do so. Even if it is frustrating, it is strongly advisable not to cross these vehicles, without seeking their permission. Few of my Pakistani friends were literally fired upon by military personnel, while they were trying to overtake a PRT vehicle, in their bid to cross Torkham Border and reach Peshawar before the sunset. But they were lucky enough to escape the bullets.

One notices a string of small shops, across the highways, selling everything from mouth watering kebabs to dry fruits and Afghan carpets—from the grapes of Chara-kar to the famous potatoes of Bamian. You can catch the locals sauntering and enjoying an easy pace of life; some busy farming in the roadside arable fields, while others shopping in the local markets. Another refreshing picture is to catch a beeline of students, especially, girls in their white scarves, thronging to or from school. Everything seems normal, warm and peaceful from the tinted panes of the Land Cruiser. It makes me want to believe that Afghanistan has a future and most Afghans want to live a normal life. There is nothing different about the way the rural folk live here compared to anywhere else. They are for peace and development. They want to work hard, send their children to school and enjoy their evenings surrounded by the warmth of their family. Someday hopefully the Taliban would get tired of war and let the country catch up with its own share of dreams.

One of the most exciting and memorable experience of my life has been crossing the Salang Tunnel. The Salang Pass is the major mountain pass connecting northern Afghanistan and the Kabul province. It is named after River Salang, which originates from the mountains nearby, and flows down south. The tunnel was constructed by the Soviet Union in 1964. It is approximately 2.6 kilometres long and is located at a height of 3,400 metres above sea level. In the peak of winters the beauty of this pass is unsurpassed. The high mountains and its massive horizontal spread, completely covered with snow, is nature at its best. When an occasional burst of sun reflects off the snow, it gleams, like a tongue of fire, trailing its way to the River Salang. Nature and science of refraction, both at its best! Till the seventies, a lot of foreigners visited Salang to ski, spending most of the day on the ski-slopes, which cover nearly one third of the mountain. But with the deterioration of law and order, the adventure snow tourism has come to a complete halt. However, occasionally you may still find a few expatriate professionals trying hard to catch up with their lost skiing skills, on the slopes.

The Salang Tunnel however, has a horrific past. On 3 November 1982, during the Soviet occupation of Afghanistan, there was a huge fire inside the tunnel, which at that time was packed with Soviet military convoys. Considered as one of the deadliest road accidents of modern times, 64 Soviet soldiers and 112 Afghan civilians were killed in the accident. During winter the Salang Pass is hit by multiple avalanches—the magnitude of such avalanches can be beyond ones imagination, at least for someone from a tropical country. The avalanche impedes the overtly busy Salang traffic, which has over 2,000-3,000 vehicles crossing through it on a daily basis. Avalanches may look enthralling when seen from a distance or on the celluloid. However, every year avalanches lead to a massive loss of property and human lives. I have had the occasion to experience one of the worst, ever.

While travelling through the area and admiring its beauty, little did I know that I will be caught up in the same and madly looking for an escape from it. On 20 March 2007, I was returning to Kabul after a fortnight long field trip. Our vehicle, along with sixty others, got suddenly stuck in the Salang Tunnel when a huge avalanche hit us, blocking the tunnel from both ends. It was a no-go situation. This meant that we had to spend all our time inside the narrow tunnel till the snow got cleared by bulldozers. It was a freezing cold day with the temperature slipping below -20°C. A rather carefree traveller all my life, let alone food, I do not even carry basics, like potable water, during travel. I never knew I had to withstand an acid test for this reckless and disorganised way of travelling, someday.

In Afghanistan rumour travels faster than the speed of light. Stuck inside the tunnel I was soon overhearing all types of rumours. Some said that the avalanche was the biggest in the century. Others said it was beyond the capacity of the existing bulldozers to clean up the mess created by it. Rumours were, of course, fed with a share of fear and I heard that a similar incident had killed fifty people, in the past. While I have learnt that one should not attach much importance to such rumours, the stories milling around were hard to ignore..

The freezing temperature ensured that everyone had to be inside their vehicle only with the slightly brave taxi drivers stepping out once in a while, to apprise us about the situation. My biggest worry was to survive without water and food, should the avalanche continue to show its wrath, as it still continued to snow heavily. Close to midnight, I had a parched throat and was craving for a sip of water. With every passing day, every crisis in Afghanistan has managed to generate a new idea in me. I have become more innovative than ever. I suddenly remembered that the Afghans were very fond of green tea. So was I. But, unlike me they always kept a cup along with a flask of green tea which they usually finished during the first hour of the journey. I managed to grab one of these cups and started collecting the falling snow into it. It was a eureka moment for me when the cup full of snow soon melted to pure water, over the factory fixed air blower in our vehicle. By then we could see the bulldozers briskly moving across, their speed suggesting some serious business at hand. We felt reassured and started hoping that the road would be cleared soon. Having solved the problem of potable water I had to attend to cries of an empty stomach. It started making all kinds of noises with the hunger pangs growing stronger by the minute. Despite trying hard, I failed to come up with any idea to assuage my hunger. I justified my inability and concluded by saying that an empty stomach does not ignite innovative thinking.

There are always a motley band of individuals, who try to make the most of any crisis and this theory, actually, cuts across, gender, religion and geographic boundaries. In the wee hours of morning, we saw a few policemen selling biscuits and fruit juices, at a rate almost five time higher than the prevailing market prices. They were our only hope and the lenders of last resort.

Not entirely sure, if the avalanche would prolong our stay inside the tunnel, I decided to hedge for an exigency, and requested for an extra pack of biscuit. The security personnel expressed his inability to entertain my request, as he had to cater to the needs of all the people stuck in the jam. A lesson in equity that impressed me! I appreciated the idea of a security personnel teaching it to a development professional, in such unequivocal terms. Over the years, I faced many instances where a layman would reinforce the concept of equity, to me, in various forms. The security personnel might have been fishing in troubled waters, by charging an exorbitant sum, but for once I was able to pardon them, as there was a noble cause attached to the act. I could not grouse them the profits of their hard work, at a time when it was needed the most.

It was twenty-four hours at a go, and our vehicle had not moved an inch. The biscuits were disappearing fast, and our condition was getting bad to worse. After twenty-seven hours, the convoy finally, started rolling forward. There was a collective sigh of relief as we made our way out of our temporary prison. We noticed piles of snow on both side of the road, through which the bulldozers had cleared a narrow passage, to facilitate one-way traffic. We also noticed a few vehicles below in the gorge presumably hit by the avalanche. This is also not an uncommon sight in the Salang Pass. Every year approximately 10 to 20 vehicles slip down the gorge, particularly during the winters. These vehicles are never pulled up by cranes, as the cost of facilitating the same would be higher than that of the vehicle. I fear that eventually after a couple of decades, Salang may look like a dump yard of vehicles.

Crossing Salang during winters is very dangerous and risky. All my friends, who keep crossing it frequently, have more adventurous stories to tell about this place. Everyone has had some sort of miraculous escape from death in these parts. That day it took us thirty-six hours to complete a stretch of 260 kilometres. In Afghanistan one has to stop counting the hours or notice the speed while travelling, as the roads are mostly unpaved and pass through torturous mountain terrain. But this is a record, which none of the expatriate professionals in my organisation have been able to break.

Another fascinating journey I used to take frequently was along the Kabul-Faizabad route, passing through Salang, Pul-e-Kumri, Kunduz, Taloqan and Kishim. This entire stretch, at one time would take two whole days with a night halt in Taloqan. Beyond Taloqan, the road was unpaved and rocky and would take the entire next day. This is something I had to undertake time and again for routine programme review and planning. One can well imagine the pain of travelling 160 kilometres over one full day.

Over the years, things have changed a lot in the area of road transportation. The stretch from Taloqan and Faizabad is metalled today, and you can easily complete the journey between Kabul and Faizabad, in a single day. And Taloqan to Faizabad takes only a couple of hours. For any country, this can be a decent indicator for progress and development. However, the same cannot be said about Afghanistan, with as much confidence. With the growing presence and influence of the Taliban in northern Afghanistan, these roads are sporadically taken over by them. The once heavy traffic of Pul-e-Kumri to Kunduz has turned into a trickle today. All the INGOs have imposed restrictions on road travel on this route. One hears about targeted terror attacks on this road almost every other day. Even while writing this chapter, I heard that a police check post has been attacked and eight Afghan policemen have been killed. This incident was covered in all international print and electronic media.

What is the advantage of having a metalled road when you cannot use it? This is the dilemma of development in Afghanistan. Security is critically linked to development. Despite all developmental process in progress, lack of security puts a spanner, every now and then. One always operates under this confusion of whether we are moving ahead in Afghanistan or not. Development is happening at its own pace; however, we are not able to extract the full scale of benefits in the interest of its people. This is one of the reasons why one has raised strong reservations against the existing US military strategy and emphasised on peace building as the chief priority in Afghanistan in the earlier chapters.

A question often asked is whether indeed, our efforts are making any positive changes in Afghanistan. I am working with civil society and governance structures that deal with people directly. I have clear evidence of improved capacities and leadership among the democratic civil society and governance structures. I can see that they are trying hard to make a sense of Afghanistan. A number of them have taken up an expanded set of roles and responsibilities with higher capacities. All the actors within their given capacities are making concerted effort to build durable peace, in their respective domain. Hence, I encounter this confusion, of whether we are moving forward, less than others. Rather, I feel very charged and excited and strongly believe that a strong civil society and government can finally tame the Taliban. I am confident that our work is moving very well in the right direction. My peers wonder what gets me so excited about Afghanistan. And, how or why, even after so many years, I do not show any signs of fatigue. I surmise that my faith in good governance and a vibrant civil society keeps me going. I have taken every failure as a challenge in this country.

As I have said earlier, common sense seems to be the most uncommon thing in Afghanistan. I have probably encountered this more often, than others. The expatriate development professional working in Afghanistan can be divided into three categories—

the managers, the technical experts and the policy makers and talkers (mostly UN, US and other multilateral agencies). The entire gamut of development professionals can be further divided into three segments: just-Kabul-based, non-Kabul-based and those who are Kabul-based, but working all over Afghanistan. I have highest regard for the latter two. They are the ones making the real difference in the context of Afghanistan. They are the ones putting their lives at greater risk to re-build the country. Their telling efforts are spinning the hope of a prosperous and stable Afghanistan. Having worked in both the categories, I know for myself what it takes to excel as a professional in this ravaged country.

This particular analysis may raise certain eyebrows among just-Kabul-based professionals, especially, the policy makers and talkers. Let me clarify. An esteemed colleague and friend has been instrumental in facilitating the creation of 1,500 saving groups in the provinces of Bamian, Baghlan, Takhar and Badakashan, over the last three years. These Self Help Groups (SHGs) are meeting the credit needs of the people and making the poor families invest in productive assets for a better future. Besides, he has built a local brigade of approximately fifty staff, who can deal with saving groups at ease. This potentially means that the activity will continue to exist and expand even after his departure. I know at least five other professionals based in Kabul, who are engaged in developing policies concerning microfinance. Without undermining their contribution, I am more excited by the former category of professionals engaged in the reconstruction of Afghanistan, directly. Similarly a brigade of Nepali engineers have fixed more than 1,000 microhydel power projects, in remote villages of Afghanistan, as a result of which rural folk are getting uninterrupted and green energy 24x7. These categories of professionals are required in larger numbers in Afghanistan, if we want to accelerate the pace and the quality of development and reconstruction efforts here. These are the professionals, who will make a difference in the lives of the common man and change Afghanistan. But, the irony is that these breed of professionals are in short supply, while the just-Kabul-based policy talkers far exceed the demand. In a war-ravaged and struggling country like Afghanistan, big time action is required at the grassroot.

However, the movement of development professionals based in the provinces (non-Kabul-based) is getting continuously curtailed due to the re-emergence of the Taliban in the recent years. The evolving situation saddens me a lot and gets me worried about the future of Afghanistan. There are only handful of development professionals, who visit villages to witness the grassroot level work. Travelling to villages certainly means that you are exposing yourself to high risk most of the time, if not always, which many are not ready to undertake.

A question I often ask myself is the relevance and rationale behind the development approaches and practices employed in Afghanistan by a few INGOs and UN agencies. A large number of development professionals working in Afghanistan have seen, experienced or read some or the other best practices, or approaches, in some other countries. They are bent upon introducing the same 'best practices' in Afghanistan, without considering whether it has any merit. Any Kabul based meeting is an ideal platform for these just-Kabul-based development professionals and experts to flag these best practices and build a case for their replication. These platforms eventually become an opportunity for them to demonstrate the depth and breadth of their intellectual abilities. This idealism and their obsession for best practices, has done some fatal damages, to some of the key development programmes in Afghanistan. I have never seen any concrete outcome from any of the meetings I have attended in Kabul in the initial years. Hence, I vowed never to attend any of these meetings again, unless I was convinced of their sincerity of purpose. In the last five years of my stay in Kabul, I have attended only ten meetings, mostly with the World Bank and MRRD, which have yielded the desired outcome. My colleagues rarely invite me to attend them, for the above reason. And they have, further, learned the tricks of the trade, and try their best to extract the most, from these meetings.

One has to understand that these best practices have emerged after several years of quality development work in other countries. The development process in Afghanistan is very nascent. How can one introduce all the global best practices in a development process, which is not even a decade old? Besides, the context of Afghanistan is quite different from the rest of the world. What may have worked in other countries, may not work here. One has to judiciously balance idealism with realism here. This is what is precisely known as contextualisation. A large segment of development professionals working in reconstruction of Afghanistan, are grappling with the process of contextualisation. They are suffering from a syndrome where they tend to overlook the context and push their agendas of best practices which are often simply irrelevant. I too, stand accused of the same, when on one such occasion I tried to replicate the Indian Administrative Services (IAS) capacity building module, for the training of the district governors of northern provinces after necessary localisation. An Afghan district governor, more or less plays the same set of roles, as their Indian counterpart. In fact, these district governors are functioning in a milieu of constant insecurity and resource crunch—which makes their job further difficult and challenging, compared to their Indian counterpart. They are, further, directly recruited without any proper training and are, therefore, hardly exposed to the art and practices of good governance. It was only prudent on my part to think of training the district governors through a series of good governance workshops. The training was highly successful in getting the message across, and preparing the district governors to improve governance processes at the district level in Afghanistan. But little did I know that most of the district governor would lose their jobs mid-way through their tenure, as the government would issue fresh circular to recruit district governors through the newly constituted IARCSC, with higher academic credentials. This potentially meant that bulk of the trained district governors would no more be holding their offices, but they might play a different set of roles in the evolving bureaucracy. The training programme had also canvassed the executives of the district governor, hence, even if the district governors left, the nucleus of good governance would be left in the hands of the executives in the office of the district governors. However, there is no denying that the programme failed to create the intended impact.

A big challenge for the development professional, therefore, is to contextualise and strike the judicious balance of idealism and realism. This is the common sense I was talking about!!!

I also went through one of the saddest moments of my life, in the process of capacity building of district governors. I once met a very bright and young district governor from the Baghlan province. In one of my training sessions, we were discussing how to fix downward accountability of a district governor. In the last two years, every district governor's office I passed through, I made it a point to discuss with the citizen, the functioning of the district governor's office. This was my share of learning from the field, and assessing the performance of the district governors. For the majority of the district governor offices, I use to hear four standard set of public complaints—corruption, bias towards the rich and the powerful, inordinate delays and issues of punctuality. Hence, this whole idea of fixing downward accountability increasingly dominated my mind. This is a relatively new concept of governance, and is rarely practiced anywhere in the world. In fact, after reading about our initiatives, in one of the leading US dailies, one of the staff members of Minnesota Municipal Corporation, blogged and suggested I come to their municipal corporation with my team, after finishing our assignment in Afghanistan.

Getting back to the discussion on downward accountability, I launched an audacious attack against the district governors, with the complaints I heard from the public about their functioning. I suggested a technique of public audit, whereby the citizens assemble and audit the performance and functioning of the district governors. While others remained silent, the governor of Nahrin district (Baghlan province) was the first to raise his hand and agree for the audit. As a governance specialist, I must say that it requires some courage and conviction to accept a public audit, wherein the district heads and their functioning are brought under direct public scrutiny. In an established democratic country, like India, I am yet, to hear of a public audit of a district collector's office. The young man in question was by far one of the most honest and able district governors. There were never any complaints about him, and he was doing his job to perfection. Anyway we moved ahead, and finalised the tentative schedule of the public audit exercise, in the district of Nahrin in Baghlan.

According to hearsay, one of the strategies of the Taliban, in the southern provinces, has been to target and kill the honest government officers, while keeping the corrupt ones alive. The corrupt officers tend to create the public dissatisfaction with the State through their inaction and corrupt practices. The public then turns to the Taliban looking for respite. In a way the corrupt officers, with their continuous misadventure, help the Taliban to win back the masses. The honest officers are seen as a threat to the Taliban, in their efforts to sway the masses in their favour. Hence, the lives of honest officers are at a higher risk.

I had no inkling that the Taliban, who were until now not very active up north, would soon be resorting to similar tactics, here. In no time the young governor of Nahrin was killed (6 September 2010), in an incident of target killing by a roadside bomb. It was, in fact, the second bid on his life and he was not lucky enough to survive this time. With him, all lessons of good governance were also gone. I cannot count the number of such honest state officials, who have been killed over the last few years. Some may have felt amused, at the emotional outburst of President Hamid Karzai in public. The Western media suggested that he might be slipping into depression. Only if you are in Afghanistan, will you realise, and experience the pain of losing brilliant state officials and military forces, on a daily basis. These are the people, who can make a difference. Their killings, in such large numbers, will seriously impede the growth and stability of Afghanistan. I can fully empathise with the president, having been through the same pain myself, and witnessing untimely deaths, of a considerable number of government officers trained by me.

The growing insecurity and lawlessness has changed the approach of development professionals, engaged in reconstruction and development of Afghanistan. A vast number of professionals today, prefer to play a waiting game, in the pretext of this changing context. They play their cards as per the unfolding situation. I somehow belong to a different school that believes in grabbing every opportunity that can make a difference in the context of Afghanistan. Such an approach will always result in a handful of actions. It may lead to failure at times, as elaborated in my case, with the capacity building of district governors. But one does not mind getting fired for doing too much. It is preferable to take certain risks than to sit idle in the name of a changing context. In fact, by sticking to this strategy there have been more successes than failures. In conflict-prone countries, failures should always be accepted, as a part of the learning curve.

Moreover, as the context remains highly volatile and keeps changing rapidly, in conflict-prone countries one hardly comes across situations where one has the leeway to design manual-centric programmes. Adapting a stereotype approach of designing a programme, as per the unfolding situation, may have worked for most countries, but it does not work so well in these settings. It delays the development process in countries that call for rapid action in all spheres of development, to render succour to its struggling citizen. Hence, it always makes more sense in proactively creating opportunities by taking calculated risks, to ignite the rebuilding process.

I must share one very interesting incident to present a clearer picture. In 2003, Community Development Councils (CDC) were being established in Afghanistan. CDCs are almost equivalent to *panchayats* in India or the lowest tier of governance in any other country. The future of the CDC was uncertain, in 2003. It was still unclear whether it was meant to be a full-fledged local governance institution, or just a local body to implement village level projects. Most of the development actors including the State, were apprehensive about investing heavily on capacity building of CDCs, given their uncertain future during that time. However, we employed massive resources and embarked upon building the capacities of CDCs, in 2005. A large number of international agencies cast doubts and aspersions, on our strategy. CDCs have, however, attained great deal of credibility and recognition as permanent bodies in the context of rural development, today. Since 2010 most of the agencies, including the State, have committed huge resources to aggressively pursue the agenda of CDC capacity building, after lying dormant and inactive in this domain for five years. Our capacity building efforts, as forerunners, have been guiding the agenda of capacity building process in Afghanistan. This is what I meant by taking proactive actions instead of playing the waiting game.

Managing the socio-cultural sensitivities in Afghanistan remains a herculean task. Afghans are very sensitive about their social, cultural and political traditions. They are not at ease in sharing these aspects in the public domain. Hence, it remains quite a profound challenge managing these sensitivities. I have been part of endless discussions, which had to be curtailed, as soon as they boiled down to their culture. Further, it is very difficult to challenge stereotypes, especially gender stereotypes, as the Afghan society still revolves around authoritative and dominant patriarchy. This obliges development professionals to acquire new skills and intelligence, essential in tackling such issues. It is always good to address the stereotypical stance without challenging the tender sensibilities of the Afghan society, largely controlled by men. I shall elaborate upon one of the major challenges that I faced, while working with the Ministry of Women Affairs, in one of the northern provinces.

There are large incidences of domestic violence in Afghanistan. A meagre proportion of these cases come to light, while majority remain unreported, due to the presence of traditional patriarchal society, with limited opportunities for women to define their own lives. The cases of serious magnitude, where the women are driven out of their homes, often spill out in the public domain. The Minister of Women Affairs was witnessing a rise of such cases, in one of the northern provinces. She was keen to address them, though in a subtle way. The ministry was able to provide some rudimentary counselling, largely unscientific, to work out patch-up terms for women, without getting their men reprimanded for such offences. Nevertheless, the effort of the ministry needs to be lauded, as they had the guts to take up such a challenging task, the first of its kind, in Afghanistan. As a governance professional, we wanted to help the ministry to address such cases with a more professional approach. After drawing an initial contract, we constructed safe homes for women in the vicinity of the ministry, and also offered professional counselling support to victims. A comprehensive design was worked out to address the issues of domestic violence with a proactive approach. As soon as the news of such a programme spread around the higher echelons of decision making, they threw a spanner in the works stating that such programmes were not included in the authorised government plan. There is an inherent resistance on part of the State to accept large presence of domestic violence in the Afghan society. Even if there is subtle subscription of the problem, by certain segments, they are of the opinion that it should be resolved within the archaic traditional systems. It has been almost two years now, the complete infrastructure is ready to set the programme rolling, but we are still awaiting the nod of the relevant ministry. We further struggled to enable the women CDC leaders to reach out to provincial ministries, to air their concern for attracting affirmative action around issues affecting their lives and livelihood. Such moves were resisted by few male

CDC leaders as well as the religious leaders, as they challenged the tenets of Afghan culture. In almost any programme, which is set to challenge societal or gender stereotypes, one faces similar hurdles. Most of the international agencies generally give up, or do not challenge stereotypes. They prefer to take the neutral approach of pursuing women development by providing basic services to women, without challenging their status quo in the society. Such an approach may provide immediate relief to the women, but it may not change their status within the Afghan society. I personally believe, while extending basic services to women, one must also challenge gender stereotypes, albeit in a restrictive way, and without threatening the Afghan culture. This may endanger our existence, in terms attracting the wrath of radical religious forces, but one still prefers to give it a try.

In Afghanistan, the development professional, more often than not, has to go through rough patches. The infamous Kabul riot, on 29 May 2006, was one such moment, which left a scar in the lives of development professionals, forever. In 2005, anger and frustration was brewing up among the Northern Alliance supporters, against the constant sidelining of their key leaders, by the incumbent Karzai government. The brief honeymoon between the Northern Alliance and the incumbent government, post Taliban, was on downslide, for sure. Meanwhile, anti-American sentiments were also brewing up simultaneously, for their inability to tame the Taliban. The people, especially, the sympathisers of Northern Alliance, were looking for an opportunity to vent their anger against the State and Western forces. A deadly traffic accident, caused by a US military convoy, provided that perfect opportunity. The accident also somehow provided a converging point, for both the Northern Alliance supporters, and a considerable part of the Afghan population who were frustrated with the inaction of the incumbent government. It sparked off a full blown anti-West riot, raging across much of the Afghan capital, leaving at least fourteen people dead and scores injured. A handful of protestors swelled into a massive mob, in no time. Largely led by the Northern Alliance supporters, they took to the streets, and went on a rampage. The first victim was, of course, the American aid agency CARE, and soon, others followed. The unruly mob even started targeting the houses of expatriate development professionals.

The Afghan security forces maybe proficient at handling terrorists, but they lack the skill and experience of mob management, especially with the use of mild force (like the use of baton, water cannon et all). In fact, this was a completely new phenomenon and a fresh experience waiting for the Afghan police. The police forces of neighbouring countries, like India, Pakistan and Bangladesh have developed excellent skills of mob management, as they routinely face such situations, in their respective countries. Due to formal training and frequent experience, they are now very well equipped in the art and practice of managing unruly mobs. Their Afghan counterpart, on the other hand, have mostly witnessed insurgency, and learned the art of taming terrorists with lethal weapons, with greater alacrity than their neighbours.

The riot resulted in the mob going berserk, and outnumbering the policemen. Seeing the large crowd, the policemen were utterly confused about their next step. They started running for cover, to save their own lives. The city was left in complete command of the unruly mob. Incidences of loot, arson and rioting, amplified at an alarming rate. Complete lawlessness prevailed in the streets of Kabul, and the situation got from bad to worse. The mob literally torched every INGO office they came across, and deliberately targeted some. The UN and other bilateral agencies had the privilege of calling special armed guards to protect their property and the lives of their professionals. But other INGOs were left to the mercy of god. Necessity is the mother of invention. While in Afghanistan, the INGOs have also learned to cope with any emergency. Most of the INGOs abandoned their offices and took refuge in civilian houses to protect their lives. By evening, Afghanistan was able to deploy Special Forces in all the nooks and corners of Kabul, to finally bring the city to order.

Fortunately, I was in Pul-e-Kumri, the capital city of the Baghlan province, during the riot. Exactly at lunch time, I was informed about the riot through a rather strange SMS. One of my female colleagues wanted us to convey to her husband, that she still loved him. I did not know whether to laugh or sympathise with her at that point. I guess they were going through a rough marital patch, and as she was not hopeful of surviving the riot, she wanted to make amends. Fortunately, she survived the riot along with the other development professional in Kabul. Later on, I found that most of the professionals had many a survival story to share—some horrific, some interesting, and some rather funny. The riot went by without the death of even a single development professional. It, however, caused large scale damage to INGO properties and brushed many with the fear of death. On the lighter side, however, I guess, it also managed to unite a few broken souls!

The following day, there was a mass exodus of expatriate development professionals from Kabul to adjacent countries, especially Dubai, as they were seriously traumatised, by the riot. Some of the agencies even employed professional counsellors, to give them the much required healing touch. And, why not! Till the other day, we thought that we had only to be wary of the terrorists. We were secure in the knowledge that the masses were on our side. The riot had broken that confidence of the development professionals. Even though there has been no rioting for the last five years, every professional lives under the constant fear of how the masses might behave in future. The popularity of the US forces is dwindling with every passing day. Afghans are no longer appreciative of their role in the reconstruction process. On the other hand the Taliban is getting stronger and is able to extend their sphere of influence to Kabul, too. The Northern Alliance has been subjected to continuous marginalisation by the incumbent government. Together, this presents perfect fodder for another riot. Kabul is perched on the edge. A small incident has the potential to spark a riot, like never before. But, this does not scare development professionals, who are committed to their journey in Afghanistan.

There is no end to the challenges of working in Afghanistan. It gives an amazing sense of satisfaction, when you see your work adding value to the lines of the people. It is absolutely thrilling to see your work contributing to the cause of Afghanistan. Like many, I have left behind my pain and have learned to relish the challenges. The positive changes have fuelled ones endeavour to strive for further professional excellence and take up new frontiers of challenge. But there is a lot more to achieve, and there is a long way to go, for us. I sincerely hope that the almighty Allah keeps us away from that ever chasing bad moment so that we continue to contribute to the growth and development of Afghanistan!

The Bollywood Connection

Despite an all out effort, the Taliban has failed to erase 'this connection' from the heart and minds of Afghans, including its own followers. It continues to weave its magic on this war-torn nation.

In this land locked mountainous country, where there is a little bit of India everywhere, one of the most surprising elements is the popularity of blockbuster Hindi movies. Bollywood's links with Afghanistan are very old and quite inseparable. It has been a virtual ambassador connecting the two countries. While its impact has irreversibly multiplied over the years, strengthening the socio-cultural ties between the two countries, its presence has, increasingly, generated tremendous goodwill for India.

Whether it is in the hostile southern provinces or the relatively peaceful northern provinces, the influence of Bollywood is palpable in the Afghan society. It is an inescapable slice of truth in an ordinary Afghan's life. Through simple correlations, one can infer the popularity of Indian actors. For example, be it the bustling roadside shops of the capital, or the local markets nestled along the muddy roads of historic Bamian, it is common to find large posters of Aishwarya Rai, Rani Mukherjee, Shahrukh Khan and Salman Khan, everywhere. Like India, the windscreen of private taxis plying in the streets of Kabul and Mazar-e-Sharif are also replete with such glamorous posters.

Bollywood movies are very popular in Afghanistan due to country's proximity to the Indian subcontinent, and the cultural perceptions they share. The common Afghan loves Bollywood films, because they revolve around fighting injustice, which is omnipresent in the contemporary society. This inevitably touches a raw nerve in them. The larger-than-life representations of the Bollywood heroes, in sharp contrast to their stark reality, provide them a vicarious opportunity to immerse themselves into the grandiose reel life fantasies. The chart-bursting music is another addictive element. For majority of Afghans, who may not fully understand the language, songs and dances, drama and action more than adequately make up for the handicap. Action and musical romantic films are, therefore, most popular among them.

More than the government, Bollywood has been able to establish a people-to-people link. Amongst the first Hindi films, to make an impact in Afghanistan was the 1956 release *Kabuliwala*, which starred Balraj Sahni, as a tough Pathan, with a kind heart. A number of Bollywood movies were filmed in Afghanistan later, including the famous *Khuda Gawah.* Even though the film bombed at the box office in India, it did stupendous business in Afghanistan. It ran to packed houses for ten weeks in Kabul alone. This film was extensively shot in Kabul, Mazar-e-Sharif and even Kandahar. It is well known that even with a civil war raging in the country, the Najibullah government took great care of the film unit because of, then Indian Prime Minister, Rajiv Gandhi's friendship with Amitabh Bachchan. Extra caution was taken by providing convoys of five tanks, guarding and escorting the unit, from both front and rear. Being a popular icon himself, Amitabh's fan following cut across the peripheries of the ruling party. It is said that during the shooting of the film, the unit received a message, from none other than the opposition leader, late Burhanuddin Rabbani, who happened to be a fan of Bachchan. He personally assured the unit not to worry about their safety from the rebels. It is also reported that Rabbani was among the first to watch the movie, when it was released.

Afghanistan was amongst the biggest market of Bollywood films until the early 1990s. Even during the civil war years, Hindi films continued to do brisk business in the cinemas of bigger cities, like Kabul and Mazar-e-Sharif. The Taliban imposed their austere moral code of conduct, and put a blanket ban on movies and music, as soon as they captured power in Afghanistan. According to the Taliban philosophy any entertainment through music and movies was blasphemous. Any indulgence in this respect was considered an act of moral turpitude. So much so the official spokesperson of the Taliban made a public announcement that those who wanted to watch a movie, and sing a song, must shift base to India. This, in fact, is a very common rhetoric used by many radical mullahs in Afghanistan-Pakistan region, who enjoy ideological leanings with the Taliban. The mullah duo, Maulana Abdul Rashid Ghazi and Maulana Abdul Aziz, of the infamous Lal Masjid incident, also issued similar warnings in Islamabad, in their bid to enforce rigid Islamic Sharia law, in Pakistan. The mullahs, with a handful of follower students of their madrassa, would blatantly raid video and CD shops in broad daylight, and burn them in full public and media glare. The victim was, of course, Bollywood and to some extent Hollywood movies and songs. The mullahs were, however, silenced by the Pakistani army in Operation Sunrise (July 2007), when their acts started bringing disrepute to Pakistan in the international community. The hardcore Maulana Ghazi was killed, while his brother Maulana Aziz was made to surrender before the might of Pakistan military.

The Taliban created a cultural force in the name of bil-Maroof to put their irrational cultural diktats into practice. One of the prime functions of this force was to completely eliminate Bollywood movies and songs from the Afghan society. However, it failed despite serious attempts. On conditions of anonymity, a government officer from the time of Taliban once confided to me that several policemen watched Bollywood movies in private, even when the Taliban was at the helm. There was, apparently, no better way of relaxing than watching a full drama and action packed Hindi movie, after a week long hectic schedule. During the trying Taliban times, it was Bollywood movies which kept the entertainment quotient high, and the adrenalin flowing, especially, among the youth. They even risked smuggling video cassettes and CDs of popular Bollywood movies, from Pakistan, to watch them privately in their houses. The present generation of Afghan youth has in fact, grown on a staple diet of Bollywood movies, like their Indian counterparts. Even for the large number of youth who migrated to Peshawar, during the times of the Taliban, their love for Bollywood films continued unabated.

The relationship between Bollywood and Afghanistan is inseparable, and even the ban imposed by the Taliban has failed to erase them from the mind and imagination of the common Afghan. They are back in Afghanistan with a bang after the ouster of Taliban, post 9/11. A not-too-successful Bollywood action film, *Elaan*, was among the first films to be screened in Kabul's Bakhtiar cinema, shortly after the Northern Alliance forces took control of the Afghan capital, after driving the Taliban away. Ever since, popular Indian movie channels, like Sony, Max and Zee TV, have been available in almost all cities through cable TV, for people to enjoy uninterrupted supply of Hindi music and movies.

The supply of movies has, recently, been aided by the massive flow of satellite dish TV, in Afghanistan. The younger among the lot is quite adept at procuring pirated new releases. The popular CD shops, in the malls of Kabul, are always thronging with customers, mostly youth. I too, stand accused of watching pirated Bollywood movies in Afghanistan, but these have been largely supplied by my local friends.

In every village that I have visited, I have been hounded with unending questions regarding Amitabh Bachchan and Shahrukh Khan. Be it the desk officer of the Star Hotel Serena in Kabul, or a village leader down south, they discuss Indian actors with the same amount of elation. In fact, in one village, I had a hard time explaining that Puneet Issar (the villain in the movie *Coolie* where Amitabh was severely injured during the filming) did not mean to hurt him purposely; it was a freak accident.

Amitabh is simply a super icon for them and dare anyone drag him in the popularity rat race. 'He is beyond any comparison', I have been told innumerable times by locals, during my stay in Afghanistan. Incidentally, my Pakistani friends have given the same status to Madhuri Dixit, in Pakistan. The most popular diva, among the current generation of female actors in Afghanistan, is however, Aishwarya Rai. She is truly the global face of Indian cinema, and rightly reckoned as 'the connector' by the journalist fraternity of CNN. A bulk of my Afghan friends, never lose time in enquiring about the new releases, of this gorgeous actress. The adventurous of the lot enquire about her marital status, and grow visibly disheartened to know she is not single anymore.

The Afghan women are a bit reserved in their public discourse about Bollywood movies. Even those, who have discarded their veil recently, are reluctant to talk about movies. However, in private discourses, they express their fondness for Bollywood actors.

One young lady from Kabul, once told me that she simply adores Shahrukh Khan. She is even 'ready to die', to be able to meet him, just once. I found her very well conversant with Bollywood movies. She thinks that India should send movies, with powerful gender themes and messages. The women can develop self confidence and draw inspiration from such films, according to her. The women of Afghanistan need to see strong gender based movies, to play a more decisive role in transforming the society, for the better, according to her. It is a wonder, if Bollywood makes such movies, anymore. The last movie with a strong gender message I saw, was *Dor* with the beautiful, ever smiling Gul Panag. A more recent one is *No One Killed Jessica*, based on the murder of Jessica Lal, a little known model brutally killed by the son of a politician, after she refused to serve liquor at a party.

The Afghans are fascinated with Mumbai. This tinsel town, the hub of all action packed thrillers and grand romantic love stories, entices them, like none other. Bollywood movies have such a huge impact on them that at times they may, even, influence their personal life. My private guard is a victim of this magic. While he is from a humble background, he is in love with the daughter of a powerful commander in Kabul. Bollywood movies have been a huge inspiration to woo his lady love, and not allow his humble conditions to disrupt his future plans of tying the knot with her. His ideal is, however, Mithun Chakraborty and not Amitabh. Mithun is a veteran, who has won his lady love in similar circumstances, in innumerable movies. He has lost count of how many times he has seen *Pyar Jhukta Nahin*, a Mithun starrer love story. He pins his hope on his movies, to guide his own love story. This is how deeply Mumbai connects with the common Afghans.

As part of capacity building, I bring a large number of Afghan officers and NGO staff, to expose them to the best practices around rural development in India, every year. I always struggle to keep Mumbai out of the map during every such exposure visit. Two of my local Afghan colleagues took special permission, during one such exposure visit, to enjoy the thrills of Mumbai, at their own cost. Later I found one of them was seriously considering throwing his hat in the show business.

Afghans love Mumbai and want to have a peek of this dream city, at any cost. They just want to revel in the thrilling ambience of the city. The younger lot craves to have a glimpse of some movie stars, in real. The fire brand leader, Raj Thackray of the Sena Brigade, MNS, may not like this, but for Afghans, Bombay can never be Mumbai. They say they find it very hard to refer to the city as Mumbai, when they are visiting their dream city. The intellectuals in Afghanistan are however, not too happy with the current generation of Bollywood films. They complain about their weak storylines and feeble social messages. Driven purely by commerce, vulgarity has also been on the rise. This saddens them no end. A professor from Kabul University once asked if India had made any contemporary movie that can match up to *Mother India* and *Sangam.* I tried hard to convince him with my little knowledge of Bollywood, which, I daresay, didn't suffice. I explained how the taste of Indian audience has changed, over the years, for both better and for worse. While a tradition of a rich parallel cinema existed and contributed to thought-provoking, well documented movies, they never made it big. Recent movies, like *Khelein Hum Jee Jaan Se,* based on the powerful history of Chittagong Uprise, had to struggle to find audience, even on its first day of release. The blockbusters are tailor made for the masses, and lacked in seriousness and are usually more frivolous. But these are times for the 'Munnis' and the 'Sheelas' (names of characters from two recent box office hits with no critical acclaim) to rotate the eyeballs of the audience and set the cash register rolling at the box office.

Music is back on the streets of Kabul, since the ousting of the Taliban. Invariably it is the Hindi numbers that you the hear most. A few musical bands have cropped up in Afghanistan, after the downfall of the Taliban. The rock band Kabul Dream, is one such band, which is becoming increasingly popular among the urban Afghan youth, and is about to create their international footprint soon. Mawj, a pop band from Kabul performed in India for the first time (7 October 2010), as a part of international music festival, when Delhi hosted the Commonwealth Games. This may sound regular in the context of any other country, but for Afghanistan it is a huge makeover. Music was banned under the Taliban regime, but now for the last ten years, Afghan music has gradually resurrected itself. It has been experimenting with all genres of music, like jazz, blues and pop. Mawj is symbolic of the new wave of music in Afghanistan which has ushered in a fresh lease of life, especially among the Afghan youth. Recently, Afghan National Music Institute has also been inaugurated in Kabul to proactively train a new generation of musicians.

Music has its own language that can break all barriers to unite hearts who love it. The sway of Indian music, and the way it communicates with most plebeians of Afghans proves its veracity. That a nation, so steeped into music, should have it banned for fanatic compulsions is really unfortunate. Afghans simply love the rhythm, the lilt and the raw pulsating energy of Indian music. Very often you will find an Afghan singing a Punjabi or a Hindi song (with great gusto and an inimitable Afghan inflection), even without understanding the language or comprehending its meaning. Daler Mehendi's 'Ho gayeji teri balle balle' for instance is a hot favourite. These songs are translated into Persian or

English and then learnt by rote. Afghan's love for music truly, knows no bound.

Beside movies and music, Afghanistan's entertainment landscape has transformed over the past few years. The country now boasts of half a dozen television channels. Private TV networks have flourished since the 2001 ouster of the Taliban (which had banned television). Their staple has been imported dramas, news programmes and home based reality TV shows. Broadcasters were smashing taboos as quickly as they could find the staff. Women read the news, male and female DJs joked together on the radio/TV, and would-be rock stars vied for attention, in a nation that once banned music.

Cashing on the Afghan legacy of love for Hindi movies, the private TV channels were enterprising enough to acquire the popular Indian 'K brand' serials of Balaji production. Their low cost and addictive appeal was a bonus. They soon became a huge hit. According to broadcaster TOLO TV the Indian serial *Kyunki Saas Bhi Kabhi Bahu Thi* alone, garnered an estimated viewership of some 10 million, which is about one third of the population. Local spin-offs, of popular television shows, such as *American Idol* in the name of *Sitaray Afghanistan*, have also found a niche market in the country, in recent times.

Bollywood may have established the bridge, but the television industry with their rightly pitched soap operas, has lent the real momentum to the historic friendship and bonhomie between the two countries. Ekta Kapoor's famous K brand TV serials, like *Kyunki Sas Bhi Kabhi Bahu Thi* and *Kausati Zindagi Kay*, have been weaving the same magic, as they did in India. Life in Afghanistan grinds to a complete halt during the prime time. During official visits to the provinces, especially the district offices, the cooks make it very clear, 'Either have your dinner at

6 pm or be prepared to be served after 9 pm. We do not want to be disturbed, while the popular TV serials are on'. I had reconciled to their ultimatum and helplessly resigned to the late 'after-nine-serving-slot'. Supper-at-six is an impossible imposition on the Indian gastronomy, but nine, after a tiring day was too late. I didn't have Ekta Kapoor's number or I would have definitely lodged a complaint.

Meanwhile, every village I visited, which aired the popular TV serials, bulldozed me with enquiries about Tulsi (Smriti Irani) and Prerna Bajaj (Shweta Tiwari). Some of my local Afghan colleagues implored me to procure the serials in bulk from CD stores in India. Afghan patience is always in short supply. It was hard for them to cultivate the fortitude to wait week after week, to witness the unfolding saga of these famous soaps. When I expressed an inability to procure the CDs, they hounded me to share with them the storyline, till the end. Such queries put me in a bind. Much as I would have liked to alleviate their plight, I was incompetent to handle this specific request. I never followed the serials myself, and had no clue of the tempestuous, ever changing, marital status of Prerna Bajaj. 'What! You do not know?' Through exasperated gasps of disbelief, I had slowly resigned to the fate of being a social outcast. I desperately sought to connect them to my better-informed Indian friends, thereafter, to salvage some self respect.

The sale of television sets spread, like wild fire in the rural areas, due to the airing of these wildly popular TV serials. In fact, the sale of both generators and televisions went up manifold after the popular TV serials came on air. So much so, during the initials days of broadcasting, it was difficult to purchase a generator from the local market in the provinces. The demand far exceeded the supply. These serials weaved the same magic in Afghanistan that Ramanand Sagar's epic *Ramayan* did in India.

The impact of this so-called Tollywood or the television industry was so ubiquitous that the fate of Tulsi and Prerna became household names, and subject of daily discussion. The teenagers took to touching their elders' feet in a very non-Afghan sign of respect. Tulsi may have been the most popular character in India, enabling Smriti Irani win loads of accolade for her gripping act in the serial, but Prerna Bajaj portrayed by Shweta Tiwari, can make her eat a humble pie, in Afghanistan, in terms of popularity and fan following. Shweta can give it a try in Afghanistan, if her Bollywood career fails to take off, after her success in Big Boss 4. In fact, during the recent elections a political commentator remarked that, if anyone could defeat the incumbent President Hamid Karzai, it had to be only Prerna Bajaj. Even though, Amitabh Bachchan maintains his iconic stature in the heart of every Afghan, I am afraid Shweta Tiwari is not very far behind, in that popularity race.

A couple of years ago the television channels ran into issues with the Afghan government. The Ministry of Vice and Virtue, banned the broadcast of Indian serials in Afghanistan, because they felt it affected the Afghan culture. It was hotly debated in the parliament, as well. A majority of the parliamentarians opined that they are anti-Islamic, and therefore, bad for the Afghan society. Apparently, nobody told the parliamentarians that during the holy month of Ramadan, the broadcaster received mass petition from viewers, to delay the evening broadcasting of the serials so as to accommodate evening prayer time. In fact, most of the parliamentarians (of first term) were viewers themselves. A few fire brand women parliamentarian were very vocal in their resistance. 'Why are you stopping women dancing on TV when you cannot stop young boys dancing for the men, who sexually abuse them?' was their argument. However, the official ban compelled two TV channels to bring down the shutters on the widely popular Indian TV serials. TOLO TV managed to resist the ban, imposed by the government saying that it was illegal and ill defined. The issue was amicably resolved at a later stage between the broadcaster and the relevant ministries.

The Indian serials are still dominating the prime time in Afghanistan. But, the broadcaster has pixilated the content of the Indian serials, they found objectionable, to buy peace with the ministry. The cleavages of gorgeous Indian actors and the famous backless bikini blouses of Komolika (the vamp in *Kasauti Zindagi Kay*), are blurred by the broadcasters in Afghanistan. Kissing and other forms of expressions of endearment are further censored to fit to the context of Afghanistan. But, they still manage to attract the same amount of viewership.

The Indian film and music industry is once again riding high and continue to further the friendship and bring these two countries together. Despite the resurgence of the Taliban, the love for Indian cinema and music goes unabated in Afghanistan. It is time for Bollywood to make big inroads in the country. Bollywood broke new grounds in Afghanistan, in 2006, with the release of *Kabul Express*, the first international movie, filmed in the post-Taliban Afghanistan. It was banned in Afghanistan due to some objectionable comments made on the ethnic Hazara community. The movie had also introduced an Afghan actor, in a key role for the first time. Bollywood must rethink about integrating Afghan actors, to take the bond and camaraderie to the next level and make this cross cultural exchange, an irreversible process.

The Forgotten Sikhs

The Afghans say they belong to India but the Indians refuse to acknowledge them. Little known and inconspicuous, 'this religious minority community', from India, continues to struggle with a split identify. Their suffering knows no end.

Afghanistan is a country with an amazing mixture of ethnicity and religion. It has four major ethnic groups: Pashtun, Hazara, Tajik and Uzbek. Almost all Afghans are Muslims, but there is also a minority population of Sikhs and Hindus living amidst them. They say, there is an India in Afghanistan. This is even more evident when you see this small contingent of Sikhs (and Hindus), in Kabul. Few people outside Afghanistan, however, are aware of the Afghan-Sikh community here—the little known, inconspicuous religious minority from India. Historically, they have grappled with a plethora of problems, emanating primarily from their minority status in Afghanistan. Their plight has been further aggravated in the absence of a healing touch—either from Afghanistan or their own country of origin, India.

I read about them, while trying to familiarise myself about Afghanistan, before I left India in May 2005. I remember reading that the Sikh community was diminishing at an alarmingly rate in Afghanistan and that they were literally on the verge of extinction. I have always been fascinated by the Sikh community and their entrepreneurial abilities. They have made it big in the US, Canada, UK and other Western countries through their sheer grit and determination. This special interest and fascination for the Sikhs, prompted me to explore more about their community in Kabul, from the moment I landed here. I was lucky to have had ample opportunities to talk to them and know more about their lives, over the last six years, while travelling through the length and breadth of Afghanistan.

The descendants of the early Sikh traders, who did business along the trade route through Afghanistan, over the last few centuries, were one of the first settlers here. Starting in Sindh and Punjab, these trade routes went across the Hindukush to Samarkand and Merv, further down to Europe, cutting across Kandahar, Jalalabad and Kabul. Bulk of these traders used to have a second home in Afghanistan. A flood of migration occurred later during the partition of India, when many Sikh families living in Western Pakistan, found it safer and easier to seek refuge in Afghanistan. Rather than risking their lives by fleeing through Pakistan to reach India, they settled for Afghanistan, as a temporary safe home. The partition of India in 1947 thus defined the lives of not only those who made the tumultuous passage to India but also of those who sought refuge in Afghanistan. Eventually most of these Sikhs made Afghanistan their first home and were issued Afghan passports.

Before Soviet occupation and the three decades of uninterrupted strife, an estimated 2,00,000 Sikhs lived in Afghanistan, many of them concentrated in the capital. According to a report on ethnic cleansing in Afghanistan, (published by a coalition of human right organisations, under the international campaign to end genocide), this country had a population of over 50,000 Hindus and Sikhs before 1992. Over the years, the number dropped to 3,000. The Khalsa Diwan puts the population far below 3,000. Just about 1,500 Sikhs live in Kabul today, who managed to survive successive oppressive regimes, including the Taliban. The ones who stayed back were those, who had either invested way beyond in Afghanistan to simply abandon it, or lacked adequate resources to migrate to another country.

Historically, the traditional Afghan Muslims have been quite happy to tolerate the presence of the Hindus and Sikhs in the country. The Sikhs and Hindus established about eight gurdwaras and three temples, during that time and were allowed to practice their religion freely. In their bid to gel with the larger Afghan community, they mastered the native languages, mostly Dari and Pashtu, blending more easily with the society. Even though in minority, a bulk of small businesses was controlled by the Sikh community, who dominated the economy of Kabul and other provincial headquarters. They even established viable small businesses in the provinces of Kandahar, Khost, Helmand and Ghazni—places which are considered traditional bastions of radical Islamic fanatics.

The Sikh community was the major pillar behind building the local economy. For many years, Sikhs were a prominent part of Kabul's commercial scene. The relative prosperity of this group, once, can be gauged from the fact that despite being barely two per cent of Jalalabad, they controlled a large part of the economy. Occupying important positions as traders, entrepreneurs and later, currency exchange experts, they remained very popular among the Afghan population. One will easily find a Sikh cloth merchant in Jalalabad city or a Sikh owned pharmacy shop in Pul-e-khumri, the provincial headquarter of Baghlan province. My monthly provision and consumer durables come from a Sikh owned grocery shop in Kabul.

Afghanistan changed rapidly with the downfall of Najibullah's government. The Sikhs suddenly found themselves marginalised during this time. They had to struggle to maintain their distinct cultural and economic profile in Afghanistan. Their fortune started dwindling soon after the rise of Mujahideen, followed by other repressive regimes, including the Taliban, in Afghanistan. The number of gurdwaras reduced to three. They are all located in Karte Parwan, in the outskirts of Kabul city today. Karte Parwan is, apparently, the main Sikh-Hindu area of Kabul. Religious intolerance and persecution of religious minority by successive repressive regimes of the Islamic fundamentalist forces literally pushed them to the fringes. Tired of complaining of extortion, intimidation, kidnapping, theft and even rape, those with means started fleeing. Thus Afghanistan started witnessing a mass exodus of the Sikh minority to India around this time.

The Taliban was not as hostile to the Sikhs, as they were to the ethnic Hazaras. The Sikhs too, apparently, learned to manage the Taliban, over a period of time. This can be inferred from the fact that they had far less complaints against the Taliban than the other repressive regimes of the past. Known for their hard work and entrepreneurial abilities they worked out a system with the Taliban popularly known as the Taliban Protection Tax (TPT). By paying a fixed amount of TPT, on a monthly basis, they saved their business and properties and received protection from the Taliban.

The Taliban introduced the famous yellow badge system during this time to identify the minority Hindus and Sikhs. Some say it was a step towards saving them from the cultural compliance force of the Taliban, popularly known as bil-Maroof. This force was entrusted with the task of ensuring mass compliance to the irrational socio-cultural diktats of the Taliban and prosecuting the errant and offenders. I was told by one of my friends, that in the University of Kabul, a college girl was served a punishment of fifty sticks on her leg for, apparently, exposing about one inch of her bare skin between the socks and the trouser. The yellow badges may have curtailed the atrocity by the bil-Maroof, but by segregating the Sikhs thus a process of religious profiling had been instigated, according to some. The Sikhs felt unwelcome and migration continued unabated even under the Taliban.

Most of the businesses and properties of the Sikhs were either lost in the unending civil war or were occupied by the powerful warlords. Even today, a large number of properties which were previously owned by the Sikh community are lying under the control of the powerful ex-commanders and warlords. The files associated with the properties are collecting dust in the state offices. The influential local commanders have ensured that the Sikhs are kept far away from these abandoned properties. But their misery does not end there. Bulk of the Sikh children stay at home and are deprived of education, because of widespread harassment at schools. Their problems do not end even after their death. Recently the plot of land, used by them as funeral ground in Kabul, was encroached upon by the urban land mafia. The Sikhs faced a huge resistance, in setting up the funeral pyres of the dead. Cremation has been a bone of contention between the Sikhs and the radical Islamists, for last few decades. According to tradition, Sikhs cremate their dead, an act considered as sacrilege in Islam. The traditional cremation ground of the Afghan-Sikhs has been appropriated by the radical Muslims. In 2003, Sikhs complained to the Afghan government regarding the loss of the cremation grounds, which forced them to send a woman's body to Pakistan to be cremated, following which the Ministry of Religious Affairs investigated the issue. Though, the cremation grounds were reported to have been returned to Sikh control in 2006, the very next year radical forces beat up mourners attempting to cremate a community leader, and the funeral had to be conducted under police protection. Till 2010, cremation in Kabul was reportedly unwelcome. The issue of cremation ground was again raised by the Sikh community during the visit of Indian Prime Minister, Manmohan Singh, in June 2011.

One thing that amazes most is how they keep their Indian connection kicking and alive, through all this turmoil. They keep visiting their kith and kin in Punjab, and are frequent visitors to the famous Golden Temple in Amritsar, which they proudly refer as the, 'Land of their Guru'. Prospective grooms and brides are also searched in India. This gives me great hope for India. It makes me believe in the potency of diversity that gives India its unique stamp of an all absorbing melting-pot, which it truly is. The manager of Ariana had realised this well in advance and initiated a Kabul-Amritsar flight, for the first time in the aviation history. But, his bad luck chased him no end. He struggled with the load factor to keep the plane flying until it was, finally, grounded due to dearth of passengers.

A large number of Sikhs have their wives and children settled in India today, while they continue to do business in Afghanistan—plying up and down only during holidays and festivals, like the rest of us expatriates. However, migration to India has not made much of a difference, or ended their misery in any way. The government of India has accorded a refugee status to the Sikhs of Afghanistan, as of now. Sporadically, a very thin minority has succeeded in receiving citizenship. A majority of their problems however remain unsolved; their self esteem battered to no end. Their predicament was best articulated by one Sikh cloth merchant, from Jalalabad. 'The Afghans say that we belong to India and Indian government says that we belong to Afghanistan. I wish there was a no mans land for us; we belong nowhere today!'

Despite a plethora of problems, the Afghan-Sikh communities are trying to rebuild their lives and livelihoods. History bears testimony to the indomitable courage of the Sikhs. They are famous for fighting to their last breath. They are certainly not known for giving up! I do not have an iota of doubt that they will once again build a thriving Sikh community in Afghanistan someday, and tie their destiny and fortune with the future of Afghanistan. The number of gurudwaras and langars, too, will increase. None better than the Sikh community understands and follows the practice of pardon. They will once again make Afghanistan their first home, forgetting their troubled past. One only hopes that the Indian government, gives a cremation ground to the Sikhs, if not a citizenship status.

Kandahar Off Limits

Kandahar is sine qua non to Taliban, terrorism and narcotics. It is said what 'this province' decides today, Afghanistan follows tomorrow. It is the litmus test of the ongoing global war against terrorism.

Kandahar has several introductions to its credit. The US military sees Kandahar as a bastion-cum-breeding ground of the Taliban and hardcore al-Qaeda militants. The international policy and strategy contingent sees Kandahar as sine qua non to Taliban, terrorism and narcotics. The international media sees Kandahar as a litmus test of the ongoing war against terrorism, in Afghanistan. And Indians see it as the laboratory of the lethal ISI and Taliban nexus. But one of my Pashtun friends from Kandahar defines Kandahar in the best possible way—'Kandahar decides and the rest of Afghanistan follows.'

Historically, Kandahar has always decided the destiny of Afghanistan. It was way back, in 1989, that the city paved the way for the Taliban and within a couple of years the Taliban captured the whole country barring Panjsher and few other strategic provinces, like Badakashan. It was Kandahar again, which sealed the fate of the Taliban, post 9/11, by allowing the US backed Ahmed Gul Sherzai forces, to overthrow the Taliban from Kandahar and the rest of Afghanistan. Kandahar is intrinsically linked to global security. In some sense, it would decide the fate of the global war against terrorism. The city has also given

Afghanistan some of the top rung political leaders, including the incumbent President Hamid Karzai and Ahmad Shah Durrani—the founder of Afghanistan.

My first introduction to Kandahar was through the great Hindu mythology *Mahabharata.* One of its key figures, Gandhari, remembered as a woman of great beauty and resilience, hailed from Gandhar, now modern Kandahar. Gandhari had not only taken the bold decision to marry the blind king Dhrtarashtra (who had renounced his throne to his younger brother Pandu, for being blind) but also as his loyal consort, chosen to remain blindfolded, for the rest of her life. Her offsprings, the Kauravas, were pitted against the Pandavas, in the mightiest war of ancient times, which produced the grand epic *Mahabharata.* Shakuni, Gandhari's brother, played a key role in this high drama. He won the kingdom of the Pandavas for his nephews, as a wager, in a rigged game of dice. This started a mighty power struggle resulting in an epic war, which eventually brought an entire nation to the brink of destruction and ruin.

Kandahar is known to most Indians for the infamous hijacking of Indian Airlines flight IC814, en route from Kathmandu to New Delhi. The aircraft, with 176 passengers on board, was hijacked by armed terrorists after it entered the Indian air space. After touching down in Amritsar, Lahore and Dubai for a while, the hijackers finally forced the plane to land in Kandahar. The hijacking was a strategic ploy employed by the Pakistan based militants to negotiate the release of hard core Islamic militant Maulana Masood Azhar, who later founded Jiash-e-Mohammed, then languishing in a jail in Indian Kashmir. The Bhartiya Janta Party (BJP), led government headed by the versatile Atal Bihari Vajpayee secured the safe release of all the passengers on board, by meeting the demand of the hijackers.

The Maulana along with his key accomplices were sent to Kandahar on a special flight, along with, then External Affairs Minister, Jaswant Singh. Many saw this as a meek surrender of a state to terrorism by the so called hardliner BJP. The image of India as a soft state was reinforced through the act of Jaswant Singh. However, he was only carrying out the decision of the government of the day.

While the hijack crisis was brought to an end by securing the safe release of the passengers, the political fallout continued to spiral. Kandahar popped up in public memory, after every terrorist attack in India. The hijack episode became an integral and inseparable part of Indian politics that kept hounding the BJP, even after they lost power to Congress, in 2004. Prevention of Terrorism Act (POTA) brought by the BJP when they were in power was the first casualty when the Congress assumed power. The BJP, blaming lack of tough anti-terror laws, for everything was easily silenced by the incumbent government which pointed out that terror attacks happened even when POTA was in force, thereby dismissing the need for special anti-terror laws. The Congress never forgot to rub salt into the wounds of the BJP by constantly reminding them about the Kandahar debacle, and see them squirm at its mere mention. However, it is a wonder, if things could have been any different under the Congress, had they handled the Kandahar debacle. The only option they could have availed was to send the terrorists and the minister in two different planes, instead of one.

India has failed to leave Kandahar behind, even after more than a decade. The new generation of Indians, immediately, connects to this remote place of Afghanistan over the ongoing political skirmishes on the hijack episode. They, however, know very little about the historical significance of this city.

Historically, Kandahar has always been a kingdom of high strategic and economic relevance in South Asia. Many empires have fought long wars to control the city for its geostrategic location along the popular trade routes of Central Asia. It provided a vital connection to the lucrative markets of the Middle East and Persian Gulf. Besides being the gateway of attractive international trade routes, Kandahar has been a major centre for sheep, wool, cotton, silk, tobacco and fresh and dried fruits. It produces one of the best variety of grapes and pomegranates in the world, too.

Before Alexander discovered it in 330BC, the city was the provincial capital of the Achaemenid Empire. Mahmud of Ghazni captured Kandahar in the 11th century, followed by the Ghurids of Ghor. Genghis Khan and his Mongol armies invaded Kandahar in the 13th century. It was a part of Timur's (Tamerlane) Timurid Empire, from the 14th century to the 15th century. In the late 15th century Kandahar went to the Arghuns. Later Mughals attempted to capture Kandahar, in their quest to prove their economic and strategic supremacy. Tamerlane's descendant, Babur, the founder of the Mughal Empire, annexed Kandahar in the 16th century. Babur's son, Humayun, lost it to the Shah of Persia. Humayun's son, Akbar, regained control of Kandahar, but by the early 18th century subsequent Mughal emperors lost the territory once again to the Persian Safavids.

In 1748, Ahmad Shah Durrani, founder of the Afghan Empire made Kandahar its capital. However, one of the later rulers of Afghanistan, thereafter, shifted the capital to Kabul. During the Soviet occupation, Kandahar witnessed heavy fighting. Soviet troops surrounded the city, and subjected it to a heavy artillery and aerial bombardment, in which many civilians lost their lives. After the Soviet withdrawal, and the fall of the Najibullah government in 1992, Kandahar fell into the hands of a local Mujahideen commander, Gul Agha Sherzai. The Taliban uprooted the powerful local commander as they captured power in Kandahar, and made it the capital, in 1996.

It is the second largest city of Afghanistan, nestling a populace of about half a million and is located to the south of the country at about 1005 m (3297 ft) above sea level. Kandahar is referred as the pride of Pasthuns. It is the heartland of the Pasthuns, who form a majority of the Afghan population. However, in scattered pockets, there are Tajiks and Hazaras living in this region too. Kandahar, apart from its international significance, is strategically located, from the domestic perspective, too. It provides extensive road links with Farah and Herat to the west, Ghazni and Kabul to the north-east, Tarin Kowt (another Taliban infested area) to the north, and Quetta in Pakistan to the south.

A natural inquisitiveness to find out how this strategic marketing-hub, holding enormous potential and promise once, turned to be the hot bed of terrorism, drove me to learn more about Kandahar. What represented modern Kandahar? What led to the transformation of this city, into becoming one of the most dangerous places in the world? What had been the difference between the pre- and post-Taliban periods in the lives of an ordinary Kandhari?

Hence, when the opportunity of working in Kandahar appeared, I grabbed it with open hands. Very few people ever opted for a job in Kandahar, those days. Travelling in the city is a constant brush with the jaws of death. For an Indian, it is simply stepping into a death trap. I have mentioned, several times in this book, how one bad moment separates life from death in Afghanistan. When you are in Kandahar, you are inching fatally closer, to that bad moment. I am not sure if our flagship state insurance company, the Life Insurance Corporation (LIC) of India, would even provide insurance to cover Indians visiting Kandahar. Let alone the LIC, most of the private Indian banks have a policy, of not lending to Indians engaged in rebuilding Afghanistan and Iraq. I had great difficulty in securing a loan for purchasing a modest house in Kolkata, in 2006. It is an irony that the same bank held my NRE account, for the last so many years. When it comes to providing loans, however, they see us as potential candidates for a loan default. After every terrorist attack Prime Minister, Manmohan Singh, would re-emphasise on how a resolute India would keep serving Afghanistan. The state institutions would, however, see the same Indians as risk elements, impeding their fiscal performance, and adding to their non-performing assets. These are small inherent contradictions within India that one learns to live with, over a period of time.

Meanwhile I kept travelling to Kandahar quite frequently. In the course of my parleys with the common man and government officials, my knowledge of the locality gradually improved. In fact, I did not lose a single opportunity to investigate, explore and expand my new horizon of learning. I got plenty of opportunities for prolonged open ended conversations, with a wide range of stakeholders, which were more than illuminating, at times.

On my first trip to Kandahar, 'the mainland of the Taliban' in military parlance, in March 2008, I was certainly a little nervous. I witnessed a beeline of fighter jets and F16s lined up at the Kandahar Airport hanger, for assaults on the Taliban. My eyes were wishfully longing to capture a glimpse of the mysterious drones, which were shrouded in secrecy. Driving from the airport to our office I kept gazing through the window. Life looked normal, except for the long military convoys bringing traffic to a standstill, ever so often. Every such moment was a reminder, of being in an extremely troubled part of the world. The driver would always stay away from such convoys, as they were the favourite targets of any terrorist attack.

The exhaustive list of do's and don'ts that I was handed over, as I stepped into our modest office, might have compelled any newcomer to take a return flight to Kabul. But adherence to the list was a must, if one had to work and more importantly survive in Kandahar. I learnt that quite early, within my next few visits.

During my second visit, I got a real taste of Kandahar. As soon as I landed at the airport, I was warned by my security advisor to wait inside, until further instructions. Apparently, three suicide bombers had sneaked into the city, and were looking for potential targets. It was only after three hours of agonising wait that I was given the green signal, to leave the airport. The three suicide bombers had, meanwhile, blown themselves up outside the premises of the governor's office. Such incidents of volatility have been so much a part of Kandahar that no one attaches much importance to them, anymore.

During my subsequent visits to Kandahar, I endeavoured to explore the city and its undercurrents. Even though visiting the local market in Kandahar is a serious breach of security norms, I took the risk of flouting it. Draped in a typical Kandhari dress, covering my head with a scarf to lower my visibility, I would persuade my counterpart in Kandahar to accompany me to the market. Being well conversant in Urdu (almost a second language in Kandahar), I would talk with the shopkeepers, at ease. In the markets, I discovered the bonhomie an ordinary Afghan shared with the Indians. Irrespective of the Taliban agenda of fanning hatred against India, these people had high respect for Indian culture. The shopkeepers would eventually figure out my place of origin, from my typical accent. They would flood me with questions, thereafter, particularly about Bollywood. The youngsters would never fail to enquire about Aishwarya Rai, Rani Mukherjee and also about Salman Khan and as to why he ended up in jail so often in real life. Frankly, I did not have an answer to that latter question. The only submission I could make on Salman's behalf was that he certainly seemed to have matured over the years.

Amid the busy streets another familiar observation was the sound of Bollywood songs, hitting the high note, with unfailing regularity. During the Taliban times there were diktats against playing any music, especially, Hindi music in Kandahar. This open demonstration of love for Hindi songs spoke volumes of the changing times, and specially peoples' choice in Kandahar. India has been seen as a very close ally, irrespective of the hatred campaign engineered by the Taliban. Indian commodities, especially, pirated CDs and music cassettes of popular Hindi movies, sell openly in the market, like hot cakes. I was surprised to witness the availability and popularity of the dish TV in Kandahar, which I could fix in my guest house within an hour. I wonder if their Indian counterparts could do it with as much alacrity. The markets are also flooded with Chinese goods, which are popular among the Afghan customers for their throw away prices.

The market places are completely dominated by men, and you can hardly see any female customers, on the street. At times, you may wonder if any women exist in Kandahar. History bears testimony, women in this city have suffered the most, compared to any other part of the world, courtesy the rigid and dominant patriarchy imposed by the Taliban, during their regime. The irrational diktat had pushed women to the periphery of the society, consigning them to household drudgery—completely eliminating their role from the domain of public life. There was an absolute ban on women's activity outside the home, unless accompanied by a *maharam* (close male relative such as a father, brother, husband, or an adult son). The city has also witnessed several incidents of public stoning of women, accused of infidelity, in the past. I am told that even after the fall of the Taliban, post 9/11, such incidents have sporadically happened, in certain remote pockets of Kandahar province.

The Taliban had also imposed a complete ban on male doctors attending to female patients, in the past. A Swiss doctor, working with an international health focused NGO, once narrated the pathetic tale of a pregnant woman, who died unattended despite being in the district hospital. Her husband did not allow her to be operated upon by a male doctor, despite delivery complications; and so she was forced to die slowly in front of the helpless doctor.

Whether it is nail paint or brightly coloured dresses, women have been banned from adorning themselves. I am told a few women with painted nails have had their nails ripped out under the Taliban regine, by the bil-Maroof. There was a blanket ban imposed on women studying in schools, universities or any other education institutes, too. Such reported harassments were, merely, evidences of the tip of an iceberg. The everyday plight and suffering of women in their houses and society, I am told, were unimaginable.

The condition of women started improving after the downfall of the Taliban. Women rejoined colleges and universities to resume their studies. They started taking up jobs in the government and NGOs. Today, one can even find beauty salons for women, in this heartland of the Taliban. But, this only depicts the broader changes, which are in no way indicators of the real status of women in the society. The pitiable situation of women based in rural Kandahar has shown no sign of improvement, as they still remain under the proxy control of the Taliban.

Women have to go a long way to assert their pending rights, and voice their choices and preferences, around issues concerning their lives and livelihood. Any woman, who has tried to take up the cause of women in Kandahar, has been silenced by the Taliban in no time. The fearless and senior most woman police officer, Lt Col Malalai Kakar, was killed by the Taliban as she was about to leave for office, on 28 September 2008. Malalai, in her early forties, was known for fighting abuses against women. Likewise, a very vocal female provincial council member, Sitara Achakzai, was murdered on 12 April 2009. She was famous in the political circle of Afghanistan for promoting women rights.

Other than the 'invisible' Afghan women, I had a certain curiosity about the youth of Kandahar. I wondered how the young people were growing amidst the turmoil. In the course of my visits to Kandahar, an interesting observation one made was their love for cricket. One would often find young boys playing cricket in the barren streets of Kandahar, which is otherwise a very common sight in India and Pakistan. This penchant for cricket in Kandahar has permeated from the Baluchistan side of the Pakistan border. Once, during a development discourse with a senior Afghan representative of a UN agency, I inquired about the kind of support the youth of Kandahar needs today. He was quick to respond, 'If you are from India, please get us a cricket coach! I assure you, half the Kandhari youth would clap for the Indian cricket team in a typical high tension Indo-Pak encounter.' I later learnt he was a key representative of the Kandahar Cricket Association. The gentleman was right in his assessment. It may surprise a few, but when India locks horns with their arch rivals Pakistan, there are Afghan supporters who clap for India, in Kandahar. The interest in cricket among Kandhari youth is picking up gradually after the success of their national cricket team in international circuits, in the 2009 and 2010. The national team even won the ACC Trophy Elite Panel, in 2010, by humbling Nepal. It is even more exciting to note that Afghanistan is in the process of convening their first female cricket team.

The gentleman shared another incident which happened in 2007, when he was away to Bahrain as part of the ICC cricket officials training. He was being repeatedly teased by his Pakistan and Indian counterparts in the workshop. 'When did you learn to hold the bat instead of the gun?' they would ask, with all the participants in the workshop bursting into laughter. He had retorted, 'You will get a fitting reply by our cricket team'. The Afghan cricketers did, eventually, defeat Pakistan team in the Asia Cup in 2010. Let there be not an iota of doubt that Indian cricket team will also meet the same fate, sooner or later. I was told that the best of an Afghan (and especially, a Kandhari) comes, only, amidst challenge. This incident proved its veracity.

During my conversation with the coach, I realised the importance of the apropos investment, that needs to be made towards generating political and civilian goodwill in Afghanistan, and holds high strategic interest for Indians as well. It could be achieved in small meaningful ways, like sending a cricket coach, in this case. Winning the hearts and minds of youth in Kandahar could be an investment worth a hundred thousand dollars. One however, failed to trigger the same amount of enthusiasm among the Indian embassy officials posted in the consulate, at Kandahar. Call it my political naivety, my idea was not strategic enough to merit support from the Indian government.

I didn't give up my inherent weakness for working with the youth, though. I visited the Kandahar University to explore the possibility of engaging with the students. I was given two interesting proposals by the Vice Chancellor. One was to initiate a faculty of economics in the University of Kandahar, and the other was to enrich the course curriculum, of their existing electrical engineering faculty, by introducing an element of renewable energy, especially solar energy. Education liberates the mind from the fetters of ignorance, and helps one judge between good and bad. Most of the Taliban recruits, as one knows, are illiterate. It is always easier to fan jihadi leanings among the illiterate youth. There cannot be any contribution more relevant than educating the youth, in a place, like Kandahar. However, one has already learnt a lesson. It will be a mistake to pursue the government of India anymore, on this.

Kandahar has so much potential to reclaim its glorified past, but its deteriorating law and order situation is holding it back from its journey towards peace, prosperity and development. Development responses have been modest, and often plagued by insurgent attacks and growing threats against development professionals. With the Taliban getting stronger, with every passing day, the process has naturally been crippled, and now almost brought to a grinding halt.

With the high threat perception, most aid agencies working in Afghanistan have put a blanket ban on the travel of expatriate development professionals to Kandahar. Most INGOs manage their severely downsized operation with just a bunch of local staff. Barring a few UN officials, there are only a handful of expatriate professionals, working in Kandahar today.

For Indians, it has been particularly difficult because for the Taliban, who comply with the ISI operative manual in Kandahar,

Indians are strategic targets, more than any other nationals. Ask any Indian embassy official posted in the Kandahar consulate—they have spent more time in the specially designed bunker (in the basement of the building), than their respective desks, to avoid the recurrent rocket attacks. The staff of the Indian consulate can hardly move out of their citadel, and walk in the streets of Kandahar, without military escorts.

The Kandahar consulate has been the bone of contention between India and Pakistan. Pakistan feels that the consulate would be used by the Indian government to fan the Baluch unrest. The local media of Kandahar has brushed aside such allegations, calling it a figment of Pakistan's imagination. But the Taliban faction, owing their allegiance to ISI, keeps the rockets flying to the office, welcoming Indians. I am sure that most of the consulate officials count the days of their posting in Kandahar.

One of the Indian embassy officials I met, way back in 2008, expressed his serious displeasure with my decision to visit Kandahar. Before I could probe his feelings, he was honest enough in admitting that he was there out of compulsion, rather than choice. After having served the government for so long his choice was limited. He could not leave the government job and foray into the private sector anymore. He emphatically suggested that young guys, like us, should never get into the Kandahar imbroglio. He was correct, to a certain extent. Kandahar is like walking on a razor's edge, especially for Indians.

From gaining supremacy in Afghanistan, to their downfall, post 9/11, it has been quite a roller coaster journey for the Taliban. The rise of Taliban, from a handful of mullahs under the leadership of Mullah Omar, is an interesting tale. They could sense it well in advance, during the early nineties, that Kandahar would pave their way to the throne of Afghanistan. Hence, a bunch of mullahs, under the influential leadership of Mullah Omar, started camping on the Baluchistan side of the Pakistan border to spread their Afghan agenda, in the early nineties. Few madrasas were initiated on both sides of the border to pursue their design. Tacit support of the ISI, at that point of time, enabled them to be more aggressive in pursuing their Afghan dream.

After the Soviet withdrawal, and the collapse of Najibullah's government in 1992, the city fell into the hands of a local militia leader, Gul Agha Sherzai. The process of development had virtually come to a standstill around this time, building frustration and disillusionment in the people of Kandahar. Rampant corruption under the leadership of Sher Gul Aga Sherzai, further, marred the process of governance. He was, however, controlling only parts of Kandahar province, with most of it, still, under other powerful Mujahideen commanders.

By early nineties, it was a perfect opportunity for the Taliban, under the influential leadership of Mullah Omar, to start planting the seeds of dissent in the minds of the ordinary citizen. They did so by selling the dream of a new Afghan society, based on the principle of equity, justice, esteem and security. The tenets and practice of pure Islam was cardinal to this new dream. The Holy Book of Koran was often employed to sell their Afghan dream. Kandahar was set as the central stage, to kick off the new revolution, to create a model Islamic State of Afghanistan. The Taliban employed the Kandahar based mullahs, to propagate this message of a new Afghanistan, to the masses in Kandahar and adjacent southern provinces. The entry of the Taliban to Kandahar was a cake walk as there was only handful of local commanders, providing minimal resistance. In fact, Kandahar welcomed them with open arms. In November 1994, the entry was greeted with much fanfare and joy by the masses. People poured into the streets with a hope of change that would reverse their misery.

A large number of Kandhari youth, queued outside the police headquarters for jobs in the new Taliban administration. I was told by one of the youth that he and hordes of others, from relatively better economic backgrounds, were prepared to work voluntarily. Few households even pledged their gold ornaments to make them financially strong. The atmosphere of hope and optimism was palpable in the streets of Kandahar. The Taliban were able to organise ordinary citizen, with a dream of a new Afghan society based on the tenet of Islam. Everybody was ready to subscribe to the Taliban dream of a new Afghanistan.

After consolidating their foothold in Kandahar, the Taliban captured the remaining southern provinces, with little or no resistance. Mujahideen commander Ismail Khan was the lone combatant, who put up a brave face against them, in Herat. He thwarted the Taliban offensive in 1995, but was forced to flee to Iran, eventually, with his 8,000 followers. The Taliban never looked back after driving Ismail Khan to exile, and captured the bulk of Afghanistan, barring Panjsher and few other provinces like Badakshan, within the next couple of years. Thereafter, Ahmed Shah Mehsud, popularly known as the 'Lion of Panjsher', was the sole resistance, who single handedly resisted the Taliban in Afghanistan. He valiantly fought them to his last breath.

The tacit support of the ISI started becoming more overt with the consolidation of the Taliban position in Afghanistan. By September 1996 they became a new regime to reckon with, in the highly volatile and ever changing power equation in South Asia. Kandahar was finally made the capital of Afghanistan.

However, with the passing years, the dream of a new Afghanistan dissipated more quickly than one imagined, in

Kandahar and the rest of Afghanistan. The plight of the poor man got from bad to worse. The process of governance started tottering. The administration remained plagued with massive corruption, especially, among the rank and file of the Taliban. The rule of law collapsed with every passing day. Instead of focusing on governance and development, the Taliban went hammer and tong to pursue their cultural agenda. They wanted the masses to comply with their version of Islam. This resulted in serious cultural persecution of the common man. A series of irrational diktats like putting a ban on watching television, not listening to music, establishing a stringent dressing code etc. were issued for the masses. A special cultural protection force called bil-Maroof was created to ensure mass compliance to the diktats. This created a divide between the masses and the Taliban, which only became wider with every passing day. The suffering masses desperately looked for an opportunity to flee the oppression mostly by migrating to Pakistan and Iran. The period of the Taliban thus resulted in mass exodus of Afghans to these neighbouring countries.

The Taliban may have had a dream, but they did not have a framework to deliver that dream. The same Taliban, that enjoyed enormous support of the masses initially, plunged into unpopularity at an equally alarming speed. Seething anger within the masses looked for an opportunity to retaliate. Post 9/11, an attack on Kandahar was imminent after the refusal of Taliban to handover Osama-bin-Laden to the US. This was seen as a perfect opportunity by the masses, and the rebel Mujahideen leaders to express their angst. On 21 October 2001, as a part of Operation Enduring Freedom, the US Navy began hitting the city with precision guided cruise missiles, from the Persian Gulf. They targeted the airport and the building that was occupied by the Taliban. Within a fortnight the Taliban started surrendering to the private militia that had been formed by Gul Agha Sherzai, with the backing of the US. It was widely reported that the common man of Kandahar celebrated the exit of the Taliban with the same ardour that they had welcomed them with, in November 1994.

Kandahar once again fell into the hands of Sherzai, who controlled the area before the rise of the Taliban. He was credited, with the same charges of corruption and misgovernance which had initially fuelled the growth of the Taliban. Sherzai was transferred in 2003, and replaced by Yusuf Pasthun, until Asadullah Khalid took the post in 2005. The current governor of Kandahar is Tooryalai Wesa.

Historically, it takes a lot of time for a country to make its transition to peace. Countries which have achieved fast turnarounds took nothing less than a decade. This transformation has always been based on approaches that suited local conditions. However, in the case of Afghanistan the path of peace and development would emanate from Kandahar. As stated earlier, Kandahar would decide the fate of global war against terrorism.

Kandahar is the bastion and traditional stronghold of the Taliban and al-Qaeda. Overt support from the ISI, coupled with the uninterrupted flow of Pakistan based militants through the porous Afghanistan-Pakistan border, make it an irreversible breeding ground for terrorism. Kandahar is the place where all cross-border signals of terrorism converge and translate into nefarious terrorist designs. Hence, Kandahar remains the focal point for the US and the NATO forces in its efforts to eliminate terrorism from the whole of Afghanistan. The Pentagon knows that they have to curb terrorism in Kandahar, to make any significant dent in the overall scenario of terrorism in Afghanistan. It is here or never!

President Obama sensed it well in advance. In his entire presidential campaign he increasingly talked about a military upsurge in Afghanistan. He kept his pre-electoral promise, and expanded the military capacities in Afghanistan as soon as he stepped into the White House. While to the world it may seem the military upsurge was meant for Afghanistan, as a whole, it was essentially Kandahar, where the US military build-up went up by five fold. The Pentagon think tank was well aware that Kandahar would turn the tide for them. The city was soon transformed into a war zone with deployment of heavy weapons and artillery. Kandahar Airport was transformed into a military airbase with sophisticated and ultra-modern fighter jets, lined across the dominant part of the airport. The usage of the drone increased for hitting militant hideouts in remote and inaccessible areas within Kandahar, and adjacent restive southern provinces along with the infamous terrorist corridor, lying across the Afghanistan-Pakistan border. Experts dubbed the drone the 'Beast of Kandahar' after photographs of the mysterious unmanned aircraft emerged in the media.

The Afghan National Police is supposed to control the basic law and order situation in the city with the assistance of Canadian and the US forces. The US and the NATO forces are rushing to quickly expand the Afghan police force for the prevention of a possible Taliban comeback in Kandahar.

However, despite massive police and military build-up, the US has not been able to contain terrorism in Kandahar or tame the Taliban for that matter. In fact, the terrorist activities are spiralling higher than ever in an unprecedented scale, and getting from bad to worse by the day. The Taliban engineered a jail break episode, freeing 500 of their ex-accomplices through a tunnel, from the high security prison of Kandahar. Analysts see the jail break as a disaster, and a serious blow to stabilise the volatile southern provinces. This was followed by the Taliban seizing strategic office buildings of the government, killing scores of security personnel and civilians. Targeted killing of high profile officials goes on unabated. Ahmed Wali Karzai, the half-brother of the president, the police chief, the mayor, and the deputy governor of Kandahar are the latest, whose names have been added to the list. US military has designed a massive operation in Kandahar to weed out the Taliban. The much awaited showdown or the final assault is still to come. The impending operation is seen, by many Western experts, as the end war, as they believe it is going to seal the fate of Afghanistan in general and Kandahar, in particular.

How important is Kandahar from the military standpoint? Listen to Mike Mullen, the ex-Chairman of Joint Chiefs of Staff of the United States Forces, who visited Kandahar in March 2010, to assess the military situation. He said, 'Kandahar is the centre of gravity in the Afghan War'. He compared it with the surge in Iraq in 2007, and how that had helped the allies to win the war. Kandahar will assume the same importance, in Afghanistan, he said.

But, initiating a structured military operation in Kandahar is not going to be a cakewalk for the political leadership and they know it. President Karzai had travelled twice, in 2010, to meet the tribal and religious leaders of the Kandahar region. The meeting highlighted the need for support of the ISAF forces, to undertake a concerted attack against the Taliban and al-Qaeda militants, to stabilise the province of Kandahar vis-à-vis southern Afghanistan. The West may see it as a humble submission with the president travelling all the way to Kandahar to seek approval of the tribal chiefs, for the pending operation. Afghanistan, in fact, operates at a different level. Decisions are driven more by the context than pre-set manuals on public administration and military science. Here, the rules of the game are set by the powerful tribal chieftains. The local populace owes their allegiance to these traditional leaders more than the State. Historically, a considerable section of such leaders have always been soft on the Taliban and al-Qaeda due to their ideological leanings, and overlapping of religious interests. Hence, it becomes imperative for the State to win over the tribal chieftains and key religious leaders, before initiating any concrete action against the Taliban and al-Qaeda nexus in Kandahar.

The city is, as if, sitting on a time-bomb. The intelligence reports say that the Taliban has assembled in the remote pockets of various districts of Kandahar, and are preparing their strategy for the forthcoming decisive war. Even though the military believes that the operation in Kandahar would seal the fate of the Taliban, once and forever, it can be guaranteed that the much hyped and awaited operation would far from eliminate terrorism from Afghanistan.

The Taliban are well aware that they cannot withstand the might of American military; hence, they would prefer to play a waiting game, and employ guerrilla tactics at large. A bulk of them may slip into the Pakistani side of the border, and wait for their turn to strike against Western interests. This would also provide them with the required time to re-group and re-arm. And hordes of radical mullahs, on the payroll of the ISI, would leave no stones unturned to sharpen their jihadi leanings, and prepare themselves to take up the Western forces upfront, with the passage of time. At best, the US would claim that the operation has killed a few thousand terrorists. In the US military history, this would be seen as one of the most successful military campaigns against terrorism. The problem of terrorism would be far from over, but this would give the desperate US forces, a window of opportunity to exit. The layman from Kandahar sees the impending military operation as a quick fix arrangement rather than a long-term solution. It is also reported by certain sections of the media that the US is contemplating a change of plan! Instead of a massive military operation, the US may toe the idea of a sustained and coordinated operation to establish security bit by bit, and drive away the Taliban. Along with sustained operation, the US commanders have ordered the NATO troops to join civilian development experts to create competent governance, where none exists. But, have all such efforts in the past shown any results, so far? So why is the situation in Kandahar getting from bad to worse, despite the massive military build-up, and sustained military operations in Kandahar? Why have Western military forces with all their military might failed to tame the Taliban in Kandahar? It may be very easy to criticise the Western forces, but one has to understand the complexities of Kandahar, and, especially, the undercurrents.

One does not have to be an insurgency expert to fathom the reasons behind the burgeoning trouble and unrest in Kandahar. There are a variety of reasons behind the failure of the ISAF troops, so far. The first and foremost is the influence of the Taliban in Kandahar. Being the birth place of the Taliban, they enjoy a considerable amount of local support, especially, in remote districts, bordering Pakistan. The local support is sporadic in nature, but it provides a perfect logistic support for the militants to deceive the Western troops. This support from the scattered and remote hamlets of strategic border districts of Kandahar enable the militants to strike against the Western forces, with consummate ease. In the recent years, the Taliban militants have developed mastery in striking against the Western military forces from remote villages inhabited with local populace. They keep on attacking with unfailing regularity, and cross the porous Afghanistan-Pakistan border after every attack. Perhaps, it needs to be mentioned here that a large number of militants come from the other side of the border, and take refuge in these pockets.

The action of the military forces is in some sense becoming counter productive, too. In order to dissuade the local populace from harbouring militants, the Western forces round up the entire village, especially youth, and subject them to sustained interrogation, after every such attack. The whole village is stamped as offenders, instead of the peripatetic militants. After a series of interrogation, a few young people are usually detained. They languish in jail for undisclosed periods of time. The military forces do not comply with laid down legal procedures and systems in such cases. The released youths have to, further, clear their names from the list of suspects in the government files. On conditions of anonymity, I was told by a few victims, that they had to bribe the local police and army officials to get their names cleared. Such shakedowns instead of uprooting the growing militancy largely turn the rural populace against the Western forces, and make them Taliban sympathisers. The support for the Taliban, mostly prevalent in the form of a nucleus, in remote villages, is thus growing with every passing day. It is quite obvious that such support would step-up the process of local recruitment for the Taliban, in Kandahar. The apparent gap between the terrorist and the remote villages of Kandahar is only closing with the approach of the Western military forces. In fact, the Taliban militants are strategically using this ploy to alienate the masses from the Western military vis-a-vis the State of Afghanistan to increase the scale and scope of their logistic support.

Besides, the Taliban is very familiar with the geography and climate of Kandahar, which is very different from the rest of Afghanistan. It is hotter and located near a visible desert. The militants can carry out long gun battles without the support of ice bags beneath their stomach. The local intelligence gathering system of the Taliban is also far superior to the US forces. Militants do not need any advanced technological system to locate the movements of the Western troops. They rely on their traditional system of seeking intelligence through their trusted network of sympathisers lying within strategic locale. Together these put them in an advantageous position to strike in guerrilla style raids. They are fully familiar with the terrain, and can test the perseverance and skill of the Western military to the maximum.

In addition to the knowledge of the local area, they are equipped with the latest range of guns, explosives and rocket launchers. The Taliban of 2010 is very different from the Taliban of 2001. The present day Taliban has started relying on technology apart from its committed soldiers. The larger question is the source from where these militants procure the latest range of military machines. In the late seventies, CIA and ISI equipped the Mujahideens to resist the Soviet occupation. The traditional sources of arm supply have continued even when a considerable section of the Mujahideen has donned the cap of the Taliban with passage of time. A bulk of the arms held by the Taliban today is procured from the thriving arms black-market of Pakistan, run under the full knowledge of the army.

The analysis of the Taliban strength would be incomplete without mentioning their daring and die hard attitude. In 2006, the British government decided to send additional contingents of troops to another volatile southern province, Helmand (adjacent to Kandahar) to weed out the Taliban, as a part of their ongoing military assistance to Afghanistan. Then southern commander of the Taliban, Mullah Dadullah, boldly announced to the media that they would make most of these soldiers sleep in the British cemetery in Kabul. This cemetery was built as the final resting place of the Britishers, who died in the Second Anglo–Afghan War in 1878. Perhaps it needs to be mentioned that the Afghan fighters defeated the British soldiers in both the First and Second Anglo–Afghan Wars, fought in 1839 and 1878 respectively, and sent them packing on both occasions. Both the wars culminated in large scale deaths of British troops. Helmand was one of the locales of the war. The Taliban commander had snidely added that since the grandfathers of the existing lot of British soldiers must be missing them, the Taliban would ensure that they receive the opportunity to sleep beside their grandfathers, in the British cemetery in Kabul.

It is unbelievable, but the Taliban had brutally killed 380 British soldiers, by the beginning of August 2011. The leaked mail, of the fired British General, has clearly underlined the inability of their current military contingent to tame the Taliban in Helmand, anymore. The British government has already announced their departure schedule from Helmand, and a majority of these soldiers are counting their remaining days. I wonder who was right in their assessment. The British soldiers or the Taliban. Who has achieved their goal, between the two?

I have said before, in the chapter 'The Peace Game', military operations alone cannot silence terrorism. It is a common understanding, two terrorists spring out of every terrorist killed by the Western forces, in Afghanistan. In the last nine years of military operation, one has lost count of the number of terrorists killed in Afghanistan, especially, in the southern provinces. But the Taliban stands stronger today, with swelling numbers.

Especially down south, their numbers are increasing at an alarming rate.

The local support for Taliban also emanates from the inability of the present day government to deliver basic amenities, to assuage the plight of the common man. The government of Kandahar is paralysed, and cannot extend and expand development services to the remote districts of Kandahar due to the proxy rule of the Taliban in most of the districts in Kandahar. The development process in Kandahar is largely confined to the periphery of Kandahar city, and the relatively safer districts of Dand and Daman. Of late, the citizens residing in the city of Kandahar have started getting services, like better electric supply and safe drinking water from the provincial government with international assistance. This is a welcome change, but certainly not going to make much difference in the context of the battle at Kandahar. The provincial government has to reach out to the remotest districts, and address the plight of the poorest of the poor communities.

The development services offered by the INGOs are the only source of support for the poor and vulnerable section of the society, nestled in the remote villages of the remaining districts within Kandahar province. The food support of World Food Programme (WFP) is the lifeline for the poor families in the remote districts of Kandahar. Due to alarming deterioration of law and order, most of the INGOs have either suspended or severely downsized their operations. The radical faction of the Taliban has even attacked the trucks of WFP carrying wheat for the poor families in the remote districts.

I have always believed that the INGO community innovates amid crisis only. Sensing blockades in their movements, these INGOs have started relying on local Kandahar based NGOs to reach out to the poor and needy communities. The broader INGO community is outsourcing bulk of activities through the local NGOs that are the lenders of last resort for the extremely vulnerable families living in remote volatile districts. The Taliban has, so far, desisted from attacking the NGO representatives as they want the development services to reach out to the poor, in a limited scale. But the development programmes are subjected to minute scrutiny by the Taliban. They have somehow struck a tacit deal with the Taliban to provide development services to a considerable number of villages in the province of Kandahar. They have, however, touched their capacity ceiling, and therefore are able to offer only a limited range of services. Hence, potentially the INGOs too have reached a ceiling in terms of extending development services. Further, the support provided by the INGOs in collaboration with the local NGOs is insubstantial, when compared to the scale and diversity of human needs in Kandahar.

Few progressive INGOs have been investing heavily towards building capacities of the local NGOs to build up the development sector in Kandahar. The rewards of such efforts, however, shall only be perceived in the long run. The need of the poor communities is more immediate. Before it leads to a catastrophic situation, the development actors of Kandahar, the State in particular, have to find a solution. Afghanistan cannot hold the Kandahar community together on promises of nationhood alone. The State has to offer public services, and effectively perform its duty to win the heart and minds of the struggling citizens and bind them in the fabric of a nation.

Inaccessibility of basic services is frustrating the common man, and turning them towards the Taliban, slowly. Hence, the State is locked up in a typical cyclic development debate, where it is unable to offer services due to the threatening law and order situation in Kandahar. And the inability of the State to provide services to its citizen is turning them towards Taliban which is getting stronger, and aggravating the law and order situation with their nefarious terrorist designs. This is, further crippling the sporadic development process of Kandahar. One would never have come across any manual on public administration or military science which is prepared to deal with such a grave situation. This is Kandahar!!!

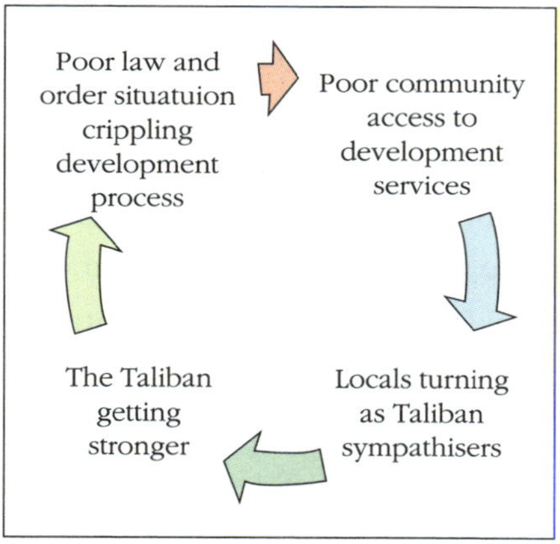

The Taliban understands the context of Kandahar far better than the government, the international forces, and even most of the INGOs. They are aware that development can pacify terrorism. Hence, they have brought the development process to almost a grinding halt. They are conscientiously stifling the reach of development services to alienate the masses from the State, to gain from the status quo in Kandahar.

While writing about status quo, I reckon that no one is really ready to challenge the situation in Kandahar. I can understand why the Taliban may not be too eager to challenge the status quo—it is their raison d'être. I am, however, incapable of understanding why the INGOs and the State in particular have been reduced to such placid acceptance. In Kandahar, you get a feeling that everybody has resigned to fate, as if there is not a ray of hope, and no option, but to endure the status quo in passive silence. The deteriorating law and order situation is a common explanation for such inaction. I had a harrowing glimpse of it when I wasted nearly four months trying to launch our development programmes in Kandahar. Striking a meaningful collaboration with other agencies in Kandahar seemed impossible. I realised I had very little time for action and could not afford to lose it over unproductive inane meetings. A bulk of provincial departments is happy providing services to the Kandahar city and its adjacent districts, which are relatively safer. It took me two years to finally convince the Department of Women Affairs, to extend their services to rural women, beyond the peripheries of Kandahar city. It took another year to start a formal computer training centre for the women in Kandahar. As the Taliban is against women's education, technical education of women is strictly prohibited!

Nearly nine years into the US led war, Kandahar is still served by a few corrupt Afghan officials and marred by poor governance. What little governance exists in Kandahar is overshadowed by a cabal of Afghan hustlers, who have milked their connections with high ranking government officials to earn illicit fortunes. A US Congressional subcommittee in 2010 said that Afghan warlords have siphoned millions of dollars, through protection rackets involving security escorts for the NATO convoys.

Beside poor governance, corruption is impeding the flow of development services to the needy communities in Kandahar. An average Afghan in Kandahar cannot get his work done unless he pays a bribe to the clerk, the officer and the political bigwig.

The Taliban has been gaining ascendancy greatly because of the rampant corruption in the provincial government—something widely reported by the national and the international media.

Endemic corruption has also played a large role in alienating the ordinary Kandhari from the State, and driven them towards the Taliban. Once a senior UN official, posted in Kandahar told me how he had been informally asked by a senior police official to share half of the wheat meant for poor families. When he refused to accept his diktat the wheat truck was burnt down by the official's henchmen. These volatile, rabid reactions of powerful office bearers deeply damage the US efforts to bring Kandahar under control.

I was told by one of the senior government officers, on conditions of anonymity that the Taliban allows the corrupt officials to thrive. Inaction coupled with corruption alienates the masses faster from the government, and turn them to the Taliban for an alternate solution. The alternate solution has, however, been elusive. Despite the claims the Taliban initially made, they have not been able to follow through their promises. They have planted spies in the government system, the officer confided, to routinely report about sensitive and confidential issues. This information is released carefully to influence and sway the masses, in their favour.

Despite rampant coverage of corruption in the government, I would caution people not to draw a conclusive opinion about all government officials working under the tiring and trying circumstances of Kandahar. I personally know some very honest senior government officers working in Kandahar. Every time I meet an honest officer I pray to god that he stays alive. These are the people, who can easily drive the Taliban to the throes of marginalisation, with their credible work. While the Taliban has allowed the corrupt officials to thrive, they have wasted no time in killing those known for their impeccable integrity, obviously for strategic reasons. I have lost count of the government officers killed over the past few years. The Deputy Governor of

Kandahar, Abdul Latif Ashna was killed in a brutal suicide attack in broad daylight on 29 January 2011, in Afghanistan. The Taliban claimed responsibility of this attack. He was one of the daring representatives of government, who was widely popular among the masses, and known for his honesty and professional integrity. It is a real pity to witness these government officers sitting, like lame ducks, with minimal security in their offices, almost waiting to become the next victim of the Taliban. I am always warned by my security advisor to avoid visiting these offices in Kandahar. Once I asked a senior official as to why he was risking his life, working with the government. Pat came his reply, 'So that my son can proudly say that he is from Afghanistan.' I was moved. In the last six years, I realised that the dream of any ordinary literate Afghan youth is to migrate to a developed country, and lead a comfortable and peaceful life. What the government officer meant was that he wished to reverse that trend.

The whole strategic community is watching Kandahar, and waiting to see how it unfolds with time. Kandahar is silent on that score and not showing any sign of change. The Taliban has already started weaving a fresh dream of Afghanistan, especially, in the southern provinces, including Kandahar. They are mobilising mass discontentment around the weaknesses of the existing government. Limited reach of development services, misgovernance, corruption and escalating hostlity of Western forces are helping them to fan public hatred. Before the Taliban manage to rally the masses connecting them to their dream once more, the legitimate development actors must present a better option to the masses in Kandahar, and elsewhere in the southern provinces. The US and the NATO forces are caught between the devil and the deep sea. Of late, efforts are getting around at fixing governance and development issues. Even if it is too little, one can only hope it is not too late.

Acknowledgement

The author and his work can seldom surpass the energy of the setting that stimulates it or the people who orchestrate it, and the loving support of a close network of family and friends, who sustain the process of recreating it. I have each one of you to thank who, consciously or unconsciously, contributed to my adventurous attempt at decoding the myth of Afghanistan, from the lens of a developmental professional.

This book is dedicated to my diligent team and scores of grassroots leaders, who despite a constant threat to their personal well-being have been, relentlessly, challenging the status quo in Afghanistan. This book attempts to capture the rigour and pathos of their walk along a razor's edge—the tremendous dedication and sacrifice that go into building a shattered nation, brick by brick—and the enduring faith, that alone cements it. They have remained my biggest inspiration in believing Afghanistan will, indeed, surmount its perilous and fragile existence, and emerge a strong nation, someday.

The process of writing this book has been cathartic, in more than one way. This is an unfolding saga of a nation, beleaguered by a startling new crisis, every day; struggling to take a fresh step forward, after being pushed behind several notches. It was particularly painful losing a few friends (mostly government officials), and colleagues, while writing this book—people who could have made a significant difference to Afghanistan. This book intends to carry their message of hope and optimism to millions across the globe who would have never known about these unsung heroes, otherwise. A personal crisis, wherein I lost my father, who had been a driving force all along, also accompanies the completion of this book, making this mission, even more significant for me.

This book would not have been possible without the support of my immediate and extended family that encouraged me to follow my heart and pursue my dream to contribute to the rebuilding process. I would like to also extend my sincere thanks to my employer for providing me the opportunity to serve in Afghanistan.

Built around the subtle perceptions and experiences of the common man of Afghanistan this book is an attempt at narrating the everyday tale, which goes unnoticed by the frenetic media. But for my roommates Yatesh, Abdullah, and closest buddies Akhtar and Bashi, among others, I would have never got a chance to hone my story-telling skills. But for my wife, Anindita (my strongest critic and my biggest source of strength), and Ishaan, who wanted to see his father as a writer, I would not have picked up the quill to finally scribble the first few lines. I am, especially, indebted to my literary agent, Kanishka, but for whose indomitable spirit this book would not have got past the publishing mire to see the light of the day. I also wish to thank Niyogi Books and its editor Jyoti for helping me connect with my dear readers. Finally, my sincere thanks to my journalist friend, Jaya, for overall assistance in making this project a success.

A special thanks to one and many, who contributed to this book, whose names I cannot reveal due to reasons of personal safety and security. Thank you all for encouraging and enriching me with your valuable inputs, and for consistently supporting me through this journey in search of a new Afghanistan, which shall, hopefully, continue.

Disclaimer: The book is purely based on my experience and perception, gained from wide range of conversation with various stake holders, in course of my stay in Afghanistan, over six years. I have written this book in my personal capacity and my employer may or may not subscribe to the perspective, ideas, opinion and analysis presented in this book.

Abbreviations

BJP:	Bharatiya Janata Party
IARCSC:	Independent Administrative Reform and Civil Service Commission
ICC:	International Cricket Council
IDLG:	Independent Directorate of Local Governance
INGO:	International Non Governmental Organization
ISAF:	International security Assistance Force
ISI:	Inter Service Intelligence
MAIL:	Ministry for Agriculture, Irrigation and Livestock
MADRAC:	Microfinance Agency for Development and Rehabilitation of Afghan Communities
MoE:	Ministry of Education
MISFA:	Microfinance Investment Support Facility for Afghanistan
MRRD:	Ministry for Rural Reconstruction and Development
MoWA:	Ministry of Women's Affairs
NABDP:	National Area Based Development Programme
NATO:	North Atlantic Treaty Organization
NGO:	Non Governmental Organisation
NSP:	National Solidarity Programme
PRT:	Provincial Reconstruction Team
UK:	United Kingdom of Britain
UNAMA:	United Nations Assistance Mission for Afghanistan
UNDP:	United Nations Development Programme
UNHAS:	United Nations Humanitarian Airline Services
UNODC:	United Nations Office for Crime and Drugs
US:	United States of America
USAID:	United State Agency for International Development
WFP:	World Food Programme

Glossary

Afghan Warlord: A warlord is a person with power who has both military (mostly private), and civil control over a certain region in Afghanistan.

Afwa: Political pardon.

Al Jazeera: An international English news channel, with headquarters in Doha, Qatar. Initially launched as an Arabic news and current affairs satellite TV channel with the same name.

Al-Qaeda: An international terrorist network, comprising of loosely affiliated cells that carry out attacks and bombings in the attempt to disrupt the economies and influence of Western nations and advance Islamic fundamentalism. The group is held responsible for 9/11 bombing.

Bil-Maroof: Department of preservation of vice and virtue. The Taliban employed the department, to enforce their rigid religious and cultural code of conduct, developed for Afghan citizens. The department was entrusted with the task of ensuring mass compliance, of the irrational diktats of Taliban, and strictly prosecute the offenders.

Burqa: A loose, usually black or light blue robe, worn by Muslim women, especially, in Afghanistan that covers the body from head to toe.

Haqqani: A Taliban affiliated insurgent group, currently based in north Waziristan, Pakistan. The network is led by the father and son duo of Maulvi Jalaludin Haqqani and Sirajuddin Haqqani. According to US military commanders, the network is the most notorious faction of Taliban and considered one of the biggest threats to Afghanistan.

Hijab: A headscarf worn by Muslim women, sometimes a veil, that covers the face, except for the eyes.

Jihad: An Islamic term considered a religious duty of Muslims. Muslims use the word in a religious context to refer to three types of struggles: An internal struggle to maintain moral and virtuous life, the struggle for spreading and defending Islam, or the struggle against injustice. However with passage of time, the Islamic fundamentalist used the term to mobilise Muslim youths to fight Western and Indian interest, in the name of freedom from injustice.

Jirgas: Local consultation meetings.

ISAF: ISAF is a NATO led security mission in Afghanistan established by the United Nation Security Council on 20 December 2001 by resolution 1386 as envisaged by the BON agreement. It is engaged in the war in Afghanistan. ISAF is engaged in intensive combat operation against Taliban and al-Qaeda militants in Afghanistan.

Loya Jirga: Grand council or grand assembly of elders.

Madrassa: A school, where mostly Islamic studies take place.

Mujahideen: A person engaged in jihad is called as Mujahid; the plural is Mujahideen. However, in Afghanistan Mujahideen is referred to as a military force of Muslim guerrilla warriors who fought Soviet occupation.

Mullah: Generally a Muslim man, educated in Islamic theology and sacred law.

Sharia: Code of conduct or religious law of Islam.

Shura: Traditional village council mostly active in the domain of conflict resolution.

Soviet Occupation: The Soviet war in Afghanistan was a nine year conflict involving the Soviet Union supporting the Marxist government of Afghanistan, against the Afghan Mujahideen and foreign 'Arab-Afghan' volunteers. The initial Soviet deployment of the 40th Army in Afghanistan began on 24 December 1979 and the final troop withdrawal ended on 15 February 1989.

Taliban: Islamist militia group that ruled large parts of Afghanistan from September 1996 onwards. Although in control of Afghanistan's capital (Kabul) and most of the country for five years, the Taliban's Islamic Emirate of Afghanistan gained diplomatic recognition from only three countries: Pakistan, Saudi Arabia, and the United Arab Emirates. After the 9/11, the Taliban regime was overthrown by Operation Enduring Freedom. The Taliban mostly fled to neighbouring Pakistan where they regrouped as an insurgency movement to fight the democratic Islamic Republic of Afghanistan (established in late 2001) and the NATO-led International Security Assistance Force (ISAF).

Sujeet Sarkar is engaged in promoting and strengthening democratic governance and civil society in fragile and conflict-prone countries, over the past fifteen years. Currently working as an international advisor, in a globally reputed organisation; Sarkar is supporting the portfolio of governance and civil society in selected countries across Africa and Asia, including Afghanistan.

The idea of writing *In search of a New Afghanistan* emerged during the phase of his active stay in Afghanistan.

Sarkar's governance related work has been considered as a frontline model in Afghanistan, and has been recommended for broader replication, in other conflict-ridden countries.

About the Book:

Where is present-day Afghanistan heading? Will the dream of a new and stable Afghanistan, elude the international community, and more importantly its own denizens, forever? On the eve of the departure of the Western forces, in the midst of a resurgent Taliban and growing speculation around the stability of this country, *In search of a New Afghanistan* takes an incisive look into Afghanistan, with an attempt to apprise the international audience about this conflict-ridden country, post 9/11. An easy-to-understand tale, for all and sundry, it is a bold attempt to release one from the mainstream rhetoric, perceptions and opinion on Afghanistan.

The book undertakes a fresh probe into the development and reconstruction process of Afghanistan, post 9/11 and provides valuable insight into the contemporary challenges confronting Afghanistan today? It provides a daring new outlook, denouncing several myths that colour common global perception of this war-ravaged country. Further, several lesser known facts are unveiled, helping to create an alternative understanding about Afghanistan, for the first time.

That Afghanistan can be a fascinating place to live in and even fall in love with, despite the ongoing hurdles, is difficult to comprehend for most. These fascinating aspects are dwelt upon, while, elaborating, the thrill and challenges of working in Afghanistan, from ground zero.